JOURNAL III, 1970–1978

MIRCEA ELIADE

JOURNAL III
1970–1978

Translated from the French by Teresa Lavender Fagan

THE UNIVERSITY OF CHICAGO PRESS

Chicago and London

This book was originally published in France by Éditions Gallimard, Paris, as *Fragments d'un Journal II, 1970-1978.* © Éditions Gallimard, 1981. The translator's note and the index are published here for the first time.

The University of Chicago Press, Chicago 60637
The University of Chicago Press, Ltd., London
© 1989 by The University of Chicago
All rights reserved. Published 1989
Printed in the United States of America

98 97 96 95 94 93 92 91 90 89 54321

⊗ The paper used in this publication meets the minimum requirements of the American National Standard for Information Sciences—Permanence of Paper for Printed Library Materials, ANSI Z39.48-1984.

Library of Congress Cataloging-in-Publication Data

Eliade, Mircea, 1907–
    [Fragments d'un journal. 2. English]
    Journal III, 1970–1978 / Mircea Eliade; translated
from the French by Teresa Lavender Fagan.
      p.   cm.
    Translation of: Fragments d'un journal II, 1970–1978.
    Includes index.
    ISBN 0-226-20408-1 (alk. paper)
    1. Eliade, Mircea, 1907– —Diaries.   I. Title.
BL43.E4A3 1989
291'.092'4—dc19
   [B]
                                      88-38070
                                       CIP

TRANSLATOR'S NOTE

Mircea Eliade kept a personal journal from 1945 until shortly before his death in 1986. We are indeed privileged to have these reflections of a unique and sorely missed scholar in the history of religions. Eliade originally wrote his journal in Rumanian, as he did his other non-academic works (novels, short stories, and his autobiography). A portion of his journal, from September 1945 to February 1969, was translated into French (*Fragments d'un journal*; Paris: Gallimard, 1973), and a selection of those entries was subsequently published in English under the title *No Souvenirs: Journal, 1957–1969* (New York: Harper & Row, 1977).

The present volume contains selections from Eliade's journal from 1970 to 1979. It, too, was first written in Rumanian, and translated into French (*Fragments d'un journal II, 1970–1978*; Paris: Gallimard, 1981) by C. Grigoresco, whose initials appear after those footnotes I have translated from the French edition. Although it is always preferable to translate a work directly from the language in which it was originally written, Eliade worked closely with Grigoresco, and, being fluent in French himself, fully approved the French translation. When possible I have used the original English text or the standard English translation of passages Eliade quotes in his journal; when I could not locate English versions of such passages I have provided my translation from the French.

I was not fortunate enough to be able to work with Mircea Eliade on this translation, but am indebted to his wife, Christinel, for her generous assistance, kindness, and memories.

STOCKHOLM, *19 August 1970*

I'm writing these lines in a café, very near the university. Hardly a half hour earlier: I realize I'm being approached in a hallway by a small, dark young man. He wears glasses and clutches an overstuffed briefcase under his arm. A young girl stands next to him. It's Franklin Pease, director of the National Museum of History in Lima and professor of Andean history at the Pontifical University. The young girl accompanying him serves as interpreter with those who don't speak Spanish. He reminds me that about two months ago he and the president of the International Congress of Amerindian Ethnology wrote to invite me to participate in the congress, and it was because I was unable to go to Lima that he has come to Stockholm, with the sole purpose of meeting me here.

All three of us speak somewhat quickly, each in the language that comes most readily to his lips. Dr. Pease takes out of his briefcase many books, brochures, and offprints from provincial Peruvian journals—all publications of which he is the author. But he also entrusts others to me: *La Sal de los Cerros* (the spirit of the hills), for example, which Stefano Varese sends me, *con admiración*. I am delighted. My arms filled with all these publications, I listen to him. I understand, or rather I guess, that he absolutely *needed* to meet me after I had written him that I was working on the second part of my study on the South American high gods. He thought, rightly, that a good number of the texts he had just given me would be unobtainable in Chicago, or, doubtless, anywhere else except in the libraries of Peru. He admits to me that *Patterns in Comparative Religion, The Myth of the Eternal Return,* and several other of my books have helped him to understand the Andean cosmico-religious conception. He'd like us to talk more at length about the symbolism of the city of Cuzco, a true "Center of the World" (it was, in fact, called *the Navel of the World*). A sacred space *par excellence:* It was there that primordial revelations took place; it was there that the population learned to cultivate the earth and to feed itself "as men" (and no longer as "savage beasts," as they had done up until that time). The construction of Cuzco equaled a creation of the world, and in fact every construction of a new city was carried out according to the exemplary plan initiated in Cuzco by the mythical Manco Capac.

For the most part I've known that for a long time. Franklin Pease was undoubtedly aware of its significance, indeed because while reading *Patterns* and *Myth of the Eternal Return,* he discovered the function of cosmogonic symbolism and the importance of the notion of "Center of the World." But the young Americanist wants us to discuss the *Nueva Crónica y Buen Gobierno* by Felipe Guamàn Poma de Ayala, from which he has published excerpts in a small volume of around a hundred pages, which he gives me and eagerly asks me to read. As a matter of fact, Pease adds, according to the Andean cosmological conception, the universe was created and destroyed four times, each destruction being followed by a period whose duration was equal to that of the primordial chaos. But Spanish chroniclers sometimes lead us to believe that there would, in fact, have been five epochs: Indeed, they distinguish the last of these periods, the fourth—that of the creation of the universe—from the epoch immediately following—the age of the Incas. Such is Guamàn Poma's thesis, for example, in which he puts forth a biblical interpretation of Andean cosmo-mythology (he speaks, among other things, of "original innocence"). Pease insists: Would it be possible for me to read the *Nueva Crónica* in the next few days so that we could then discuss it together?

UPPSALA, *20 August*

A small, very old church, the oldest in the entire region. I had already visited it in November 1957 in the company of Stig Wikander. The tombstones in the little garden around the church were at that time covered with just as many flowers, and yet it was then the end of autumn. Once again regret at not having noted anything in my journal during these two weeks spent in Uppsala. But what haven't I omitted to note! These ravens wheeling tightly in flight around the bell tower, mostly at dusk. Stig had found me a room in a pension right in front of the bell tower. This room pleased me all the more since from my window I could follow the flight of the ravens, hear their indefatigable croaking.

Lunch at one of the famous "student houses," which are the envy of all European students. But in what other university town in the world—as our guide in the bus proudly reminded us—do students constitute the majority of the population?

Next, visit to the cathedral. I leave Christinel in the company of Alice and Chuck Long and go walk alone in the attempt to bring my thoughts together. Widengren has asked me to say a few words at the reception at the university in response to the rector's welcoming address. I will speak in a personal vein, as a professor who has taught at Uppsala. I stroll in the park, stopping every once in a while in front of rocks covered with runic inscriptions, trying to control the flow of my memories. I rest in the sun on one of the benches near the cathedral. Fascinated by the incredibly blue sky without a trace of clouds, I note once again to what degree I am ill-suited for this type of "occasional discourse." As soon as it is no longer a matter of communicating ideas, facts, or methods, I no longer have the slightest talent.

While returning from the café, I meet Franklin Pease. The young girl who accompanies him takes our photograph together on the sidewalk, not far from the cathedral: him, with his book-stuffed briefcase in his hand, and me, with my coat over my arm, smiling, a bit ill-at-ease since, as I was telling him, I had not yet been able to begin reading the *Nueva Crónica*. I ask him to excuse me for not being able to talk to him right then, since I have to meet Widengren.

I continue my walk in the park. I decide to give my "talk" a light tone. I could begin thus: *Et in Arcadia ego!* by recalling the courses I gave at this university in 1957; I could talk about Uppsala as a lofty place for studies in the history of religions, while adding that such a place is always linked to a certain cult, to a certain mythology. I could then speak of the "Cult of the Mythical Ancestors" of historians of religion, from Max Müller to Nathan Soederblom, and especially of their respective "mythologies." I could recall certain "Uppsalian myths" which I had heard in my youth, this one, for example: In a train in which Nyberg was traveling in Asia Minor, around 1920, there were also people from a fair number of countries, and all sorts of languages were being spoken. The great Orientalist, who had not introduced himself and whom no one knew, spoke all the languages, from Persian and Arabic to Urdu, Cyprian, and Turkish. One of the travelers finally exclaimed, "If you are not the devil, you most certainly must be Professor Nyberg!"

I could also recall what Wikander told me one day: Widengren, a great specialist in Semitic languages and a great student of Iranian language and culture, had begun studying Sanskrit. One fine day he complained to Wikander, "I've been learning Sanskrit for two weeks, and there are still texts that I can't understand!"

But who could tell all the "myths" that are connected to university life in Uppsala! Like the ravens wheeling around the bell tower: They are the souls of those who, at over fifty years of age, have not yet obtained their doctorate and are now pursued and persecuted by their professors. But I hesitate to mention what I was told at a congress a long time ago, namely that Uppsala is the only place in the world where the tradition of human sacrifice has been maintained intact, and this from the pre-Christian era up to the present (Saint Erik was martyred there in 1160), when human sacrifice is rarely practiced any more except, figuratively speaking, in university settings.

I could conclude by expressing the wish and the hope that such mythologies will never be demystified . . .

In fact, I said only very little of what I had proposed to myself to evoke. At five o'clock we were all gathered in the meeting hall of the rectorate; the rector said a few words, emphasizing the spirit of tolerance and the universalism that governs our discipline today. Widengren then invited me to take the floor. In order to be seen and heard by everyone, I had to climb up on a chair. The preceding addresses having been given in English and German, I delivered mine in French. But I was constantly afraid of falling, and while I spoke I supported myself against the wall with my right hand . . .

STOCKHOLM, *21 August*

After our return from Uppsala, last night we went to the Hultkrantzes'. They live outside Stockholm, rather far from the city. Despite our fatigue, I don't regret having accepted the invitation. The Parinders and Andreys Johanson arrive shortly after we do. Well-known ritual of a Swedish evening "get-together": coffee and cake first, followed by alcoholic beverages.

In the course of the conversation, an animated discussion on Strindberg. Without knowing why, I suddenly find myself in the midst of delivering an indictment against Swedish literary critics: To date there doesn't exist a complete critical edition of Strindberg's works; all sorts of studies appear, of course, but almost all are devoted to his life, his relationships with his family, his friends; very few studies on the artistic value of the author's own creations. I admit to having the impression that even today Swedish critics have still not forgiven Strindberg. They are angry with him for having been what he was, for having dared so much and in so many realms. His encyclopedism, his extravagant incursions into the realms of occultism, alchemy, and mysticism irritate or upset. In the end, who can boast of having read and understood the body of Strindberg's nonliterary writings?

When I have a free moment I continue reading the *Nueva Crónica y Buen Gobierno.* Pease was right: This Guamàn Poma de Ayala, born around 1585, descended from the Incan aristocracy (his mother was the daughter of the Tupac Inca Yupanqui), having become a high ecclesiastical official (the auxiliary of Cristobal de Albornoz, "the demolisher of idolaters"), has left us what is perhaps the most interesting document on Andean religion, and this despite the difficulty and the dryness of the text. There will be many commentaries to make on the efforts he put forth both to understand the world as a good Christian and to write perfect Spanish—while all the time remaining an authentic Incan—but also to succeed in conveying to us the "version of the vanquished" when he needed to express himself on the tragedy of colonization. His presentation of Andean mythology and cosmology, considered, however, from the perspective of Catholic theology, reveals Guamàn Poma's faith in a near-future Latin American spiritual synthesis.

But the discussion of such issues has no place in this notebook. I would only like to note a few of the more recent trends among South American ethnologists. First of all, the growing importance they are placing on autochthonous theology and mythologies. Everywhere, whether it be in Pease's commentaries in the margins of texts by Guamàn Poma or Francisco d'Avila, or in the studies by Stefano Varese on the Campa populations of the Peruvian *selva,* or in the publications on Amerindian ethnology owing to researchers from Argentina, Colombia, or Guatemala, I rediscover this same *objective passion* for the spiritual traditions of the aborigines. Current studies, undertaken with unequaled scientific passion and precision, deal not so much with the creations of "primitive" tribes as with those of Andean and Central American civilizations. But what seems most significant to me is this effort to integrate these values into the cultural history (and above all into the *present*) of the South American continent.

For a long time already poets, writers, plastic artists, and choreographers have been tackling this process of assimilation, revaluing, and synthesis. Obviously, their creative efforts were limited to the actualization of pre-Columbian artistic traditions. At present the phenomenon is much vaster and more complex. They are trying to recover aboriginal culture in its entirety, without for all that falling into the defense of "primitivism" and of the extravagant, spectacular, or emotional elements that are connected with it; but rather through a hermeneutics mindful of pre-Columbian theology, mythology, and ethics. I can only rejoice at such a trend that confirms, once again, what for around thirty years I have maintained in all my work in the history of religions and the philosophy of culture: The spiritual universes that are revealed to us by archaic and Oriental worlds are not dead museum pieces. Their study and the lessons we learn from them can bring about cultural *alterations* and *metamorphoses*.

STOCKHOLM, *22 August*

Two-hour boat excursion with Christinel. What is the use of attempting to describe here the islands, lakes, canals, parks, houses, villas, and palaces, about which our guide, thank heaven, only tells us what he knows we are interested in hearing.

Joe Kitagawa informs me of the death of Professor Robinson. God has finally had pity on him. Around forty years old, he was one of the most talented American Orientalists. He knew Sanskrit, Chinese, and Japanese and had specialized in medieval Buddhism. He was not happily married, and for several years he had been living with an Indian woman, but his wife postponed their divorce indefinitely. Just recently, however, she had finally agreed to it. Robinson had rented an apartment, had installed his furniture, his library, and his "fiancée" in it. One evening, having gone down to the basement, he struck a match to find the light switch, and there was an enormous explosion around him; the landlord or the former tenant had undoubtedly not shut the gas off properly. Robinson escaped with his life, but he was horribly mutilated; he subsequently became blind and had an arm amputated.

His fiancée had to notify his ex-wife, from whom he had been separated for several years. Before leaving Chicago I had heard all sorts of stories telling of tragicomic scenes that were practically unbelievable. It seems that the unfortunate man, who lay blinded and mutilated in his hospital bed, tried to explain to those around him that his fiancée was his true wife. Fortunately God had pity on him.

OSLO, *23 August*

Arrival at eight o'clock in the morning. The day promises to be superb. Copious breakfast at the Hotel Bristol, then we wait, in vain, for the bus in which we are to visit the city.

I stroll, alone, in the vicinity of the hotel. Nearby there is a square where a statue stands, symbolizing maternity. In a little street an old woman stops short in front of a shop window: I walk over, and I, too, look at what she's looking at—alarm clocks. She must be waiting to hear them go off. When I go by again, five minutes later, the old woman is still there.

We have lunch in a garden after having visited the port and admired the town hall, the *Radhuset,* dedicated in 1950, nine hundred years after the founding of Oslo.

I regret not having asked Zwi whether the exaltation of eroticism in all its forms, and the publicity uproar in favor of pornography, are not in fact a "modern" actualization—that is, one that is accessible to Western man today—of the mythico-ritual complex, *vagina dentata.* Basically, the unlimited and uninhibited pansexuality that triumphs today in Western societies exhibits the inevitable ambiguity of "initiatory trials": There exists on the one hand the risk of being "killed" (at first, quite obviously, on the spiritual level alone) by the omnipresence and aggressiveness of sexuality. But on the other hand, the courage and intelligence needed to confront, defeat, and transform this incandescent irruption of telluric forces into an experience of paroxystic vitality amount to a true initiation of a "heroic" type. While by hundreds of thousands the "profane" (that is, the naive, the immature) who let themselves be "blinded" and "consumed" by sensual pleasures, by this same force whose mystery should have "enlightened" them, work hard toward their spiritual death while at the same time preparing their physical death, simultaneously, then, a minute number of others reach that level of existence that traditions call "heroic." And this in a completely similar way to that spoken of by Tantric authors: "The yogi gains his liberty through actions that are exactly like those for which others burn in hell for millions of years." But with this difference: The orgiastic experience, which, according to Tantric tradition, is accessible only at the conclusion of a long initiation and involves innumerable risks, is today within the reach of anyone. This is why it seems to me that the myth of the *vagina dentata* type can be applied to the current situation more adequately than can Indian erotic mystical theology.

There would still be much to say about that. This, for example: In the history of the spirit it sometimes happens that the repetition of exemplary situations on an increasingly coarse level hides or corrupts a paradoxical creativity, "paradoxical" because it is unexpected and above all "unrecognizable," absolutely imperceptible to contemporaries.

The bus finally arrives at the beginning of the afternoon. We drive across the city and make our way into the Bygdøy Peninsula. In a park as vast as a forest, near the Royal Farm, is the Folk Museum: some hundred and fifty old wooden houses from all the provinces of Norway. We stop in front of a splendid house dating from 1737, remarkable for its exterior ornamentation, whose roof has been gradually taken over by moss. A little farther, a small wooden church, without windows—like, by the way, all houses constructed in Norway between the eleventh and the thirteenth centuries. The first peasant house we see with glazed windows dates from 1670.

But what is the use of noting such details, which can be found in any guidebook? There are completely other reasons for my fascination with these venerable testimonies to the civilization of wood. It is mainly due to the presence of a motif that I rediscover in each corner of these houses, at the point of intersection of the beams, a motif that would give birth to the *Endless Column*. It contains an image that was to become familiar to Brancusi, one which he had often encountered in the Oltenia of his childhood, for it is found in wooden peasant houses. Elsewhere, too, notably in the component formed by the "pillar of the house," often made out of diamond-shaped blocks of wood. But for Brancusi memory gave way to creative imagination, and this same motif, liberated of its concrete shackles, rediscovered its primordial function as "central pillar" and *axis mundi*. This ordinary motif, common in all civilizations of wood, like so many others slept a lethargic sleep for thousands of years until it was suddenly yanked out of its torpor, ennobled and transfigured by the wave of a genius's wand.

We leave this park where more than a hundred old houses are assembled, and we head towards the Viking Museum on the other side of the road. The spacious, well-lit rooms house boats dating from the ninth century and admirably decorated four-wheeled wagons. What to say about this head of a man from which emanates such an expression of suffering that one might believe he had just been tortured? Every time I try, for my own interest, to understand the Viking phenomenon, I can't help experiencing a feeling of frustration. There is in that phenomenon an enigma that no historian has yet succeeded in solving. But what is most serious is that this enigma resides in the Vikings' destiny. They loomed up in history at the end of the eighth century, went from conquest to conquest, pillaged, destroyed, founded dynasties, swarmed into Iceland and Greenland, and discovered North America. The Viking era lasted for two centuries. Aboard ships similar to the one I am contemplating, they launched themselves onto all the seas of the North, attacked England, Ireland, France, crushing the kings and princes who attempted to resist them, taking their places, established the kingdoms of Iceland, Norway, and Denmark. For a time they dominated England, carved out a fief in Normandy, extended as far as Spain, and made their way into the Mediterranean. Eventually, those in Normandy went as far as Sicily, where they encountered the descendants of other Vikings, the Varangians, who, having left the Baltic, headed toward the east, conquered a portion of the Slavs, established the kingdom of Gardarike with the two famous cities of Kiev and Novgorod, and then traveled down south on the great Russian rivers. Some of them reached as far as the Caspian Sea and had dealings with the caliphate of Bagdad. Others, in greater number, headed towards Constantinople, where they joined the armies of the Byzantine emperor. It was from there that they ventured as far as Sicily.

Around the year 1000 all their leaders were converted to Christianity. Some of them returned to their respective lands, imposed the new religion on their subjects, reclaimed their thrones or devoted themselves to trade. By 1030, the Viking era had met its end.

Quite obviously, the spirit, the institutions, and all that the Vikings had brought about had a profound impact on all medieval Nordic culture, and the Viking era is an integral part of the history of all Nordic nations. This heroic and orgiastic exuberance, this debauchery of bloody violence, energy, and creative genius such as were known from 800 to 1000, never again reached such heights. After 1030, the "Viking factor" disappeared from history. Under the circumstances one can't help thinking of the Mongol era, except that the followers of Genghis Khan succeeded in remaining in the empire of the steppes that they had carved out for themselves, whereas the Vikings dissipated their efforts in multiple unique, disordered, or eccentric undertakings. Their adventure brings to mind that of the Polynesians, who in a few centuries swarmed onto all the islands of the Pacific, bringing their civilization with them.

In the Viking adventure what stands out most clearly is the omnipresence and the weight of destiny. It is sufficient to recall that in the year 1002 the famous Leif Erikson discovered and colonized a territory that he called Vinland, and which was most probably none other than the present-day Newfoundland, for recent archeological digs there have brought to light vestiges of Viking establishments. Some of the colonists then traveled south and went as far as the region of Rhode Island. The connections between Vinland and Greenland persisted up until around the middle of the fourteenth century. What eventually happened, we don't know. The fact remains that at the end of the fifteenth century there was no longer any trace of Norwegians, descendants of the Vikings, on American shores.

It would be useless to wonder, or to imagine "what would have happened if . . .": If, for example, Leif Erikson had landed on these same shores, not between Labrador and Virginia, but several hundred kilometers farther south and had thus discovered the rich territories that six or seven hundred years later would feed the dreams of thousands upon thousands of colonists from England. How would world history itself have evolved if the discovery and the colonization of North America had taken place *before* the discovery of firearms, and in an age, therefore, when it wouldn't have been as easy to get rid of the autochthonous populations by displacing or exterminating them, a confrontation and a symbiosis between the two civilizations still being possible.

When I was young my friends and I had endless discussions on the fatality inherent in minor, provincial civilizations, a fatality which willed that their creative genius would be exercised to no purpose in rediscovering ideas or technical developments that had already been discovered and had been in use elsewhere for a long time. Just as if someone reinvented the bicycle twenty or thirty years after it had begun to be mass-produced in the West. But even more tragic is the destiny of individuals or nations whose unique genius is wasted on creations and discoveries made *before their time,* and much too early. Thus the apparent futility of the efforts, sacrifices, courage, and intelligence of a Leif Erikson, who only needed to discover America three or four centuries later and three or four hundred kilometers farther south . . .

Quick visit to the *Kon-Tiki* museum, where the adventure of Thor Heyerdahl and his companions is admirably evoked: One can see there the balsa-wood raft with all its riggings and even the supplies found on board during the crossing. On the walls, very evocative photographs, and in the basement, in a false aquarium, a representation of the fauna of the seas on which the raft sailed.

And yet I experience a certain discomfort. Perhaps because of the publicity uproar surrounding the expedition of the *Kon-Tiki,* engineered first by Thor Heyerdahl, then by the Norwegian authorities themselves.

The courage of the navigators cannot be doubted, but Heyerdahl's pet argument, namely, that Polynesia was colonized by prehistoric populations originating in South America, remains a hypothesis that has yet to be proven, despite the *Kon-Tiki*'s successful eight-thousand-kilometer crossing. And it so happens that the museum, created in principle to preserve and display the boat, in fact contributes to the glorification of Heyerdahl and to the implicit establishment of his theories. Visitors are invited to purchase not only *Kon-Tiki*, the book that contains the extremely picturesque tale of the expedition, but also Heyerdahl's very scholarly monograph, *American Indians in the Pacific: The Theory behind the Kon-Tiki Expedition* (1952). I can't help thinking of the serious objections it has raised, notably on the part of Robert Heine-Geldern and Joseph Haekel. But how could nonspecialists, who make up the immense majority of visitors, realize that it is, in any case, merely a matter of a simple hypothesis? When the "authorities" make up their minds in an academic controversy, one fears that in reality something else entirely is at stake, and in particular an "ideology."

We return to Oslo at the end of the afternoon and go see the paintings in the cathedral; very quickly, for the six o'clock service is about to begin. Then we set out for the Munch Museum, just recently opened (1963).

It is quite simply extraordinary. The building was specially built to preserve the thousand or so paintings and the some eighteen thousand watercolors, engravings, drawings, and sculptures by Edvard Munch. The artist died in 1944, but he had already been appreciated for at least fifty years. It was he who in 1898 did an ink-drawing portrait of Mallarmé. Only two hundred of his canvases are exhibited in the rooms, but they are sufficient to show to what point Munch was obsessed by death, sickness, and love. His paintings form a sort of spiritual autobiography. He lost his sister when he was five years old, and his mother a few years later. These two tragedies pursued him for the rest of his life. He was never able to forget those images of suffering and dying, and above all of physical death, of those forever inanimate bodies; whence his attraction for all that concerned the morphology and drama of death. He painted two versions of the death of Marat (*Marat' Dod*). Another obsession: self-portraits. I haven't counted them, but there must be more than twenty.

I promise myself to return here, for I would like to decipher the universe of these immense cosmogonic, mythological, and eschatological canvases that take up a complete wall of the museum, and which I discover at present with all the surprise and admiration of the neophyte. From time to time a surprise: for example, this portrait of Stanislav Przybyszewski (1897), one of the several personalities on whom I would really like to do some research. He was a friend of Strindberg during his Berlin days. They would meet at the famous Zum Schwarzen Ferkel tavern and would drink there until dawn, supposedly to be able to see the sun rise through the little colored windowpanes. Stanislav was obsessed by sex and death, and would also have liked to write, to be a "creator." He succeeded, I believe, in publishing a few pamphlets.

Our driver has taken courses in English literature at the university for several years and has traveled quite a bit, from Spain to Syria. He absolutely insists on showing us everything we would have seen this morning if, due to a mistake made by the hotel doorman, we had not missed our bus. Thus we cross the city once again and take the winding road that climbs through pine forests up to the top of the mountain where the best ski slopes, those that are used in international competitions, are found. We look at the slopes, as well as at the device used for ski jumping. A marker points out the place where the last record was set: ninety-seven meters.

Of course, each one of us takes advantage of the occasion to more or less briefly tell an anecdote. I, too, would like to tell the one I heard from Iurasco, our minister in Lisbon in 1941. It was a story of two lovers who, after twenty years of separation, found each other in a shelter for skiers on the outskirts of Oslo. But it is too beautiful to be told briefly, and I abandon the idea . . .

At sunset we go see the groups of statues in Frogner Park, the work of the sculptor Gustav Vigeland. I doubt there exists anywhere else anything like this. The park, immense, spreads out in terraces covered with flower beds surrounded by great trees. Upon entering at the main gate of Kirkeveien, one is struck by the genius of Vigeland's work, if only from witnessing these wrought-iron gates where a whole reptilian universe is teeming. But the more we proceed into the park, the more we admire the sculptor's audacity and imagination. We cross a bridge where 58 groups in bronze portray the different stages of the life of man. They are flanked by 4 other groups in granite representing reptiles. On the playground reserved for children 9 bronzes illustrate the progress of growth, from the foetus up to the first years of childhood. No other sculptor to my knowledge has verged so close on the limits of the grotesque, the pretentious, and the ridiculous, but without ever reaching them. There is also the fountain, whose central basin is surrounded by 60 bas-reliefs and 20 groups representing the entire cycle of life, from birth to old age and death. Around the fountain, a labyrinth of white and black rocks, and farther away, a seventeen-meter-high monolith, an enormous granite pillar where 121 human bodies are intertwined, twisted, superimposed, in a supreme effort to reach the top, the light . . . The impression is extraordinary. And it is further reinforced by the 36 groups of granite that surround the monolith and portray the trials, the anguish, the emotions, and the conflicts inherent in every human life. The spectacle is beyond comment. I must obtain a most complete catalogue of these groups and figures of a surprising variety of expressions. I lack the time to contemplate at leisure these sculptures of women, mothers, old people, the dying; but I notice, almost at the top, two patriarchs with flowing beards.

It is almost eight o'clock in the evening. The sun is setting, but the flowers still retain all their brilliance. We regretfully move away from the Wheel of Life, the last work we are able to look at, perhaps one of the most entrancing, and we leave the park by the left gate, under the trees in whose shade we again find the cool of the evening.

OSLO, *24 August*

We left Oslo this morning. The sky is not long in clearing. The torrent that flows on our left alongside the road suddenly reminds me of a landscape I once caught sight of in the Carpathians. But where? When? I search, I await my own answer and abandon myself to this delicious quietude that envelops me each time I penetrate into the labyrinth of my past. Perhaps I would have been able to identify that moment of the past experienced at the foot of the Carpathians if our guide hadn't alerted us that we would soon be within sight of the lake of Tryfjorden, one of the largest, and most abounding with fish, in Norway.

We all look at it. Then I notice that Zwi has closed his eyes and is trying to sleep a few moments, as he often does.

Last night, it was not without some emotion that I listened to him talk about the situation in Israel, that which we are all aware of. In that country where everything could disappear overnight, men do, however, live; they work, go about their business, raise children, and make plans as if nothing were the matter. But what else could they do? It is History that wills it so. At least the History of today.

Out of that a question came quite naturally to me, and it wasn't for the first time: Suppose that "History" were issued from the religious genius of Israel, at the same time as prophetism and messianism; mustn't we see, in the very existence of Israel—perpetually threatened— an example and a warning? It is indeed quite possible that Israel today foreshadows the fate that all nations and all states will share tomorrow. The lesson we can learn from Israel's example will perhaps help us to bear, in a more or less distant future, not only the "terror of history," but also that of the apocalypse that threatens us.

We pass by Hönefoss. The mountain road takes us to the banks of the lake of Sperillen. For a good twenty kilometers the road is bad and reminds each one of us of other landscapes, other regions, and even other times.

Numerous pine forests, and no less numerous paper factories, the only economic activity of this relatively poor region. The road continues its twisting climb. From time to time a summit upon which a tower stands out. This reminds me of Switzerland. A half hour later we begin to see houses and farms again built onto the sides of the hills.

It is one o'clock when we arrive at the Fagerness Hotel, a very recent establishment, immaculately clean and invaded by tourists. Lunch, then a stroll in the amazingly flower-covered park. Over on the edge of the lake a hydroplane hovers weakly in the sun, waiting to take flight.

We leave Fagerness at the beginning of the afternoon by the road that juts out over the edge of the lake. In the distance we can make out snow-covered mountains. After three-quarters of an hour's drive we stop at the foot of a giant waterfall. The spectacle is splendid. On the steep hillsides grow blue campanulas and wild pansies. I hear Zwi say under his breath, *"La pensée sauvage!"* and that immediately reminds me of Lévi-Strauss's stay in Chicago two years ago. Imagine his astonishment in realizing that no one, not even Ed. Leach (who nevertheless prided himself on his knowledge of French), had grasped the ambiguity of the term *la pensée sauvage*. In his very favorable review of Lévi-Strauss's book, he wondered whatever could be meant by the flowers that decorated the cover . . .

At the end of the afternoon we arrive in Nystova (Nistus Hot), where we will dine and spend the night. We are a bit disappointed. The hotel is situated between the lake and the road carved out of the side of the mountain. As a place to take a walk we have before us only a sort of vacant lot overrun by nettles. A few hundred meters from the hotel an edifice in ruins disappears under weeds. As I approach it I realize that it once served to grant hospitality—certainly gloomy, but benevolent, nonetheless (as there were enough tree trunks there for climbing)—to the giant bears that, now stuffed, stand guard in the entrance hall of the hotel.

I read these lines in an article in *Paris Match* of 15 August on the problems of tourism in France, and specifically in Lourdes: "Miracles, pilgrimages, and the Virgin, by ensuring a six-month season, guarantee profits for the hotel industry more reliably than any financial expert."

25 August

African sky, of a purity and an intense clarity, and without a cloud. One hour after our departure from Nistus Hot we stop at the threshold of the famous wooden church (*stavkirke*) of Borgund, built in 1150 in honor of Saint Andrew, and which was able to survive for centuries without serious damage or alterations. Only the ornamentation, the embroidered hangings, and the wooden statue of the saint have disappeared. Curious edifice! Viewing it from the outside, one would say that in constructing it they were content to pile up four or five roofs one on top of the other. But the whole is supported by pillars, or *staver,* which separate the central part of the nave from the aisles. This church is justifiably considered to be one of the masterpieces of construction in wood, one of the major accomplishments of Nordic civilization at the time when it was assimilating the international values introduced into Norway by Christianity. The contribution of the Vikings is considerable and is recognizable in these dragons that appear in the corners of the two superior roofs, in runic inscriptions, in vestiges of drawings that decorated the exterior walls, and which are not all of religious inspiration.

I walk away and get some distance to better contemplate this little wooden church whose legendary profile stands out on a background of boulders. This is how I wish to keep it in my memory, *just as I see it now.*

We change buses in Laerdalsöyri. A half hour later we are at the end of the journey, in Refsnes, at the very tip of the fjord where we are to embark. Our boat glides between two walls of mountains. Never have I seen bluer or more limpid waters. In about fifty years this is where one must come, to these fjords and these lakes of Norway, when one experiences the need to *listen to the silence.* One may foresee that these steep and rocky slopes will witness the construction of hotels and shelters, and that people will come here to forget, for a few days or weeks, the sonorous hell in which we are condemned to live. This is why already in Japan today splendid parks, with their miniature trees, rocks, and lakes, where noises and even mere speech have been banned, allow one to be isolated for a few hours to abandon oneself to contemplation, to regain consciousness of oneself, to rediscover oneself.

Little by little the fjord becomes wider. One hour after our departure our boat puts into port before continuing its route to Bergen. Another boat, smaller, which is to take us to Flam, calmly comes and attaches itself to our side, and some of the passengers change boats. Zwi, Joe, and I are among them, and if the sky were not so blue and so clear I would most certainly have asked Zwi why, in his opinion, no reference is made to the legend of vampires in all of Jewish literature. Is it because such a belief, so prevalent everywhere else, didn't exist among the Jews? Or must its absence from texts be explained by the censure that theologians, exegetes, and moralists would have imposed?

I could have asked him the question a bit later as we were approaching Flam if quite suddenly, after having remained alone for a while, I hadn't remembered a flood of details on the friendship that linked Munch, Strindberg, and Przybyszewski (the "Popovski" of *Inferno*). A moment later, I already regretted that my stay in Oslo had been so brief. I would like to return, if only for a few hours, to the Munch Museum to look at certain paintings again, above all *Jealousy* (which Strindberg had discussed at length in one of his articles at the time of its exhibition in Paris), but also *The Cry,* which is said to have prefigured expressionism.

But who can fathom the arcana of memory? Why, then, dazzled, fascinated by the richness, the diversity, and, in a word, by the enigma that comprises Munch's oeuvre, did I think of Strindberg yesterday only upon noticing the portrait of Przybyszewski, when I knew for a fact that Munch had done several portraits of Strindberg, and was also aware that at the time of their bohemianism in Berlin all three had been lovers of that eccentric and nymphomaniac Norwegian whom Przybyszewski would finally marry? It is only now that I remember, aside from the orgiastic amorality that left its mark on their age—an amorality that would only be found again in Europe in post–World War I Germany, and in present-day Scandinavia—the high regard in which Strindberg held his own pictorial production (hadn't he one day claimed to Munch that it was he, Strindberg, who was the greatest Scandinavian painter?), but also the dramatic and violent rupture, which reached odious and tragi-comic heights, that occurred between Strindberg and Przybyszewski. When Strindberg and Munch saw each other again in Paris a few years later, the so-called genius of painting was drowning himself in alcohol, for only alcohol, he said as an excuse, helped to protect him from the women who were all conspiring to harass him.

All these excesses, the orgies, obsessions, and crises that touched on madness form the backdrop of this terrible—and it is meant to be such—book that is *Inferno*. For a long time already it has been known that, more than an autobiography, *Inferno* is above all a work of a writer, containing facts and real personages that have been reinterpreted and recreated. But one may also see something else in it, namely, the evidence of an "initiation," whose scenario follows the well-known sequence: suffering, death-struggle, "death" and "resurrection." Writing this book was an absolute necessity for Strindberg, for it alone allowed him to ward off the madness into which he saw himself sinking. For him, madness was one of the weapons used by the "Forces" against their adversaries.

In addition, it was while writing *Inferno* that Strindberg again found the literary inspiration that had abandoned him for five or six years, not so much as a result of the disorganized and riotous life that he had led, but because of his "scientific" research and his firm belief that he had succeeded in creating "chemical" gold. He was even persuaded that the persecutions and the criminal attempts of which he believed himself to be the target originated in the resentment of the "Forces" faced with his success in chemical matters: His discovery of artificial gold threatened to ruin the world by reason of the financial collapse that could be expected from it . . .

The panorama of mountains becomes all the more vast as the fjord widens out. No trace of ruins on these precipitous peaks of rocky walls. Obvious and melancholy proof that in the Middle Ages these desolate and solitary regions did not attract a lot of people.

It is certainly not in such a place, where arms of the sea reach more than one hundred kilometers away from the coast, that I could rediscover the landscapes of *Séraphita*. This novel by Balzac would undoubtedly have never come to mind if Strindberg himself had not told in *Inferno* how the book had come into his hands "completely by chance," thereby allowing him to rediscover Swedenborg at a time in his life when he particularly needed him.

I have never managed to read a book by Swedenborg in its entirety, and I now believe I have guessed the reason for this: I was disappointed by the "naturalism" with which this great Swedish mystic and theosophist described supernatural beings and universes. Yet that is just what caused Strindberg's admiration, since he aspired to be recognized as "a Zola of occultism" and had nothing but scorn for all that wasn't concrete and "incarnate." In *Inferno* he declares on several occasions that "the spirits have become as positivist as the age in which we live," that they have ceased to manifest themselves in visions or ecstasies, and that they intervene directly in our daily lives. He claimed to have seen with his own eyes monsters, dragons, and even the Devil in person, but that he had never been frightened by this, since for him it was perfectly "natural." The fright, the terror, the fear of becoming mad—all the threats he felt, however, hanging over him—were due to the *enormous physical and political means* (that is, social, police, etc.) that the "Forces" were using against him.

What is most striking in Strindberg's alchemical, occultist, and "spiritualist" research and meditations is their deliberately materialistic character. If he saw in alchemy a "true chemistry," it is above all because, like the other occult sciences, it made it possible to demonstrate truth in the laboratory, or in the events of daily life. "Coincidences," unusual events, premonitions, etc., were "real" facts, just as for Swedenborg—but also for Strindberg—creatures of supernatural kingdoms were "real." In *Inferno* he tells how "Popovski," who had wanted to kill him in Berlin because he had once been his wife's lover, appeared in Paris, but in an occult fashion, while playing the piano in the vicinity, hidden by a curtain of foliage. Terror is provoked by concrete events, perfectly "normal" in appearance, but suspect, nevertheless. It is thus that in the Closerie des Lilas the Devil knocked over his glass of absinthe and appeared indirectly through a whole series of incidents, independent of each other, but whose accumulation was explained only by postulating a will and a finality. The "enemies," the "Forces," accompanied him everywhere he set foot—whether it was in Dieppe or in a little village in the south of Sweden. When he believed he had found a refuge, it was only to discover—in time!—those "electric machines" designed to kill him with their emanations. It would have been a perfect crime, for everything would have happened in the most "natural" of ways. He experiences an even greater terror when he realizes that he is always alone when this happens, and thus no one could suspect a thing . . .

We land in Flam and take the train for Myrdal. It will take us close to an hour to cover these twenty or so kilometers where valleys and waterfalls abound, to reach Myrdal, at an altitude of over seven hundred meters. This landscape reminds me of Switzerland, the country destined to serve as a reference for all other Alpine landscapes. Happily, it is still open to us to choose among the landscapes, to forget some of them, to mix them up together. We should rejoice all the more since that which is given to us to contemplate today will no longer exist tomorrow (or at least *not in the same way*), and since the image of it that some of us try to keep by capturing it on a roll of film will also be altered, so true it is that the beauties of nature also participate in the "epiphanic modality" that man has introduced into the cosmos.

In Myrdal we pace up and down the platform waiting for the train that is to take us to Voss. It is there, where we rediscover the tepidness of the plain, that we will take the Oslo-Bergen express, a line I have heard so much about because of the two hundred tunnels it has to pass through and the three hundred bridges it has to cross, the majority of which are on the route we are now taking.

We arrive in Bergen at sunset. What can I say about this city that wins you over even before you set foot in it? It doesn't resemble any city that I know, although it reminds me of a good number of other "Germanic" cities that have been able to conserve their charm and character despite concessions made to our industrial civilization.

Our bus lets the travelers off at the entrances of hotels where each has reserved a room. In front of the Hotel Bristol a young couple, very handsome, in rags and bare feet. The boy has the vacant, slightly off-center stare of the drug addict. Two girls stop to talk to him. All four are probably hippies from the United States. Two passersby come into view. The first undertakes to photograph them, the second to film them, and this lasts for a good two minutes. The faces of the four members of the group suddenly light up, as if their most secret wishes have been granted. Besides guitars, sex, Zen, etc. . . . to know one is being filmed counts as one of the most exciting narcotics.

We are the last to get out of the bus, ten minutes after the others, since our hotel is located outside the city. When we see it we are crushed. In a sort of vacant lot stands an enormous greyish building with nine hundred rooms. It is here, as we were later to learn, that students live during the year, the building being used in the summer to accommodate tourists. We leave and go back to the Hotel Norge, where Kitagawa and Zwi had gotten out. There is no room available, neither here nor in any other hotel in the city. We are directed to the tourist information office, where we have to wait on line behind ten or more people. We are offered, for this night only, a room in a private residence in the old city. For lack of anything better, we accept it. Our driver lets us off there a quarter of an hour later, after having looked for the name of the street for a long time. It was the last room available, and the least splendid. Other rooms in the same apartment are occupied by young American girls. It is nevertheless quite expensive, and the price doesn't even include breakfast, which in any case is not served. But according to the owner, we will be able to obtain anything we'd like at the "general store" nearby.

We go to have dinner at the Hotel Norge, where Zwi was lucky enough to obtain the "royal suite" for the night. It costs fifty dollars, but it is spacious enough to house, if necessary, a good portion of the members of our congress. All of a sudden, here we are again plunged straight into an atmosphere of scholarly society . . . It all began when Zwi, almost mechanically, claimed that today he who refuses to be a monotheist is, whether he wishes it or not, an atheist. There is no alternative, as could be the case in a civilization where polytheism is still in current practice. We argue about this for a full three hours. As usual, the position of Buddhism in this connection complicates the problem. To take up again at the time of a morphological study of religious spirit.

BERGEN, *26 August*

Last night I dreamt I was listening to an opera whose libretto was taken from *Forbidden Forest*. Flattered, but also somewhat annoyed, I wondered why no one had notified me before taking my novel and its characters for the subject of an opera.

We spent a bad night, but to our pleasant surprise, Alisa Werblowski telephones as soon as we get up to say she has found us a room at the Hotel Norge. We go across the city again by taxi. After lunch I leave alone to scour the bookstores for an entire hour, but I am unable to locate the few works on Nordic archeology that I would like to obtain.

The whims of memory are truly bizarre. As of 1934 I had begun to follow closely the publications of the Oslo Institute of Comparative Culture, from which I obtained the three volumes of the complete works of Moltke Moe, and this had inspired me to read the *Norwegian Tales* by Peter Asbjörnsen and Jörgen Moe. I have for the most part forgotten them, but I still remember certain details concerning Asbjörnsen's family. For example, I have never forgotten that his paternal grandmother led a very "daring" life for her time, and that his own mother, before sinking into madness, believed she saw spirits, fairies, and demons and gave her children accounts of her visions and supernatural adventures. On the other hand, aside from the fact that he was poor and of delicate health, I no longer remember anything about Asbjörnsen and his collaboration with Moe.

The city is literally invaded by tourists, American for the most part, and those who stand on line at the tourist office are most likely Americans, too. There are numerous hippies among them who, on the least occasion, lose no time in annoying, provoking, and offending us.

Curiously, this always makes me think of the "crisis" which Strindberg takes note of in *Inferno,* and which he analyzed to better exorcise it. This indomitable conflict between generations, to which the young appeal and which they proclaim, and which in their eyes justifies aggressiveness, the contestation of all institutions inherited from the past, of all dogmas, of all truths, and even of facts, and which above all justifies their orgiastic amoralism, the cruelty and nihilism of some of them, can't help but make me think of the atmosphere of *Inferno.* The reciprocal tortures that friends and lovers inflict on each other, the degradation through alcohol, sexuality, and excesses of all kinds, the surrender of self at the will of impulses issued from the darkest and most "demoniacal" zones of the mind (isn't Strindberg one of the precursors of automatic writing?); all of this perhaps prepares, and facilitates, the birth of a new spiritual era. Strindberg was strongly persuaded that the "experiences" of *Inferno* paved the way for a *vita nova.* For him, "the young generation was already there, waiting for something new," and in its yearning for another credo he saw a desire for communion with "invisible worlds." He even undertakes, towards the end of the book, to play the role of prophet: "Religion will return . . . but in other forms," and any compromise with the past (with the "*ancien régime,*" in his own words) is destined for failure.

As I've said above, *Inferno* is also a novel of an "initiation." When he undertook to *write a book* in which he would relate the trials that he had just undergone, Strindberg was not content simply to retranscribe into it notes and pages from his journal, so unauthentic and *inexpressive* did they seem to him. He had to make a choice, to reinterpret, even to invent, in such a way that *Inferno,* from a mere document, would be metamorphosed into a true work of art, infinitely more authentic and "truer" than if Strindberg had limited himself to the simple relating of facts. When he undertook literary creation, as when he worked in his laboratory, Strindberg meant above all to be an alchemist, not a chemist.

To better understand the evolution that led Strindberg from naturalism to what was called his "expressionism," it would undoubtedly be in one's interest to take the writer's "occultist" conceptions into consideration. Alchemy, too, is a chemistry, but "truer" than chemistry because it is not clouded by the prejudice and inhibitions of contemporary chemists. Likewise, occult phenomena, too, have some of the characteristics of Nature, and have, just like natural phenomena, their own laws. They are more spectacular, and consequently more obvious, more expressive, because they manifest *the essential,* and this in a direct, concise, almost laconic way. This is just exactly what Strindberg would later do in his plays and in his novels.

. . . But why do these young nihilists, so aggressive and provocative, obsess me so? What is the point of their deliberate slovenliness and their orgiastic exhibitionism? Are we dealing here, too, with "initiatory trials"? Would they be living, in their own way, another, even more demoniacal, *Inferno,* all the while expecting a *vita nova?* Many hippies, I know, are in search of a "new religion" and desperately endeavor to penetrate "invisible worlds." This is even the reason they offer for using and abusing drugs. I doubt, however, that these ridiculous, artificial, mechanical, ecstasies have very much to do with an authentic "initiation," not even with the one whose account we are given in *Inferno.*

PARIS, *29 August*

E.P. gives me excerpts to read from an "exemplary autobiography" which takes into account, he explains, the historical conditions that are the lot of his generation and which, therefore, doesn't contain a personal element at all. These pages are of the greatest interest to me, but they wrench my heart. The trials the country has endured have been atrocious! What is saddest is that, although it is over, the period of Stalinist terror still makes its effects felt. As E.P. writes: "The tragic paradox in which are caught up the individual as well as the nation, the man on the street as well as the leader, is that they see themselves forced to fight against the past (against Stalinism, apathy, underdevelopment, etc. . . .) using only means from the past." When you have lived for so long with "a total divorce between the spoken and the lived," you can no longer detect what is *true,* even if those in power indeed tell the truth, even if that truth no longer has to be whispered in greatest secret. When it was officially undertaken to unmask the true face of that famous "Soviet aid," when an end was put to this "divorce between words and reality," no one dared risk the slightest comment, no one dared show his satisfaction, so fearful was everyone of a trap. Whence the lack of enthusiasm in finally seeing the proclamation of this *truth* which for the twelve or fifteen preceding years had been banished from the language.

There are a number of other evocative reflections and observations in this manuscript which I will not attempt to sum up here. When the author has completed it, he must see that the book is published in the West, under a pseudonym, of course, and that copies are clandestinely dispatched to Rumania.

I dreamt last night that I was in a post office. At the counter in front of me a woman wishes to buy a recently issued series of nine Rumanian stamps. But she insists on verifying that the series she has been given is complete, and asks if they've indeed given her the stamp bearing the head of Maitreyi. "Of course," is the answer, "it's the third in the series." I think I understand that the theme of this new issue is the characters of famous novels.

1 September

I read *La Sal de los Cerros* by Stefano Varese with much interest. Chapter 3 especially ("El Siglo de la Rebelión") is particularly captivating. I learn a lot from it about Juan Santos Atahualpa, that "Messiah of God" who gave the signal for revolt and battled victoriously in favor of political and economic autonomy for the Campo natives during the second half of the eighteenth century. I recognize there the syndrome characteristic of "indigenous" messianic movements. But what is most surprising is that the movement, once unleashed, did not collapse in on itself, and that the believers did not go through those phases of total discouragement, devastating rage, or apathy which have been noted only too often elsewhere. For ten whole years the natives lived in almost total independence. It was only then that Franciscan missionaries began to risk going into the zone of the rebellion. Juan Santos was no longer there. He had died perhaps eight or ten years after the beginning of the insurrection, but for the natives, he had simply "vanished into thin air" . . .

I must point out, too, even though it might wound the pride of the conquerors, the legend that was born concerning the origin of "White People": They were not created, like the natives, at the beginning of time by the god Oriatziri, concurrently with the animal species that had been created out of men "who had sinned." The whites, on the contrary, are the issue of the waters and darkness of the bowels of the earth, similar in that to the dragon Nonki in whom originate evil, sickness, and death.

In fact this myth tells of the extermination of the aborigines by the whites, with the exception of the primordial shaman. Salvation would come, however, thanks to the heroism and wisdom of the shamans. The "knowledge" acquired by the shamans through smoking and meditation would finally triumph, the world would be purified and regenerated, and the whites would discover themselves driven back into original chaos.

2 September

When I feel weary and lethargic I experience the need to immerse myself in the *Essays* of Unamuno. It is with the same delight that I have just reread the excerpts from his correspondence published at the beginning of volume 2 of *Unamuno en sus Cartas: Antologia epistolar.* They are filled with notes and commentaries concerning what he's read—and God knows that was varied!—his projected books, his discussions with friends, whether in a cafe, at the university, or through letters. I find this book fascinating, to such a degree that I immediately write to Spain to order other volumes of Unamuno's correspondence, assuming that more has been published.

I then immerse myself in *The Agony of Christianity,* only for the pleasure of savoring again the intelligence with which Unamuno knew how to integrate into his work everything he read, all the texts that he came across. This is why in *Agony* he doesn't hesitate to refer to the voluminous *Enquête sur la monarchie* by Maurras, to the three volumes by Houtin on *Le Père Hyacinthe,* and to texts by Leon Chestov, Valéry, and by many others still which had only a small, or no, connection to *The Agony of Christianity.* But Unamuno knew marvelously how to integrate them into the debate, how to comment on them, even how to sum them up, and this is notably the case with *Père Hyacinthe.* Whence the impression of continual improvisation, of conversation in fits and starts in a library, which gives Unamuno's essays a profound unity of style. Moreover, everywhere in his works, one must expect him to cite *Don Quixote,* Oberman, Saint Thérèse, Kierkegaard, etc. . . . And even when he is dealing with a specific subject, one can be sure that he will allude to what he is reading at the time, whoever the authors may be, past or present, even if the book is only lying around on his desk.

23 September

This afternoon, in the Café de Cluny, I had a long conversation alone with Tsepeneag. The news he brings from the country is depressing. Everything is blocked. Every attempt at "revolt" has as much effect "as a punch into an eiderdown." He resigns himself to remaining in Paris, where he will work on a thesis, with Barthes perhaps, on "the hallucinatory state in French literature." I ask him to tell me about the young generation of writers. Some of them show great talent, but as soon as they are taken in by the Party, they find themselves reduced to impotence. He cites some examples.

24 September

We were speaking recently among friends about success, publicity, and the infatuation from which "superstitions," "miracles," and all "inexplicable facts" are currently benefitting. I claimed that in my opinion one mustn't trust appearances, that no publicity uproar accompanies authentically mysterious or inexplicable cases, and that modern man is interested much more in politics, for example, than in the supernatural. Indeed, who has heard of José Pedro de Freitas, a Brazilian peasant who, between 1950 and 1964, undertook several hundred surgical interventions, some of which were extremely difficult, while using only that which he had on hand: scissors, spools, penknives, knives, without sterilizing them, and without causing the slightest trauma, the slightest infection or hemorrhage. I learned this completely by chance while reading an article in the encyclopedia *Man, Myth, and Magic* (no. 8).

Pedro de Freitas was observed, followed, photographed, and even filmed in the course of his operations by numerous Brazilian physicians, all of whom testified on his behalf at the time of his trial. For of course Pedro was arrested, tried in 1964, and sentenced to sixteen months in prison for being a "bonesetter." It appears that in the Brazilian penal code "spiritual healing" is ranked as a misdemeanor. But what is strangest resides in the very origin of his medico-surgical abilities. Pedro claimed to be possessed by the spirit of a German physician, a certain Dr. Fritz. When that happened, he spoke Portuguese with a strong German accent and carried out his surgical interventions in a state of trance: He approached the patient and, using a penknife or scissors, without any hesitation and like an automaton, incised the abdomen, removed a cyst or a cancerous tumor. Even more surprising, as is witnessed in films and photographs, he was able to cut out, without preliminary anesthesia, a sort of excrescence that had formed under the eyelid of a patient. One day the film of one of his operations was shown to Pedro, and when he saw himself on the screen, he fainted.

To the extent that I can judge it, his case is truly exceptional. Pedro was followed and observed by physicians for fifteen years; no other healer to date has been the object of such credible documentation. And despite that, who has ever heard of Pedro and of his mysterious "Dr. Fritz," who not only held his hand while he operated, but in addition—and above all—warded off all risk of infection or hemorrhage?

27 September

The *cultural* importance of Greek myths (Oedipus, Prometheus, Pandora, Ulysses, etc. . . .) is to reveal to us the condition of Western man, and to prepare us to better grasp the meaning of tragedy, philosophy, and even Christianity (through speculations on the human condition, for example).

To compare with the function of myth in archaic and traditional cultures. It serves as *exemplary model* for the behavior, the condition, and the deeds of everyone.

5 October

Correspondence is perhaps the most unreliable, possibly the most misleading, source of information that one can have on a writer! In my case, for example, it happens that almost all the letters of my youth have disappeared, and there remains almost nothing of the correspondence—very abundant, however—that I wrote when I was in India. I am well aware that the letters most worthy of interest, those that I sent to my friends at the time, must have been destroyed. My letters to Buonaiuti, where I informed him of my religious "crises," have probably met the same fate.

If it happened that certain of the letters I wrote as a lycéen or a university student, or even some of those dating from my stay in India, were later to be found, what "documentary value" should be attributed to them? To what extent could it be claimed that they express "what was most meaningful and most important" during the years of my intellectual development, when obviously the letters in which I spoke of what seemed essential to me at the time have disappeared? What value, what interest, should be attributed to a random postcard, written hastily during a brief stay I made in a port in Italy or a city in India, intended for a school or university chum?

October

Abraham couldn't grasp the meaning of the sacrifice of Isaac. To all appearances, it was an infanticide, and yet Abraham knew that Yahweh couldn't ask him to commit such an act. The "sacrality" of the sacrifice of Isaac was camouflaged, not in a "profane" gesture, but in its "absolute negative": a crime. To compare with the current situation: In our time religious experience has ceased to be recognized as such, for it is camouflaged in its opposite—nonspirituality, antireligion, opaqueness, etc. . . .

How I admire X. . . . for the instinct he displays! He has a unique talent which allows him to discover before all others the books that will be talked about tomorrow, and the yet too little known authors who are destined for imminent glory! He uncovers them, cites them, showers them with praise. In 1945–1946 it was Jean-Paul Sartre and Camus; in 1960–1961, Roland Barthes; just recently it is Claude Lévi-Strauss and structuralism. He is always up to date, and his intellectual prowess is constantly renewed. Moreover, he doesn't fail to align his tastes and opinions to it.

This faith in man and in his "interior reality" that Hegel proclaims sometimes has overtones that make it border on cruelty. At one time Cato was admired for having given himself up to death and for having refused to survive the ruin of the Roman republic. Hegel criticizes him, however, "for not having known how to raise his interior reality above the very grandeur of Rome" (*Enzyklopädie*, § 406).

McLuhan's definition of the specialist: "A man who never makes little mistakes, all the while hurrying towards the biggest."

CHICAGO, *14 November*

Eric and I come to talk about Genoa and its history. The Genoese were disagreeably surprised to find that *Christopher Columbus had been right,* for they had refused to pay attention to his "theories." Commercial routes to the Orient were henceforth never the same, and all of a sudden the Genoese cartels lost their importance. It was the beginning of Genoa's decadence as a maritime, commercial, and political power. But it was also the beginning, as Wilhelm Suida showed in 1906, of *its greatest period of artistic glory*. Indeed, the golden age of Genoa (*Blütezeit*) began just after the city had begun declining as a maritime power, and it reached its height during the seventeenth and eighteenth centuries, when Genoa became a *"città d'arte."*

17 November

I see one of my students, A.F., who participated in a seminar on myth last year. At that time she came across as so timid that she couldn't read a line of her work without raising her eyes to seek my approval . . . It was she, however, who several months later with three of her female friends caused such a stir in the hallways during a meeting of the university administration that they finally had to see her to allow her to air her grievances: The women students were asking for more rights for women, demanding that one-half of the faculty be women, in conformity with their percentage in the population, etc. . . .

But today she has come to ask my advice concerning the term paper she must write, an analysis of "Master and Man," the short story by Tolstoy. Some of her ideas are truly surprising, this for example: The master who takes the servant in his arms to protect him from the cold and dies in the snow at his side would symbolize the Russian aristocracy that, knowing it was condemned by history, would sacrifice itself to save the peasantry . . .

6 December

I'm working on "Spirit, Light, and Seed," a study that is to be part of volume 11 of *History of Religions*. Later a French edition will have to be undertaken, without notes (or the least number possible), for the subject is truly fascinating. The equivalence *"spirit–light–semen virile,"* in India as in Tibet or in Iran, which was taken up again by the "lewd Gnostics," is also discovered among the Desanas, an Amazonian tribe. What strikes me most is the surprising creativity of this homology: Its formulations are not repeated; they are "open."

NEW YORK, *2 January 1971*

K.T. cited the case of a young girl whose vocabulary is limited to twenty-six words. Her inhibition is due to family-related problems: an unwanted child, parental discord, etc. . . . This reminds me of another case, the one of the child that Dr. Dolto Marette had treated. The child's parents had been arrested right in front of him and sent to Buchenwald, where they were to die. From the day the Gestapo descended upon his family's home (the child was then three or four years old) he had not uttered a word. Having become mute, he spent his days drawing strange, extraordinarily tortuous and complicated laby-rinths. I then explained to her the symbolism of the labyrinth (zone of invulnerability, refuge against demons and the dead, but also against flesh-and-blood enemies), and Dr. Dolto Marette told me later that she was indebted to me for having been able to penetrate the secret drama of the little orphan. Ultimately the child was able to regain his speech.

NEW YORK, *3 January*

In Sykes's book I read page 91: "Webern jumped when somebody dropped a fork at the next table. His sensitivity seems fantastic, but someday we'll all be as sensitive to sounds as he was." Will this really happen? In this respect I, myself, am a highly sensitive person. A glass that falls, a motorcycle that starts up suddenly behind me, are enough to give me palpitations. I nevertheless do not feel in the least particularly proud of this. Indeed, I deplore it and see it rather as an infirmity.

NEW YORK, *4 January*

I've discovered in Lisette's bookcase the book by Em. Ciomac on Enesco. The chapter devoted to the friendship that developed between Enesco and Maruca, his future wife, is fascinating. It is really a shame that their correspondence was burned in 1918! I remember my first encounters with the great, already declining virtuoso and Maruca in 1946–1947. I must put all that down in writing while there is still time to do so.

CHICAGO, *10 January*

One of my students, J.B., a pretty brunette, probably rather rich, had asked me last autumn for a bibliography on witchcraft, for the sole purpose, she said, of understanding the experience she had lived through during her summer vacation. The day before yesterday she turned in the text of her term paper for the course on initiation, which was entitled, "Admission into a Coven: A Personal Experience." The experience in question took place on Formentera, one of the Balearic Islands off the shore of Valencia, during the summer of 1970. One day after she had smoked "a large amount of hashish" with her friend, they both went around midnight to a party organized by a group of young Americans right in the middle of a forest a few kilometers from where they were staying. They had to wander for a long time in the dark before they finally saw lights and heard music. There were around twenty young men and a few girls there, all high on drugs. They proceeded to join in, but since they had already smoked quite a lot of hashish, the amount of LSD they took had an explosive effect on them. All my student remembers is having been in the presence of a tall man with red hair, nude from the waist up. He seemed at times to be thirty-five, and at others seventy, years old, and he was the center of general attention. My student, whose recollections were rather unclear, remembered only a few songs, dances, and kisses, too. The man led her away and made love to her. She came to imagine that this gathering of hippies was in reality a ceremony uniting sorcerers and witches, and that she had been the object of a "ritual sacrifice." Indeed, she sees herself again completely undressed and surrounded by unknown people. She no longer knows whether they wore masks or not.

The day after her escapade she learned that the island of Formentera was considered both in Valencia and elsewhere to be "a center of initiation into magic."

My poor student had taken my course on initiation only in an attempt to understand what had really happened to her. I sometimes noticed her in the classroom half asleep, or rather sleeping off the effects of drugs. Whenever she spoke it was with difficulty, and most often in a thick voice, without being able to make herself understood. When she wasn't under the influence of drugs, her intelligence proved very sharp and even original. Unfortunately, she has become incurable. At least, this is what I've been told by certain specialists who claim that drugs finally got the better of her. This young woman, barely twenty-one years old, didn't want for anything, and didn't even have to earn the money necessary for her annual trip to Europe. It is perhaps just that that caused her downfall.

4 February

The saints themselves can sometimes prove to be cowardly, or more precisely, unjust, towards those they consider to be "heretics." It was in vain that the Manichaean Fortunatus appealed to Saint Augustine's testimony, begging him to disprove the charges that had been brought against him: "You who have been one of us, you must know that we do none of the things we are accused of." But Saint Augustine shunned his request in uneasy and difficult terms which in addition contained malevolent insinuations: "I was but an auditor; I don't know what you others, the elected, can do when you are together" (*Disp. I contra Fortunatum* 1–3. Text cited by Simone Pétrement in *Le dualisme chez Platon, les gnostiques et les manichéens,* p. 297). What is most serious in my opinion is that Saint Augustine was effectively to add credence to the infamous slander aimed at the Manichaeans, and all other "heretics" along with them.

His conviction was reversed, even though he knew perfectly well with whom he was dealing, and had even expressed admiration for the frugality and the asceticism of the Manichaeans.

6 February

To what can the destiny of a people or a state be owed! From the ninth century B.C. barbarian nomadic tribes of Central Asia multiplied their incursions into Chinese territory, and because they were bowmen on horseback, they almost always had the advantage. Nevertheless, the Chinese refused to adopt the combat practices of their adversaries. Indeed, they would have then had to put on the short tunic of the horseman and abandon their long robes, which for the Chinese were synonymous with social status. Resorting sometimes to persuasion, sometimes to coercion, their king finally succeeded in forming an armed cavalry corps, and border defense could from then on be undertaken in an efficient way.

ALBION, *5 March*

We arrived in Albion the day before yesterday, and it was Jay Kim, one of my former students who had taken charge of lectures in the history of religions at Albion College, who drove us. I had been invited to be a "resident" there until June, and I immediately accepted, given the small number of obligations I would have: three lectures, and a few debates with students or professors.

We're staying in a huge and comfortable house on the outskirts of the city. On the other side of the road, right across from us, are train tracks where each day a few rare freight trains pass by, and one lone passenger train—only two or three cars—for Chicago.

ALBION, *7 March*

If I were only fifteen or twenty years younger I would write the history of Western culture from the perspective of the history of religions. I would discuss Orphism in it, for example, about which our knowledge is very rudimentary, given the scarcity of truly trustworthy documents dealing with its initial blossoming in the seventh and sixth centuries B.C. It has, however, incited a whole mythology among scholars and theosophists, and has thus had a profound impact on the European consciousness and imagination, first in the Hellenistic period, then at the beginning of the Renaissance, next in the Age of Enlightenment, not to mention German romanticism. It still makes its presence known today in poetic creations, but equally elsewhere, as well.

During the night of March 8–9, prostrated by a severe attack of
pericarditis, I was taken to the hospital emergency room. My
hospital stay continued until the beginning of April. Since then I have
only been able to keep up my journal intermittently, writing notes
haphazardly in my datebook, in notebooks, or even on scraps of
paper. In the pages that follow I believed it useless to transcribe those
scattered notes, such as they are. The dates are only approximate
and I most often limited myself to indicating only the current month
and year.

10 May

A summer-like day. I receive two copies of *Noaptea de Sânziene*
[*The Forbidden Forest*]. The book appears to be superbly printed. I
write immediately to Ion Cuşa, to thank him. (I don't dare to imagine
how much money this "adventure" will cost him. But, as he confessed
to me last year, he wants to link the name of his publishing house to the
Rumanian novel, written in exile, which he likes the most.)

After a while, a great sadness comes over me. I say to myself: I
should have dedicated *Noaptea de Sânziene* to Christinel. It is my most
significant literary work. I wrote it after 9 January 1949; I wrote it with
her beside me. And yet . . . How can I dedicate to her only a *part* of my
creation? All I've done since our marriage is, in a way, *her* "work,"
because she has kept me alive, she has confirmed my faith in my power
to *carry on.* Only, the first volume of my magnum opus would declare,
to all, this fact (which a great many of our friends suspect anyhow).[1]

ALBION, *20 May*

From five to seven o'clock, visit from Mary Stevenson. I thus
have the opportunity to meet this enthusiastic reader, who learned
Rumanian only to be able to read my literary writings in their original
editions. For two years I received a quantity of letters and poems from
her. She is around fifty years old, with a very open expression, and her
smile alone is enough to light up her face. She lives in Salem, North
Carolina.

1. This entry was translated from the Rumanian by Mac L. Ricketts—ED.

She decided to come see me following a dream: Having written to the university to request admission as an auditor into my autumn-quarter courses, she was told that I was still recuperating from a heart attack and that it wasn't certain that I would be able to take on my courses in the autumn. The following night she dreamt she had been in Chicago since the day before, and that she had immediately gone to the university. She was already familiar with the buildings there, having visited them a few years earlier. In her dream, everything had plunged into darkness. The buildings seemed empty, abandoned, in ruins. Weeds grew in the pathways . . . Upon awakening she decided to come meet me, no matter what. Of course, she refrained from telling me that she was afraid of no longer finding me alive. But she was so eager to meet with me . . .

Upon arriving at our place she gave Christinel a whole armful of lilacs that she had gathered on the way over.

CHICAGO, *6 July*

We've been back now for several days. Since I am still not well enough to begin working again, at least not seriously, I reread the first notebooks of my Parisian journal (1945–1950) and mark the passages that Christinel is to type. For now they aren't numerous, for I constantly ask myself how interesting they would be to a foreign reader. Basically, it is only the journal of an Eastern European intellectual, and those in the West most fortunately do not have any experience of exile.

11 July

Only geniuses and great innovators are capable of revealing to us the mechanism of scientific thought. I have reflected a lot on what Einstein declared one day to Heisenberg during a conversation: "It is the theory that decides what we must observe." Or, as I was being told one day by the mathematician Bellman in Santa Barbara, "I don't know anything more practical than a good theory!"

16 July

I will never forget Jung's indignation, nor his face, white with anger, when he told me one day, speaking of Freud: "and to think that he didn't even know Greek!"

19 July

"The world will be saved—if it can be—only by the *unsubmissive*. Without them it would be all up with our civilization, our culture . . ." (Gide, *Journal,* from a letter to Bernard Enginger, February 1946).

Happy Gide, who imagined at the time that the "unsubmissive" could get the better of the totalitarian state and its police! And despite everything, it is he who was right, for I don't see any other solution.

21 July

Nicolas Iorga would say: "Where one works, one must also sweep up. There are those whose profession is but that." To put forward in any great work.

1 August

I imagine that at least once or twice in life we have all experienced belated remorse. Why did I suddenly remember today that play I saw in London in May or June 1940 to which Vardala had invited me? We were seated in the first row of the orchestra stalls. The play seemed deplorable to me (I was exaggerating in thinking this, for it was at most only a propaganda piece). I thus pretended to be asleep, and through my half-closed eyelids I observed the reaction of the actors. They seemed fascinated by my presence and kept glancing at me anxiously. As the play had just recently opened, seeing a member of the audience asleep in the first row boded ill for the success of the play. Victim of the most acute anxiety, the leading lady kept watching me in between each of her lines, and her performance suffered from it. I was cruel enough not to open my eyes again before the curtain came down. I then stood up quickly and left the theater.

No date

Virginia Woolf states in her journal that she felt in no way enthusiastic while reading *Ulysses* (*Diary of a Writer,* p. 46). An embarrassing detail for certain histories of the contemporary novel.

What to think of that actor from Athens who, in his epitaph, asked his former colleagues to shout his name out loud and to applaud him in chorus each time they passed in front of his grave, "to give him pleasure," as the audiences that had applauded him did while he was alive? Simple vanity, or doubts about a purely "spiritual" immortality? (It is true that the inscription dates from the second century A.D.)

Admirable Lord Acton! And how well he had grasped the meaning of German romanticism! The romantics, he writes, and especially historians, were truly fascinated by "spontaneous phenomena." It was the romantics who drew attention to the value of mythology, language, folklore, and popular poetry. It is to romanticism, adds Lord Acton, that the Germans owe their interest in all that was "distant," in Oriental languages, for example, but also in the archaic literature of their own people (*Edda,* etc. . . .).

These reflections by Lord Acton made me think of Hasdeu, and of his conception of history. When in 1936 I had the opportunity to publish certain literary and historical writings by this great, unrecognized author, I made every effort to bring to light his passion for "beginnings," for "origins," and thus for all that was *primordial,* which is typical of romantic historiography. Certain critics argued that this conception, obviously out of date, was mine, as well, and that I was trying to promote it in the place of contemporary methodology. I later realized just how dangerous it was to display sympathy for, or even some understanding of, an exotic cultural phenomenon, especially if it is of a religious nature. There is always someone to claim that you are defending it and setting it up as an example, which proves that you are basically only an "obscurantist" and a retrograde.

20 August

A handsome young man with long hair and the beginnings of a beard passes in front of the bookstore on Fifty-seventh Street. His blue jeans have a large tear at the knees. Other young people who had stopped in front of the shop window seem fascinated and overcome with admiration upon seeing him pass. Those rips have positively flabbergasted them. I observe them a moment. I think they must have discussed the situation for a long time and wondered where indeed the handsome young man could have obtained a pair of jeans so artistically torn . . .

September

Pastoral poetry (the *Georgics,* the *Eclogues,* and above all their subsequent imitations), however impregnated it may be with the yearning for a simple, country life devoid of artifice, does not necessarily imply a propensity for a love of the past, nor a desire to escape from the present, nor even a return to primitive conditions existing before "civilization." This poetic genre tries in fact to calm the reader, to make him "cultivate happiness." The atmosphere that comes out of these bucolic and paradisiacal pages can only purify and humanize him, and therefore the reader of pastoral poetry will feel less inclined towards violence and aggression. In this imaginary universe man ceases to be a wolf to man, so claimed Zarathustra, and after him Plautus, Bacon, and Hobbes.

October

I would like to be able to do some research on that German historian from the first half of the nineteenth century whom Lord Acton admired so much. After having recalled that he had known the majority of German authors, from friends of Niebuhr to Harnack and Stieve, the intellectual leaders of the young generation, Lord Acton adds: "At eight universities I have never met another man whose conversation was as enthralling." One could ask him about anything, from Philo of Alexandria to the Empress Marie-Thérèse. "He had read more than Böhmer!" Lord Acton exclaims. He had "an eye for doctrines, for institutions, for politics, for literature, for police.[1] In grasp and vivid perception of past ages, he was, I think, beyond any other man." No historical document eluded his insight, and he knew as no one else how to clarify both its content and its significance. Like a Talmudist he found multiple levels of interpretation within the same text, and when one of

1. *Police* in the older sense of civil administration, public order.—ED.

them was submitted to his scrutiny "it grew in his hands like a seed in those of an Egyptian magus."

The man capable of such wonders was named Gförer. I have not seen his name cited anywhere else.

Strangely enough, Lord Acton was uncommonly attracted to documents forged from any source. "Falsification," he writes, "is a very widespread vice, found just as often among Christians as among those who pride themselves in being free spirits." And he adds, "At the origin of all societies one almost always finds falsified documents."

In this connection how can we not mention the importance accorded to letters and apocryphal texts throughout the history of Christian ideas and mythologies: the letter of "Prester John," for example, or the *Fama Fraternitatis* of which the Rosicrucians took advantage, etc. . . . But the practice is much more ancient, and from the Alexandrian period apocalypses and revelations of all sorts (mystical, alchemical, Gnostic texts) were allegedly "discovered" in temples, caves, and tombs, just like the Tantric texts in India and Tibet. This is a subject which would make a fascinating study, and which should be thoroughly analyzed.

Lord Acton's observations lead me to think of the frauds committed by mediums, spiritists, and other proponents of parapsychology. What is quite curious is that they are most often committed—unconsciously, perhaps—by persons endowed with a real capacity for paranormal phenomena.

November

What memories do I have of the three weeks I spent in the hospital in Albion? F.F. asks me. And I answer: the memory of the third-class train car which, at the end of 1928, was taking me from Madras to Calcutta.

I regret not having been able to note down, or having done so only in fragments, all the strange images that came back to me at the time. I actually *saw once again* the faces, landscapes, and little train stations flashing by which I believed had been long forgotten. I had already forgotten all that when I arrived in Calcutta and moved into Mrs. Perris's boarding house at 82 Ripon Street.

"And what else?" F.F. asks me.

I see the emergency room where I was first taken, then the very large room where I was later put, and its wall made entirely of windows. I see the snow that was falling outside, right in the middle of March, to the great dread of the birds and squirrels in the garden. I remember Marduk, Kim's dog, and its look of surprise on the other side of the window. And I still have in my ears the soothing music that was playing through the hospital intercom system.

"There must have been many other things," F.F. insists. "Thoughts, 'visions,' much more meaningful incidents which you have forgotten."

I did not want to talk about my pericarditis attack of the night of March 8–9. It was as if my heart was gripped in a vise. Or yet, I had the impression that a locomotive was crashing right into my chest. Never before had I suffered so atrociously. Yet not once did I imagine that this attack could be fatal. I remembered what Dr. Roger Godel had told me one day, namely that the heart is a very resilient organ, and at the time of an attack "one must learn to win it over," to visualize it in a way, just as I had learned to do in India, to converse with it, and to speak to it with "deference." After an hour my suffering was already more bearable. The next morning, when Dr. C. came to see me and had given me an injection, he appeared surprised at my resistance and was astonished that I was able to hold on for so long without calling for him. Quite obviously, I was careful not to tell him about my attempts at "visualizing" my own heart, or about the dialogue I had then tried to establish . . .

This troubling passage, by Montaigne it would seem: "The public good requires us to betray, to lie, and to massacre."

I would really like to know its context, but everyone I've asked has told me to consult a "specialist."

It is heartbreaking to notice the extent to which Western intellectuals appear so neurotic! They want to discover at all costs the "hidden causes''—that is, of a political, economic, or social nature, etc.—of each of the undertakings or creations unique to Western civilization. It is thus not just Orientalism that is "demystified"! Listening to them, their interest is not due to a sincere desire to know the history and the culture of that Orient whence developed Mediterranean civilizations, but is explained more prosaically by the aims of military conquest and economic exploitation. Orientalism would thus have served as a springboard for imperialism. Young people were encouraged to study Sanskrit, hieroglyphics, or cuneiform writing only in order to better serve the interests of British, German, or French colonialism . . .

The most superficial inquiry into the prestige that glorified "the Sages of the Orient''—and this from the sixth century B.C. until the end of antiquity—would suffice to show the inanity of such a "demystification" that is as summary as it is limited. But how sad it is to note this morbid need to denigrate everything, to suspect everything, and this retreat of the soul before what is most spontaneous in all cultural creations, as in all spiritual activity.

December

I think again of that famous scene that has inspired so many conversations, paintings, and reflections: Aeneas carrying his father, Anchises, on his back, fleeing a Troy that has been overcome by flames. After multiple escapades, after having had many adventures both on land and on sea, he became the (legendary) ancestor of the Romans. From the disaster in which an entire population was destroyed, and which put an end to a singularly brilliant historical period, a hero—and he alone—nevertheless succeeded in escaping. It is to his descendants, however, that Rome owes its birth. This is quite obviously a legend forged by mythologists, encouraged by politicians, and reinterpreted by poets.

It happens, however, that the legend of Aeneas has a touching counterpart in a historical event: When Titus's legions laid siege to Jerusalem, a siege that would terminate in the burning and destruction of the Holy City, a few young men, who were carrying a casket on their shoulders, asked the guards for permission to leave the city so they could bury the dead man in the cemetery. But the casket contained the very live body of Rabbi Jochanan ben Zachaï, and the young men were his disciples. Thus the life of the most prestigious thinker and religious leader of the time was saved, even though he had opposed with all his strength the fanatics who had given the signal for the uprising against the Roman authorities. Sometime later Rabbi Jochanan received permission from Titus to open *a school for children* in Yavne, near Jaffa. And it was there, in that modest school, that the spiritual values of Judaism were saved, a Judaism that had, however, been defeated on the national and political levels, and which was very close to disappearing forever.

It has been said that the true scholar (a philosopher or a historian) is he who learns from his teachers, his colleagues, and his students alike.

I will go even further and claim that one recognizes a true genius by the extent to which he brings forth in his disciples talents that are at least as great as his own.

One of my favorite students, J.O., asked me today if there were a method for learning Sanskrit "rapidly." I answered that the only method I knew of consisted of sitting down at one's desk in the morning, immersing oneself for twelve or sixteen hours straight in the study of Sanskrit to the exclusion of all other subjects, and not stopping except to take therapeutic walks in the morning and evening. After four or five months of this routine one may allow oneself to do something else on the side, although it is preferable to read nothing that isn't related to Indian history or civilization. I added that I myself had to go through this during the first year of my stay in Calcutta. I felt all the more melancholy in saying so since for some time I've felt not a little detached from what was once the passion of my youth.

"But it's different for you!" J.O. exclaimed.

"It has nothing to do with me, and I am far from being the only one to follow this regimen! Look at Angelo de Gubernatis, for example, that Italian scholar and Indianist who has been quite forgotten today. Read

Fibra, the book in which he writes his memoirs, and you will see that he learned Sanskrit in only one summer, but by closing himself up in his room in the suburbs of Berlin. He only went out to buy himself something to eat . . ."

24 December

I wonder how many priests have had the courage to cite this phrase by Angelus Silesius in their Christmas sermon: "Had Christ a thousand times / Been born in Bethlehem / But not in thee, thy sin / Would still thy soul condemn" (*The Cherubic Wanderer* 1.61).

Mystics have really had no luck. In the past churches, and above all the Roman Catholic church, suspected them of heresy or accused them of excessive emotivity. According to Anglo-American theologians of today, mystics have become, to employ the term they use, "irrelevant." For today the only problem churches have to worry about is, of course, the "social problem."

3 January 1972

Departure from New York in horrible weather. In Chicago the lake is frozen. I spend a day going through the mail that has accumulated during our absence: letters, books, and various journals. Each time I open a package and come across a book that seems interesting, my emotion is so strong that I can't help laughing at it. When will I ever find the time to read even half of the "interesting" books I receive? But I know, too, that I will never lose this passion that dates from my adolescence—or if I do, only on my deathbed.

January

American students (but also men of science) are truly bizarre. L. . . . , who was talented enough to assimilate Chinese, doesn't dare learn German. Another scholar, a specialist in Kwakiutl languages, sees in French "one of the most arduous of languages" and thinks that Latin, for all those who don't have "the genius for languages," is "inaccessible."

The resistance with which traditional theories oppose the victorious offensive of the scientific mind is truly surprising. It is thus that Van Helmont energetically refutes the concept of man-microcosm. Which doesn't prevent him from seeing in illnesses a phenomenon comparable to the formation of metals in the depths of the earth; in other words, in the heart of our Mother Earth.

Without knowing why, without the slightest apparent reason, a brief passage from *L'Education sentimentale* pursues me to the point of obsession: "It concerned the Tunisian ambassadors and what they wore." Lord knows what enigmas or repressed desires a psychoanalyst would find in this . . .

It is quite possible that it is primarily to royalty that we are indebted for the passage from *myth* to *history*. I see proof of this in the chronicles of Tibetan dynasties. Rulers are presented in them in chronological order, but in accordance with their image-model: Each one of them is placed in a well-known framework, both mythical and cosmological. However, in time information of a historical nature begins to appear. For example, such and such a king had bridges built; another showed lands that had previously been considered infertile to be of value; a third established systems of weights and measures, etc, etc. (Cf. Haarh, *The Yar Lum Dynasty,* p. 122 *et seq.*)

Of course we've known for a long time that historiography, as it was known among ancient peoples, was in no way an objective science, and that it is rich in falsehoods and legends. But the Tibetan documents show us that historiography is constructed from a mythological model: Each new creation (the building of bridges, the clearing of virgin lands, the establishment of systems of measure, etc.) is added to the cosmogony and the sacred history that precede it. It is nevertheless true that these new expressions of traditional mythology prepare for the advent of historiography.

The always incomparable Goethe: "I have never permitted myself to appeal to intuition."

The mystery—or enigma—of conversions: Not so many years ago, Alec Guinness played the role of a priest in a film. Between shooting two scenes he went for a walk and ended up in a street that he thought was deserted. He was, however, approached by a small child who took his hand and walked for a while by his side. The confidence the child immediately showed in a "priest" made such an impression on Alec Guinness that the memory of this encounter remained with him always. Some of his friends even claim that it was not unrelated to the actor's conversion.

However, I will never again risk telling this anecdote to a theologian if I remember the indignation of Father M. when I told it to him. He accused Guinness of "excessive emotionalism," and myself, too, while he was at it. And yet, what wouldn't he have discovered by reflecting on the story, among other things that the mystery of conversion is hidden behind the mask of banality, and even of "emotionalism"!

28 January

Today I gave Victor Turner a copy of *Australian Religions: An Introduction*. It is a collection containing articles that were already published some time ago in *History of Religions*. It will appear in the series Turner is editing for Cornell University Press: *Symbol, Myth, and Ritual*.

I realize that I will never finish *Primitive Religions*, the book I had begun in the sixties. I feel somewhat sad about this, but also somewhat relieved. This work, undertaken so many times, weighed on me like a cadaver I was carrying on my back.

February

Jules Renard notes on 17 August 1896: "I am only lacking the taste for obscurity." I don't know to which sort of obscurity Jules Renard was referring, but I endorse what he says without any hesitation. In all I've been able to write, and even in my books on the history of religions and the philosophy of culture, "I lack the taste for obscurity." And I have long understood the price one must pay for such a lack.

Aborigines: men who are one with the land, and who consider themselves "born" in the place where they live. It has been said that such beliefs are characteristic of sedentary, agricultural populations. But the same idea is found among hunting peoples, among the BaMbuti, for example, a pygmy tribe living in the forests of tropical Africa: "We are called the men of the forest. . . . When the forest perishes, we will perish, as well."

For the BaMbuti the forest constitutes an authentic *Terra Mater.* It is of the forest that they were born, and it is the forest that feeds them, just as a mother would do. In a certain sense the BaMbuti are still in an infantile state, and will never go beyond it. They depend wholly on the resources of the Mother Forest. When she disappears, they will disappear.

This example illustrates perfectly the "mythologization" of the feeling of dependence vis-à-vis Nature. And far from remaining *pueri eterni,* the BaMbuti have shown extraordinary maturity, both physical and mental. They have not only succeeded in surviving in an environment that could hardly be more hostile, but they have in addition developed an original culture of extraordinary richness.

23–24 February

Stefan Banulescu and Marin Sorescu, both writers in residence, arrived yesterday with their wives from Iowa City. They are our guests at the Quadrangle Club. I met them for the first time in Rome in the summer of 1968. They were the first of the young generation of Rumanian writers I had met. And coincidentally, they were also the only ones whose works I had read. I had very much liked *Iarna barbatilor (The Winter of Men)*, the collection of short stories by Stefan Banulescu, as well as the poetry of Marin Sorescu. Up until then I had tried several times, but in vain, to immerse myself in the new literature of "socialist" Rumania. A lost cause: The novels, short stories, collections of poems, were the fruit of a lamentable *"prolet-kultur."* All the same, in the years 1966–1967 a beginning of liberation had allowed certain authentic writers to come forward. Sometime later the vise closed again, soon after the Soviet invasion of Czechoslovakia. We know the rest.

Impossible to summarize our long conversations: I put both men through a battery of questions about my friends and colleagues who remained in the country, about the new generation of writers, etc., etc. . . . The miracle of a culture that persists in creating and enriching itself during the rare moments of peace History accords it, once every ten or twenty years, if not once a century . . .

March

I again come across this confession André Gide made to "la Petite Dame" (4 March 1929): ". . . I am filled with weakness, I am without resistance before others, without resistance before sympathy."

I would give a lot to know whether André Gide really understood the complete significance of this proposition: "without resistance before sympathy . . ."

"Where there is symbol, there is creation," said Mallarmé. Quite obviously, poetic knowledge grasps the essential. But it will have taken dozens of years and unceasing research for the statement dear to Mallarmé to have begun to be understood.

13 March

Dinner at the Mid-America Club, where we are the guests of Edward and Kate Levi. Among my colleagues, how many are there who are truly aware of the passion with which Edward propels, directs, and defends the University of Chicago? He knows as no one else how to wear the masks that resemble him—but only in part. I remember the ability, the sense of humor, and the spirit of decision he showed several years ago when a handful of "specialists" and a few dozen rowdy and naive followers occupied the university administration building. To all the provocations from which the "specialists" counted on his calling in the police, Edward responded with an enigmatic smile, and he asked his associates to display those two elementary virtues: patience and imagination . . .

I also remember that evening in a French restaurant where I saw Edward look at his watch and sigh with relief in seeing that it was past ten-thirty. "I've narrowly escaped!" he said. That same night a group of protesting students had decided to show a pornographic film in the university movie theater. They expected someone would call the police, whence a scandal, arrests, television, etc. . . . Edward had added: "I couldn't have objected to police intervention, since pornographic shows are within the jurisdiction of the vice squad which has the constitutional right to operate in all public places."

March

Alexandre Dumas retains infinitely more admirers than certain historians of literature could have predicted. I happened to meet some of them. However, not one of them knew of this passage in a letter from Dumas to Hyacinthe Meynier, who persisted in resisting his advances, notwithstanding the unbridled courtship the young author pursued. Dumas wrote her: "Hyacinthe, my love, I wouldn't have believed that you could make a man so happy by refusing him everything . . ."

I sometimes fear that my decision to condense as much as possible *A History of Religious Ideas* is forcing me to leave out a good number of reflections and commentaries that are nevertheless useful and worthy of my readers' interest. What inspiration, indeed what passion, I believed to have put into my numerous courses on Vedic religion! The pages I wrote this week, in which I dealt with the gods Varuna, Agni, and Indra, seem hastily written and too summary to me. But if I were to develop them all, the book's economy would be compromised, and I would have to go back to the chapters already drafted, rework and develop them, as well. And I would never see the end of it . . .

Arsène Houssaye maintains that Dumas didn't fear death: "It will be sweet to me," he said, "because I will tell it a story."

I hope this anecdote isn't apocryphal. In any case, the imaginary universe (of archaic and popular structure) revealed by the anecdote is characteristic of Dumas's unique vision. The ordeal of death is considered to be a "passage," and at the same time death is anthropomorphized and takes on the characteristics of a woman still young enough to be sensitive to the charm—that is, to the magic—of a tale.

23 March

I am paid a visit by a young man who is writing a thesis on "Jesus in the Work of Mircea Eliade." I have yet to convince him that in the thousands of pages I have devoted to the history of religions, I have never broached the subject of Jesus, apart from a few thoughts on "cosmic Christianity" as it has been experienced in Eastern Europe.

8 April

Lunch at Edward Levi's with John and Evelyn Nef. John has remained just as I've always known him, perhaps because he and his wife get along admirably well, and he is entirely absorbed by the book he has in progress. Back in my office at Meadville, I look for the notes I had taken between 1957 and 1960 at the time of our first conversations and those memorable dinners where John brought together, twice a month, the members of the famous Committee on Social Thought. It is not without emotion that I reread what I had written on our encounters with Jacques Maritain, Jean Hippolyte, Julian Huxley . . .

12 April

I committed the imprudent act of accepting to talk, during the monthly student-faculty luncheon, about my literary activity, and more specifically about the relationships, and above all the tension, between the rigor demanded by research in Orientalism and the history of religions, and the "creative imagination" of the writer. I spoke for almost a half hour, after dessert. Only towards the end did I realize that the subject was as fascinating as it was rich in discoveries. I must review all this in detail—but when?

13 April

I have immersed myself again in my journal notebooks to choose the passages Luc Badesco will translate. I sometimes have the impression that I am sacrificing the most "personal" pages: recollections, conversations with living persons, opinions on certain works and certain authors. I wonder whether I'm not on the wrong track. A journal must be presented to the public, if not in its entirety—for repetitions are frequent—at least in massive doses. But what publisher would accept four thousand pages of notebooks, which would represent about twenty-five hundred typewritten pages? But what if I lost these notebooks, just as I've lost so many other manuscripts? As imperfect as my choice may be, it is still for me the only way to save my journal, if only in part.

April

When I think about the dozens of pieces of paper that pile up on a corner of my desk—notes, remarks, citations, bibliography—I have the urge to throw everything into the wastebasket. I then remember Nicolas Iorga and his mania for using everything that came into his hands for taking notes, whether it was the back of an envelope or any old scrap of paper. In his classes, when he discovered one of them by chance in his pocket, he would look at it with surprise, hesitate, and finally put it back where he had found it. It is probably this memory I've kept of him that prevents me from getting rid of my innumerable scraps of paper.

Certain precisions, even secondary ones, when a more or less obscure colleague knows how to place them judiciously and at the right moment, sometimes suffice to establish his scientific authority. Martin tells me about having once attended a thesis defense at an American or Canadian university on Schelling and his precursors, if I remember correctly. After three hours of discussion the jury and the candidate were exhausted. Suddenly, one of the professors, who up until then had maintained a caustic silence, spoke up: Why, he asked, had the candidate failed to cite the Scottish doctor John Brown, author of a famous book in its time, *Elementa Medicinae,* in which he put forth his hypothesis on "stimulants" and the "total reaction" of the human body? An erroneous theory, to be sure, but one which nevertheless had the merit of suggesting to Schelling his romantic conception of polarity and totality.

The professor's intervention lasted only a few minutes, but, Martin said, it made a "very strong impression" on all his colleagues. A few months later he discovered by chance that Brown's influence on Schelling is cited in all works in the history of medicine.

IOWA CITY, *21 April*

We are met at the airport by Stefan Banulescu, M. Sorescu, and their wives. We are the Banulescus' guests, and they have found two rooms for us in the university housing reserved for married students and foreign writers in residence. It's a pity the building is several kilometers from the city.

In the evening we have dinner at a Chinese restaurant and then go visit a young Greek professor who speaks perfect Rumanian.

IOWA CITY, *22 April*

Stroll in town. Then we climb the hill located behind the university buildings. Discussions, tales told, evocations of memories. Useless to try to relate everything here in haste; a whole volume would be necessary to leave to future generations, if there are any . . . In the evening, discussions with other "writers in residence," a Japanese, a Yugoslav (from whom I learn that *Myth and Reality* came out in Serbo-Croat translation two years ago).

24 April

Yesterday, outing in the car to Amana. We have lunch in an admirable restaurant, the Ronneberg, antiquated and melancholy.

Today, return to Chicago. All evening, and until late into the night, sadness invades me. I hardly dare to think of the only hope I have left. I try to convince myself that all the current trials and humiliations of the Rumanian nation are perhaps the price it must pay for its subsequent spiritual alteration. I want to believe that what is true for individuals is equally true for peoples.

1 May

Admirable confession by Kepler, thrilled to have discovered the third law of planetary motion: "The thing which dawned on me twenty-five years ago before I had yet discovered the five regular bodies between the heavenly orbits . . . ; which sixteen years ago I proclaimed as the ultimate aim of all research; which caused me to devote the best years of my life to astronomical studies, to join Tycho Brahe, and to choose Prague as my residence—that I have, with the aid of God, who set my enthusiasm on fire and stirred in me an irrepressible desire, who kept my life and intelligence alert, and also provided me with the remaining necessities through the generosity of two emperors and the estates of my land, Upper Austria—that I have now, after discharging my astronomical duties *ad satietatum,* at long last brought to light. . . . Having perceived the first glimmer of dawn eighteen months ago, the light of day three months ago, but only a few days ago the plain sun of a most wonderful vision—nothing shall now hold me back. Yes, I give myself up to holy raving. I mockingly defy all mortals with this open confession: I have robbed the golden vessels of the Egyptians to make out of them a tabernacle for my God, far from the frontiers of Egypt. If you forgive me, I shall rejoice. If you are angry, I shall bear it. Behold, I have cast the dice, and I am writing a book either for my contemporaries, or for posterity. It is all the same to me. It may wait a hundred years for a reader, since God has also waited six thousand years for a witness. . . .'' (cited by Arthur Koestler, *The Sleepwalkers,* New York: Macmillan Co., 1959, pp. 393–94).

3 May

Following our long discussion of last evening, during which we mostly spoke of how it is henceforth impossible to listen to Bach or Mozart as their contemporaries did, since our ears have also become accustomed to the sonorities of Wagner, Schönberg, Bartok, etc. . . . , tenacious insomnia: knowing that all cultural creations and all beauties of nature change their appearance, and thus *disappear* irretrievably, because the human intellect invents, transforms, and adds to its own history. Total, nuclear destruction is but the ultimate, definitive result of the historical process.

HANNOVER, *24–26 May*

On 24 May we fly to Boston. One of my former students, Hans Penner, comes to get us at the airport. Two-and-a-half-hour car ride to get to Hannover. The town is immediately enchanting. We get out at the Hannover Inn, then go to the Penners'; they live in a dream house, right in the middle of a forest. Champagne. Hans and I recall my first courses in 1958–1959. Hans is grateful to me for having inspired him to learn Sanskrit.

The next morning Christinel and I visit the town. At three-thirty, lecture ("The Sacred City"). At five o'clock, debate with professors. At six-thirty, dinner. Back at Hans's at eight-thirty, where our discussion goes on until after midnight.

This morning at eleven-thirty, conversation with students, during which we cover the most diverse subjects. At twelve-fifteen, leave for Boston on board a small tourist plane. Arrival in New York around four o'clock. Wonderful.

NEW YORK, *28 May*

I should have taken notes in Hannover during our discussions on "methodology."

At four o'clock we leave for the airport. In Chicago it's hot and humid. A big storm is forecast for tomorrow.

I look at my agenda: starting tomorrow and for the whole week, tests, meetings with students, and a number of little chores, none of which I can possibly get out of (a long review for the *Encyclopedia Vallecchi* on religions, etc., etc. . . .).

May

Leigh Hunt, that intelligent and courageous journalist who was the first to recognize the genius of Keats, didn't like Homer. And he knew why: When he was younger, during a fit of anger a professor of his had broken one of his teeth by hitting him in the face with a copy of *The Iliad*. From that day Hunt has preferred Aristotle and Tasso . . .

Certain pages of my *Autobiography* are unfair to me. Talking about my adolescence, I was afraid of exaggerating by commenting on my abilities of that time. I tried to minimize them, or spoke of them in an amused tone. I wasn't aware of my mistake until it was too late, well after the book was published. Jowett was right in saying that the greatest danger that preys on one who is writing an autobiography is *self-depreciation*.

Adalbert von Chamisso: "I am everywhere a foreigner." For me, just the opposite is true.

"Axiomatic bases for theoretical physics cannot be drawn from experience. They must be freely imagined." This is what Einstein thinks (*Ideas and Opinions*).

And this is what J. Bronowski thinks: "The step by which a new axiom is added cannot itself be mechanized. It is a free play of the mind, an invention outside the logical processes. This is the central act of imagination in science, and it is in all respects like any similar act in literature" (*American Scientist* 54, no. 1 [March 1966]: 6).

When I think of X or of Y, or of one or another of my colleagues who have devoted their lives to the humanities, but suffer from the inferiority complex of the "nonscientific," and henceforth wish to be "objective," separate themselves from the values they study, and dream of the day when they will be able to call upon computers to help them in their work . . .

When I think . . . But the "science" they have in mind has never existed in that form. What existed, on the contrary, during the second half of the nineteenth century, was a certain positivist ideology in which only certain literary types and amateur psychologists believed. It was enough so that through novels, and thanks to a few popular writers and to some so-called scientific popularizers, an outdated ideology still makes its effects felt and inspires inferiority complexes in the name of "scientific rigor." "Humanists" are terrified at the idea of not being taken seriously, and of finding themselves accused of "doing literature."

5 June

Constantin Noïca has finally obtained his passport. He will first go to England, where his wife Wendy and his children have been living.

He'll then stop in Paris for a two-week stay, and we will of course go see him. It's been thirty years since we parted company! It will be one of the greatest days of my life, and in addition it will confirm what I've said again and again, i.e., that as long as we're alive, anything is possible. I can't forget that in the 1960s Noïca had been implicated in a "cultural" conspiracy and was sentenced to twenty-five years of detention with hard labor. I didn't even dare hope that he would survive it, for I knew that he had had a tuberculous kidney removed when he was barely thirty years old. And yet, he managed to survive . . .

June

If I were only ten or fifteen years younger I would set to work on an anthology of those whom I once called "secular mystics," from the pre-Socratics up to Nietzsche. I would like to begin it with these thoughts by Einstein, which I've just read in the book Philip Franck has devoted to him, *Einstein, His Life and Times* (New York, 1947, p. 284): "The most beautiful emotion we can experience is the mystical. It is the power of all true art and science. He to whom this emotion is a stranger, who can no longer wonder and stand rapt in awe, is as good as dead. To know that what is impenetrable to us really exists, manifesting itself as the highest wisdom and the most radiant beauty, which our dull faculties can comprehend only in their most primitive forms—this knowledge, this feeling, is at the center of true religiousness. In this sense, and in this sense only, I belong to the rank of devoutly religious men."

18 June

We spend the evening in the company of Ovidiu Cotrus. Our conversation goes on until two in the morning. His memory is absolutely prodigious. When he was in prison he gave lectures on Rumanian, French, and Russian literature. He cited from memory not only passages but entire pages from novels, which he then commented on. I had learned this from certain of his fellow prisoners whom I met in Paris. I entreat him to record his recollections—those of prison, of course, but also any others—on tape, here or in France: It would be an exceptional document. Only he, endowed with such a prodigious memory, has the opportunity to be in the West. I could never summarize all that he told me. I hope that it has been noted down by the numerous people who have approached him.

Cotrus lives only by miracle. The doctors who have examined him can't explain how he can still be alive. He has every imaginable illness. His liver and heart are affected. In addition he has pulmonary tuberculosis and chronic colitis, etc. . . . Yet despite all that he is overflowing with vitality, always seems happy and well, even after ten hours of uninterrupted discussions. He smokes like a chimney, eats everything, drinks hard liquor, and pays no attention to the diets that are prescribed for him.

19 June

An afternoon wasted in writing many letters. Happily, we're spending the evening with Cotrus. We're preparing an interview for a journal of Oradea. But Ovidiu has doubts as to its publication . . .

20 June

Lecture at the Lutheran School of Theology on the role of the history of religions in today's culture. The subject is fascinating and would deserve a book written on it alone. But when would I be able to write it? My office is cluttered with files and boxes stuffed with notes and papers—and there are just as many manuscripts in the works. With a little luck I'll dot the final *i* in *A History of Religious Ideas*. I continue to believe that once more luck will stay with me all the way to the end.

NEW YORK, *21 June*

This morning I finish with my correspondence. Then, departure for the airport. Our flight is scheduled for six o'clock. We arrive in New York in the rain. Since our flight for Paris leaves early in the morning, we decide to spend the night in a nearby hotel. All night long the wind blows like in *Wuthering Heights*. We have difficulty sleeping.

PARIS, *22 June*

Arrival in Paris at eleven-thirty in the evening. Sibylle, Giza, and Dinu T. are waiting for us at the airport. On place Charles-Dullin we chat with Sibylle until two in the morning, Paris time. But in Chicago it is still only seven in the evening, and we're not sleepy. We should take a sleeping pill, but neither Christinel nor I wants to, so great is our horror of barbiturates.

23 June

Noïca came to see me this afternoon, and we spoke for three whole hours. What is most noteworthy in what he told me? Everything about him seems extraordinary to me, beginning with the fact that we're meeting again after thirty years of separation, and he seems unchanged to me, still just as optimistic and full of confidence in the future, and also in History, even though this "History" treated him to ten years in prison. And yet he tells me again and again that those ten years were "the happiest of his life," especially those he spent alone in a cell, without a book, without a sheet of paper, without even a nub of pencil . . . "Time belonged to me!" he told me. "I could meditate at leisure, not be hurried. I thought of all that I had read up until then. That is how I remembered the entire history of Western philosophy, from the pre-Socratics up to Husserl . . ."

He repeats what everyone who, like he, has experienced prison has confided in me, that is, that prison is the great revealer of individual virtues which without it would remain ignored or would be hardly noticeable. It is in prison that one discovers that men are better, more courageous, more "authentic" than one would have believed. His great discovery was the extraordinary strength of character which many Rumanians showed, when they would otherwise have been judged to be petty, superficial, or mediocre. In this connection I remember what Cioran had told me one day: that while he was listening to the stories and the accounts of those who had been in prison or the extermination camps of the infamous Danube–Black Sea canal, he felt proud to be a Rumanian.

What is most striking is Noïca's faith in the creative potentialities of Rumanian culture *of today*. I wonder, however, how such "possibilities" could flourish in a rigorously and systematically politicized society, and whether an original philosophy could be expressed *in broad daylight* in a culture controlled by censorship.

26 June

Noïca and I meet almost daily, and it is practically impossible for me to give more than a glimpse of our long conversations. I settle for jotting a few notes in my notebook and plan to write, as soon as I get back to Chicago, a meticulous account of Noïca's ideas and suggestions regarding the "cultural collaboration" he advocates between those in exile and the current regime.

30 June

Saw *Macbeth* with Rodica and Marie-France Ionesco. I'm delighted by the daring with which this old, well-known story has been redone without, however, sacrificing the Shakespearian universe.

After the play we go to the Ionescos', where Eugène is waiting for us. Naturally we speak of Dinu Noïca and of what I've learned from him.

2 July

Last meeting with Noïca, at Marianne and François Parlier's (where we were invited to dinner last evening with Noïca and the Lupascos). My notebook is filled with notes taken that evening. Later I pick up *Faust*, part 2, which I hadn't reread for a long time. I find the book as fascinating as before, and since sleep escapes me, I turn the light on, get dressed, and continue reading. I think I could perhaps organize a seminar on *Faust*, part 2, with a Germanist and a specialist in comparative literature. For my part I will try to comment on certain passages from the perspective of the history of religions.

3 July

My meeting at the Café de Cluny with Sorin Titel leaves me drained (the tragedy of the Rumanian writer of today), but on the other hand gives me a certain confidence: Constrained to creating under current conditions, it is not inconceivable that certain writers will succeed in discovering writing styles or a new poetic language allowing them to short-circuit the censors, and will thus indeed manage to publish works which written in their usual styles would never see the light of day.

5 July

This evening Sorin arrives from Amsterdam. Virgil and Monica Ierunca have invited us to dinner, and we don't stop talking. When I walked into the restaurant Virgil and Monica were frightened by my haggard appearance: "What happened? Why such a face?" I then tell them about my meeting with Z. that afternoon. For two hours he spoke only of himself and of his successes. For years I've hoped, and even believed, that in this battle between his angel and his demon of pride, the angel would come out ahead. But today, after having heard him hold forth just as he's done for years, I understood that I had been deceiving myself. My disappointment was so strong that I preferred to remain silent. It is as if I had just learned of the death of a brother, of a lifelong friend . . .

6 July

Long discussions with Sorin. I'm writing the gist of them in another notebook. In the evening Eugène, Rodica, Marie-France, Cioran, Virgil, and Monica come to see us. They are all experiencing the emotions resulting from our reunion with Noïca. So many enigmas that catch us unawares. We are only sure of one thing: He has managed to assimilate his prison experience, in other words, to accept it without revolt, and even to find a meaning for it. He came out of that horrible ordeal more mature, more accomplished, and especially ready to take up his role in the current historical conditions in Rumania. He intends to give the best of himself only in these few areas that are still tolerated. In a word, Noïca, to whom Hegel's philosophy is so familiar, submits himself to History, knowing well that any other course would end only in silence, sterility, or neurosis.

CHICAGO, 7 July

Departure from Paris this morning at nine o'clock. Giza, Dinu T., and Sorin accompanied us to the airport. Stop in Montreal. Arrival

in Chicago at four o'clock local time, but it is eleven in the evening in
Paris.

8 July

The weather is radiant. I spend the morning going through my
mail. Memories come back to me, those of summers of my youth, in
Bucharest, in the Carpathians, or in the delta of the Danube. But it is
especially a line by Ionel Teodoreanu that keeps surfacing in me to the
point of obsession: ". . . like a summer night in Iassy . . . !" That
must refer to around 1928. He, his wife, Ibraileanu, and a few friends
sometimes spent entire nights in the garden, drinking cup after cup of
coffee and talking enough to run out of breath. I feel I can still see the
image dear to Teodoreanu of those houses glowing milky white in the
light of the moon, suddenly lit up by silver rays of light. I've
contemplated the same scene many times in Calcutta, Jaipur, or
Fatehpur Sikhri, and I wonder why in fact that line by Teodoreanu
obsesses me so. Perhaps it is because I know so little of Iassy, and that
in any event I've never spent a summer's night there. Is it because of a
profound, incurable regret at not knowing one of the high places of
Rumanian culture, this Iassy of Creanga, of Eminescu, of the *Junimea,*
of *Viaţa românească?*[1]

SANTA BARBARA, *11 July*

We arrived yesterday, invited by Robert Hutchins and the Center
for the Study of Democratic Institutions. We're staying in a motel with
a pool that is surrounded by trees in which liana winds itself. I've
brought along my files on Buddhistic texts and a few books. I've finally
decided to begin writing the chapter on the Buddha and Buddhism in
India which I've been preparing for so long. Also invited to this
colloquium are the Austrian historian Heer, Garaudy, the former
minister of culture of the Dubček government, and many others.

1. *Junimea:* literary movement of the second half of the nineteenth century, originating
in Moldavia, of which Iassy is the capital, which grouped together the greatest writers
around T. Maiorescu, the creator of Rumanian literary criticism.—C.G. [*Viaţa
românească* (Rumanian life): also a literary movement.—ED.]

13 July

This afternoon, while contemplating the eucalyptus trees of the center, I remembered that autumn day, in 1959 or 1960, when I was explaining to my students the reasons that had caused the Buddha to be made the "king" of therapeutists. I seem to see once again those large trees, and especially that oak in the university quadrangle that was losing its golden-yellow leaves one by one, and which fascinated me so much that I feared not finishing my sentences due to looking out the window . . . Why was I thus so impressed by the context of my talk (autumn, falling leaves, the decline of all vegetation) when I was analyzing "the therapeutic structure and function" of the message of Gautama Buddha? I was saying that for the Buddha, all men ("beings") are sick people who can be cured only by the Buddhistic message. The healthy state is that of the absence of evil (*arogya*), and this term is the very one used to qualify Nirvana. I had cited one of my favorite texts: "Following metempsychosis, the beginning of which no one knows, all beings are tormented by illnesses of the passions, and no one has yet succeeded in curing them. . . . But I have finally come, I, King of the therapeutists, and I have gathered together all the remedies of the Law . . ."

But what problems arise from this simple passage! Beginning with that of the illnesses from which Gautama Buddha himself suffered, the doctors who treated him (and most especially Jivaka, a layman), the fact that he died of indigestion from pork or truffles . . . All that deserved explanation. The young F. couldn't help thinking that he was faced with an obvious contradiction: On the one hand Gautama told the hermits, the *bhhikus,* to treat each other amongst themselves when they fell ill (on this point it is necessary to specify that Buddha didn't admit into his order those who were seriously ill, for these individuals, in fact, wanted only to be treated by their companions); and on the other hand, these same disciples were forbidden to study and practice medicine, "a secular activity . . ." They were even forbidden "verbal" therapeutics. I recalled the case of the monks who recited a sutra containing recipes for healing. The laymen protested: Why then don't they recite the Buddhist sutras that cure illnesses of metempsychosis? Any *bhhiku* who ostensibly gave medicine to one of his companions was accused of violating discipline.

Evidently, we must see in these attitudes vestiges of the Brahmanic tradition of the impurity of doctors (cf. *Manu* 3.80, 4.212: Taitiriya Samhita forbids Brahmans to practice medicine). Certain texts specify that the two *Açvin* had been immediately excluded from the sacrifice of the *Soma* only because they were called "doctors." But there would have been so much to say about this, and above all that if we want to understand the role of the doctor, the thaumaturgist, and the spiritual leader in traditional cultures, it is indispensable to know in detail and to understand the extremely complex function of the shaman in archaic societies.

16 July

"Adam"—that's his nickname—is one of the most surprising of young men. I met him last evening, and I only wish I could see him again. Unfortunately, he has to leave this very morning. One of his two grandmothers has just had an attack, of hemiplegia it would seem, and he wants at all costs to see her again before she dies, if only to be able to learn from her the exact moment he came into the world, since Adam wants to construct his own horoscope . . . He is endowed with an absolutely prodigious memory. I had on hand a copy of Conze's *Buddhist Texts,* and he tells me that he hadn't yet managed to read more than the first thirty-two pages of it, but that he had very much liked the passage dealing with the conversion of Anathapindika. And to better convince me he began to recite without hesitation the text of *Vinaya-pitaka* 2.154–59: "The tenant farmer Anathapindika, who had married the sister of a banker from Rajagaka . . ." I had to interrupt him, laughing, but I was astonished. A few moments later he explained why he had only read the first thirty-two pages. His reasons would be too difficult to summarize, for they have to do with a theory of numbers inspired by the Kabala. But, he specified, in the form he practiced it, it was an entirely personal creation. He also told me, among other things, that one of "the most tragic and most sinister" days of the twentieth century was that of 24 January 1914, for it was on that day that André Gide admitted his anti-Semitic beliefs in his *Journal.* And he recited, without stopping to catch his breath, the two pages where André Gide, from the portrait he draws of Léon Blum, affirms that "there is in France today a Jewish literature, which is not French literature," etc.

20 July

These past few days I've had the opportunity to have several conversations with Robert Hutchins. I must one day write an account of this man who was for nearly twenty years president of the University of Chicago. He was barely thirty years old when he was offered the position, heavy with responsibilities, and he immediately instigated one of the boldest reforms in all of university education. He was practically the only person to fight at the time against the dominant tendency for students to specialize much too early, and to insist on the primordial importance of the humanities and of a "basic education," which alone could assure that general culture without which scientific discoveries and technical progress risk resembling a proliferation of cancer cells.

To my great regret he was no longer president of the University of Chicago when I was appointed there. This Center for the Study of Democratic Institutions, founded by Hutchins in Santa Barbara, has its merits, but it hasn't the stature nor the possibilities of influence that a great university has.

22 July

I spent nearly two hours this afternoon recording a conversation with Wilkinson on decisive moments in the history of religions. I don't know whether the text will be of any interest, since I still much prefer to listen to Wilkinson rather than to engage him in dialogue. What I like about him is that no matter what subject is being discussed, whether it concerns time and space in post-Kantian philosophy, the American Constitution, the political situation in Africa, pop art, or ecology, when he asks to and begins to speak, he is always just as disconcerting, but never ceases to be captivating.

23 July

Ileana Marculescu and her husband come to get us in their car for a three-hour ride in the mountains in the backwoods of Santa

Barbara. I try to persuade Ileana to be more prudent, more "humble" in dealing with her colleagues—philosophers, sociologists, psychologists— who could easily take offense at her knowledge. In any case it is not only their prestige she is compromising, but also their "beefsteak." Ileana studied biology in Moscow for four years, but she later became one of the great specialists in phenomenology and one of the experts in Rumania in the dialogue on "Marxism-Christianity." It is this, moreover, that brings her to the United States. During an international colloquium on this theme she approached an important Catholic figure and said to him point-blank: "I would like to write a metaphysics, but it isn't permitted in Rumania . . ." For the time being, instead of writing a metaphysics she's working at the center and frequents a good number of philosophical groups and societies. And when the opportunity presents itself she doesn't hesitate to strongly criticize the incompetence or the superficial character of certain "authorities" who are, however, the pride of American universities. I tell her to be careful, because knowledge as rich, varied, and profound as hers is not forgiven, especially here in California . . .

CHICAGO, *14 August*

Mary Stevenson came especially to see us. She is staying with a friend who lives on campus. I notice with surprise that she speaks Rumanian remarkably well. She even suggests translating my stories and some of my novels. All the same, I doubt she will find a publisher. In the United States, as in Europe, I am known and accepted uniquely as a historian of religions. And if my literary works ever saw the light of day, even if only in part, I fear they would at first shock and would then alienate me from the publishers of my works that are considered to be "serious."

25 August

While counting the pages that have already been typed, I realize with horror that there are already more than 500, not counting the 105 pages of critical bibliography. And to think that I have not even finished with half of the first volume! I will therefore have to divide *A History of Religious Ideas* into three volumes, and not two, as I had originally planned. I could obviously resort to another solution, which would consist of condensing even more the chapters I've already written. But just the idea of cutting the text once more repulses me: I've already done it twice.

Here are a few examples cited by Goldzieher on the importance of *writing* among the Semites:

"All knowledge that isn't [bedded] on paper is lost."

"What is kept only in memory is destined to be lost. Only what is written will survive."

But opposing this, Abu Ali al-Basri, in the ninth century, states: "Whereas men of little science know nothing they haven't first read in a book, I, on the contrary, I dominate them all by my zealousness in making my ear a writing-desk, and my heart the receptacle of knowledge."

August

In his study *On Medieval Hebrew Poetry,* Shalom Spiegel insists that in the Middle Ages many original creations were "drowned in biblical exegesis." Medieval thought was most often expressed, therefore, only through a commentary on the Holy Scripture: "Even dissent and revolt are clothed in what is in name or shape but a commentary." (Cf. Finkelstein, *The Jews,* p. 860 *et seq.,* New York, 1960.)

This is a characteristic of all traditional religious cultures. Those of India, China, Tibet, are in the same category, just like Medieval Christianity and Islam. In the reigning indifference to all personal creation, true "originality" consisted above all in a better and more profound interpretation of the formulas inherited from the primordial Revelation.

What an admirable literary critic André Gide was, even at the early age of twenty! Looking at his reading notes (*Le Subjectif*), this note on Balzac: "He has the unbearable cheerfulness of a traveling salesman after a meal." One would think it a line of Cioran's! And this other, on

Paul Bourget (*Mensonges*): "He explains too much, as if he were writing for imbeciles." Goncourt, in *Manette Salomon,* "sees nature like a merchant of colors, sizing up the mixtures of ocher, sienna, and tar rendered by the tilled fields."

In a letter to Paul Valéry regarding *Narcisse:* "We will tell this story again. Everything has been said before; but since no one listens, one must always begin again."

PARIS, *10 September*

   I leaf through my datebook to see how the previous two weeks were spent. For several days before leaving Chicago I wrote letters by the dozen and sent packages of books to Rumania: Let's hope they reach their destinations . . . Departure from the airport on 1 September. We were supposed to take off at five o'clock, but at eight o'clock we learn that our flight has been cancelled due to engine failure. We have dinner and spend the night at the Sheridan South Hotel at Air France's expense. The next day we're informed that the new engine won't arrive before midnight, so we return to the hotel. In the evening we go to the bar, already filled with people. We recognize travelers from our group at nearby tables. Pilots, stewardesses go through the bar, as well as other people, and I believe I recognize familiar faces that I've noticed briefly in films, in other bars, in other hotel lobbies. Imperceptibly I feel myself overtaken by the atmosphere that surrounds me. One would think that all the people present in this bar are old acquaintances, and what's more, that they belong to the same, somewhat esoteric, community of which one cannot become a member immediately and without formalities; one must first go through certain initiatory rites . . .

We finally leave in the afternoon of 3 September. We arrive in Paris the next day, after stopping in Montreal. Sibylle is waiting for us at the airport. At home, place Charles-Dullin, I already find a pile of letters, many of which are from Rumania. On 6 September I finish correcting the translation of the *Journal* which Badesco has just completed. That evening I dine in the neighborhood with Al. Rosetti, and we chat together until around eleven o'clock. He is still just as pessimistic. According to him, we won't be able to do anything as long as the great neighboring empire is invulnerable. I remind him of what Blaga said around 1950, that is, that Rumania has entered into the shadows of a new barbarism, and that this could last another thousand years. Blaga was nonetheless optimistic, so certain was he that the nation would this time again be able to rise above the ordeal. But without the elite? Without freedoms?

I have the good fortune of being able to spend the entire afternoon of 8 September at the Orangerie viewing the impressionist exhibition. I returned comforted, almost happy. As long as such joys are available to us, we haven't the right to despair. In the evening we call Bucharest. My mother is surprisingly serene. She maintains all her faith in life, in the future. Whereas my sister Corina's voice seemed sadder than usual.

Spent two whole days, September 9 and 10, rereading *Fragments d'un journal* in the excellent translation by Badesco.

PARIS, *14 September*

Every day I see more friends again. The past few evenings we've dined at Sibylle's and at the Ieruncas', where our conversation went on until around two in the morning. It was with them, on the evening of 12 September, that I learned of the death of two Rumanian writers. Yesterday, 13 September, promotions work at Payot for *Australian Religions,* the first since 1956! I then go to Cioran's, where I run into Vasko Popa.

Today, for four hours with Luc Badesco, complete revision of his translation manuscript.

15 September

G. Sturdza came to see me. We hadn't met since 1938.

18 September

The Soviet historian Boris Hessen asserted in an article published in English in 1933 ("The Social and Economic Roots of Newton's *Principia*") that the theory of universal gravitation was only a by-product of mercantile capitalism in the seventeenth century. Hessen disappeared sometime later during one of the numerous Stalinist purges.

21 September

This early Paris autumn is splendid. Upon awakening I hardly feel my never-ending arthritic pains (this time localized in the sacrum); I don't need more than an hour to forget them. But every movement is torture for me, especially in the morning.

22 September

This evening, at Leonid Mamaliga's, I give a reading of my story *Uniformes de général*. I don't know if they liked it. In any case, it is much too long to be read in a single sitting. I wonder whether I was still being listened to after an hour and a half of reading out loud.

27 September

Received a visit from Constantin Tacou, whom I hadn't seen in some fifteen years. He's currently the head of Editions de l'Herne, and would like to devote one of the next *Cahiers* to me. He asks me to help him and to give him the names of those who should be invited to collaborate on it. He also asks me to prepare the iconography and to choose a few letters I would consider of interest among those I've received from Papini, C. G. Jung, Ernst Jünger, etc. . . . but above all to prepare my bibliography.

I suggest he offer the preparation of the *Cahier* to Jean Varenne, who could solicit the collaboration of Orientalists and historians of religions, and to Marie-France Ionesco, who could contact both French and Rumanian writers, as well as certain critics.

28 September

We were invited to dinner last evening at Madeleine and Georges Dumézil's. It is not without melancholy that we remember the autumn of 1969 and the beginning of 1970 that we had spent together on the University of Chicago campus, and that almost familial atmosphere that is the charm of American universities. We were able to see each other then at least once a week, at dinners in the homes of our mutual colleagues. And what more can be said of our interminable after-dinner discussions, where we dealt not only with theology (and even the "God is dead" theology), but also literary criticism, prehistory, or Indo-European linguistics . . .

CHICAGO, *5 October*

Arrived at five o'clock local time. We are broken with fatigue. To our great surprise our house is freezing, for the first time since we've been living in the United States. Usually we rather complain of being too warm . . .

6 October

The weather is bad, grey and cold. An enormous amount of mail awaits me. I must also immediately prepare the collection of my complete works for Japanese translation. There will be fourteen volumes. My literary works obviously are not included.

I receive a copy of *Auf der Mantuleasa Strasse* in the excellent translation by Edith Silbermann, published by Suhrkampf Verlag. It's the first translation of *Pe strada Mântuleaza* [*The Old Man and the Bureaucrats*]. I will be very interested to know whether the book is successful.

October 1972

I have finally obtained a copy of *My Autobiography* by Max Müller. I find a wealth of fascinating details in it about the Orientalists of the middle of the nineteenth century, and I finally understand why Roth and Müller were on such bad terms. The author of *My Autobiography* candidly explains it himself. On the occasion of some festal event or another, Müller, Roth, and two other students as young as they went to celebrate in a restaurant. "To me," writes Max Müller, "with my limited means this was a great extravagance, but I could not refuse to join. Roth, to my great surprise and, I may add, being very fond of oysters, annoyance, took a very unfair share of that delicacy, and whenever I met him in after life, whether in person or in writing, this incident would always crop up in my mind; and when later on he offered to join me in editing the *Rig-veda,* I declined, perhaps influenced by that early impression which I could not get rid of'' (*My Autobiography, A Fragment,* New York: Charles Scribner's Sons, pp. 171–72).

What a fascinating study one could undertake by comparing the methods of these two great scholars of Vedic philology, and their respective visions of the mythology and religion of ancient India! The first detailed and systematic investigation into Vedic divinities and mythology was done by Roth in 1846. Max Müller's lengthy analysis, *Comparative Mythology,* would only appear ten years later, but was to know unprecedented success. But it would be most interesting to examine the extent to which Max Müller contrasts his own methodology to the conclusions put forth by Roth. As he himself admits, he hadn't the least confidence in Roth's scientific objectivity; and that image of that plate ''where oysters continued to pile up'' contributed more than one could have imagined to the glory of Max Müller, if only because it forced him to bring to a successful conclusion—and *alone*—his monumental edition of the *Rig-Veda* . . .

Serious dangers threaten us when we spend too much of our time on a study that is not very interesting. This is what I've noticed among many of my colleagues. But the most tragic example of this is furnished by Burckhardt (*Weltgeschichtliche Betrachtungen,* p. 64) who cites the case of the famous Buckle, who found himself ''mentally paralyzed'' at having expended too much effort in studying the sermons of seventeenth- and eighteenth-century Scottish preachers.

14 October

The article I've promised for the *Mélanges Puech* must go out within the next few days, and I plunge back into the documentation I've accumulated on the legend of the Mandrake. I hadn't reread them since I'd written *Gayomard et la Mandragore,* my contribution to *l'Hommage*

Widengren. Under the circumstances I decide to write a short article, "Adam, le Christ, et la Mandragore."

Of all that I've written, nothing deserves more to have the adage *"Habent sua fata libelli "* applied to it. I began to be interested in the myth of the mandrake when I was still in India. I remember those afternoons in 1930 that I spent in the Imperial Library of Calcutta reading the studies by Berthold Laufer, and copying down entire pages from them, for I knew that the *Sino-Iranica* and the collections of the journal *T'oung Pao* couldn't be found in the libraries of Bucharest. My first articles on the mandrake appeared in 1932. A few years later I had assembled abundant information on miraculous plants, as well as on the myths relating to herbs, trees, and fruits believed to guarantee immortality, longevity, or a new youth. Around 1938 I had already drafted several chapters of a book that was to have as its title *La Mandragore: Essai sur la formation des légendes.* Some of them appeared in *Zalmoxis* and in the *Revue des Fondations royales.* I had promised Al. Rosetti to finish my book by the summer of 1939. But the war broke out, and I had to leave for London. My manuscripts and my notes on the mandrake and the myth of miraculous plants were the only files I took with me. When I was appointed in Lisbon, all this documentation, which I had in the meantime completed at the British Museum, was evidently retained at the airport in London. I had lost all hope of retrieving my documents when, several months later, they finally arrived in Lisbon, along with other files.

After so many years of research I had radically altered my initial project. If I had decided to use all my documents, I would have had to write at least two or three volumes. I could only congratulate myself on the decision I made upon arriving in Paris to definitively give up on the *Essai sur la formation des légendes,* just as I had given up on so many other works begun between 1938 and 1941, such as *Anthropocosmos, Symbolisme du labyrinthe et rites initiatiques, La Physique et la métaphysique de l'orgie,* etc. . . .

19 October

I've just finished reading the autobiography of Allan Watts. I remember the first lectures on Zen he gave here in Chicago. I had found them quite simply extraordinary. However, at the time, in 1956, I had not understood his "message" very well. I can only want as evidence of this Christinel's and my surprise when, having come to see us one morning, and when we offered him some coffee, Watts asked us whether we didn't have some vodka instead . . .

25 October

It is truly difficult to predict how History will judge certain contemporary events. Julien Green writes in his journal on 7 November 1956: "The fate of Hungary, crushed by the Russians, has caused considerable emotion. It will not be forgotten any more than was forgotten the division of Poland in the eighteenth century." And yet it took only a few years for the events in Hungary, and those in Czechoslovakia, to escape the memories of men, both in the West and in the United States, just like the fate of all the victims that have succeeded them. On the other hand, the Western and North American intelligentsia never forget the "victims of capitalist imperialism." A touching thought!

28 October

The day before yesterday, L.S. came to see me unexpectedly. Interminable conversation, boring and depressing. I could have perhaps gotten out of it if I had remembered that line by Max Planck: "The worst that could happen would be for someone to devise a philosophy on a physics that no longer exists."

6 November

First public lecture in a series of four devoted to prehistoric religions. I've already given courses and led seminars on this same subject, but this time I intend to present a synthesis that will serve as a basis for the first two chapters of *A History of Religious Ideas*. For years I've been enthralled, and even fascinated, by the study of prehistoric religions. It is true that we only possess a few scattered objects: bones, sepulchers, weapons, etc. . . . and, for more recent eras, engraved signs and drawings. I like to consider them to be authentic documents despite the "semantic cloudiness" that characterizes them. And yet the most insignificant object, the most banal drawing—a spiral, a point, a line—have a very precise meaning and are integrated into a language. Freud's genius was to prove that which seems obvious to us today, that is, that all the phantasmagoria of dreams which, until him, were considered to be purely gratuitous, are in fact a coded language. It's possible that one day we will succeed in deciphering that other code represented in prehistoric documents. It is truly a shame that scholars are so fearful and don't try to use the ethnographic documents at their disposal. It is true that the first researchers confronted prehistoric remains and ethnographic documents a bit randomly, and without any method. When we are finally able to connect those universes of multiple meanings that are revealed to us by prehistory, ethnography, and folklore, the history of religions will be the only history capable of opening up onto a universal history of the human spirit.

11 November

I finish correcting and work on the index for *Australian Religions: An Introduction,* which Professor Victor Turner is getting ready to publish in the series *Symbol, Myth, and Ritual* (Cornell University Press). This short treatise is only a small part of a history of primitive religions that I began almost fifteen years ago. Apart from Australian religions, I have only succeeded up to now in drafting the few chapters dealing with the religions of South American tribes. All the rest, that is, my documents on North America, Africa, Oceania, and northern Asia, sleeps in my files. I sometimes wonder why I still keep those hundreds of pages and thousands of notecards that are yellowing and getting covered with dust on the shelves of my bookcases. But I have only to be tempted to rid myself of them by burning them to immediately refrain from doing so, thinking that I might someday need them in the event that I give courses on primitive religions.

14 November

I begin drafting the first chapter of *A History of Religious Ideas:* "Magico-Religious Behavior of the Paleanthropians." Besides this chapter I have two more to write, one on the religions of the Neolithic, the other on the religions of the Megalithic. The rest of the manuscript is already corrected and typed. I can hardly imagine that the first volume of the *History* might see the light of day in a year or two.

17 November

I went to Columbus Hospital to visit Vasile Posteuca who, suffering from cancer, is in agony. We had not seen each other for almost five or six years, ever since he had persuaded himself that I had ceased to be "a good Rumanian" and he had dressed me down in all exile publications. I didn't read them, but I learned from others that Posteuca called me a . . . etc., etc. . . .

He lay suffering on his bed, emaciated, his face a very pale, waxy yellow. I took his hand and asked him how he was, as if nothing were wrong and our last meeting had been only a few days earlier. He answered with a few words which I barely understood, so difficult was it for him to speak. A moment later he signaled to a nurse, who quickly came to hold a basin for him. The doctor took my arm to pull me away, but I nevertheless had time to see that he had vomited up an impressive amount of bile, and he continued to do so several times—every three or four minutes—during the quarter of an hour I spent with him.

Posteuca only survives by a miracle. He refuses to die until he sees his daughter and son again; they were little children when he had had to flee Rumania, and are now in their thirties. Several American congressmen made many attempts on his behalf, the newspapers wrote about him, and a television crew even came to film him here at the hospital. The Rumanian authorities finally consented to issue the much-desired passports, and Posteuca expects his children any day now. But the doctors are more cautious. They don't understand how their patient manages to survive, and they doubt he can hold on one more day.

He speaks only with superhuman effort, and is most often unintelligible. I nevertheless understand that he is absolutely persuaded that he will see his children again, that he forgives all his enemies, even the communists who have brought on the misfortune that has befallen his country.

(Vasile Posteuca finally died on 21 November, a few hours after having embraced his children. He asked to be buried in Vatra, on Rumanian land.)

20 November

When one hears about the famous "American optimism," it's necessary to keep in mind that most nineteenth-century writers stressed, on the contrary, the negative aspects of American society. It is thus that Nathaniel Hawthorne is obsessed by "that pit of blackness that lies beneath us, everywhere. The firmest substance of human happiness is but a thin crust spread over it. . . . It needs no earthquake to open the chasm. A footstep, a little heavier than ordinary, will serve; and we must step very daintily, not to break through the crust at any moment. By and by, we inevitably sink!" This passage is taken from *The Marble Faun*. In *Clarel, a Poem and Pilgrimage in the Holy Land* (1876), Melville describes the idyllic scene of a mother rocking her child, then adds: "Under such scenes abysses be dark quarries where few care to pry. . . ." Melville is horrified at the approach of the "dark ages of Democracy," which will witness the New World—America—"grow old and fall sick." From that time, "no new world to mankind remains!"

And the "optimist" Whitman himself, in *Democratic Vistas* (1875–1878), goes as far as predicting the price that America will have to pay for letting itself get caught in the trap of imperialism. The United States will also know "the struggle, the traitor, the wily person in office, scrofulous wealth, the surfeit of prosperity, the demonism of greed, the hell of passion, the decay of faith, the fossil-like lethargy, the ceaseless need of revolution."

November

I've known for a long time—undoubtedly from the books by J. H. Fabre—about the existence of the nuptial ceremony among scorpions. During their "engagement" the male and female stroll around "holding each other by the pincers," and these walks sometimes go on for an extraordinary amount of time. A few days ago, having had the opportunity to meet L.V., the great animal behavior specialist, I asked him for a few specifics. With an ironic smile, L.V. assured me that this nuptial ceremony, although effective, hasn't the importance we attribute to it, we dilettantes who have only too great a tendency to consider animals' sexual instincts in an anthropocentric way. The "engagement" is only a prelude to the sexual union. The "waltz-promenade" does indeed take place, but it is we and we alone who grant it the function and value of a dance, etc. . . .

Obviously I was a bit disappointed. While thinking about it later, however, I saw that he was undoubtedly right. Specialists in the history of chemistry sometimes proceed in just this way when they see in alchemical experiments only a foreshadowing of the science that would succeed it. In reality, the alchemists had aims quite different from those of eighteenth- and nineteenth-century chemists.

1 December

I've begun a short article on the *caluşari* for the *Hommage à Theodor Gaster*. I know the subject interests him. He has already alluded several times to that cathartic Rumanian dance. In any case, I wouldn't have time to draft a complete study. Moreover, I am only entitled to twenty-five typewritten pages in all. I must nonetheless one day set to work on this fascinating subject. It is, in effect, an authentic "living fossil" and the vestige of an archaic initiatory scenario in which elements even more ancient than those that have already been identified in hobby-horse dances and military dances, the *Schwerttanz,* for example, still survive.

But for the moment, while filing my documents and rereading the notes I've accumulated over numerous years, I keep repeating to myself that I must not go over my allotted twenty-five pages, and that my article must be written very quickly, within a few days.

6 December

Received a visit, followed by dinner at the Quadrangle Club, from Mircea Zaciu, literary critic, historian of literature, and professor at the University of Cluj. We mostly talk about contemporary Rumanian writers. I ask him what has become of such and such a novelist, and what new books have been published. During these meetings with writers, professors, or intellectuals living in Rumania I always experience a strange sensation of unreality. I have the impression that they and I are actors in a play, very well known and even banal, so often has it been performed, but never to its conclusion. All the same, I must not give up my role, for then the meetings and conversations I can have with writers who have come from Rumania and who want to meet me would have no meaning. They all, without exception, assure me that in Rumania I am the widest-read, the most admired writer, etc. . . . And despite this, as far as the history of modern literature goes, I quite simply do not exist, as no article has ever been written on my books, neither on the earlier ones nor on those I've recently written. Of course, I'm aware that under the current circumstances it is impossible to *write* about me, and I must consider myself lucky that at least I can be *spoken* about. But the sensation of unreality I experience has as its origin the realization I've already come to several times, that is that in Rumania I belong to the *oral* culture, just like characters in folklore, or like a hero of a popular ballad. I in no way deserve that "glory," which in essence proves nothing, for it crowns an extremely famous writer, they say, but one whose works remain unobtainable.

9 December

The young G.G. comes to tell me about his latest "discovery," which deals with the Moslem precursors of Dante. He has just read the English translation of *La Escatologia Musulmana en la Divina Comedia* [*Islam and the Divine Comedy*], the work of the great Spanish Orientalist, Asin Palacio. In fact, he only read the first fifty pages of it, but they seemed convincing to him. He opens his notebook and summarizes for me Asin Palacio's thesis on the similarity of images relative to the mystical ascension (*miraj*) of Muhammad. Accompanied by the archangel Gabriel, the Prophet takes off "like the wind" or "like the arrow" towards his Throne of Glory. Comparing the two texts, Asin Palacio observes that Dante uses the same images. Dante, in effect, arrives "like the arrow" (*come saeta: Paradise* 5.91–92) in the sky of the moon and the planet Mars. The souls of those who come to meet him in the sphere of the planet Venus fly "like the wind" (*Paradise* 8.22–24a), and "like a whirlwind" (*turbo*) those of the sky of Saturn (*Paradise* 22.99).

G.G. closes his notebook triumphantly and asks me what I think. I answer that as soon as he presented it, Asin Palacio's thesis caused many discussions and controversies. Today, Islamic scholars who accept it in its entirety are rare. But that's not what's most important, I added. Basically, the methodological problem is the following: Does the similarity between two groups of images authorize us to see in it indubitable proof of borrowing? I remind him that the symbolism of the arrow is one of the most archaic and is basically quite complex. I look for one of my articles, *Notes on the Symbolism of the Arrow,* and cite a few examples for him. Thus according to certain Indo-Tibetan traditions, the soul that escapes from the *brahmanandra* (invisible opening at the top of the skull) flies away "like a bird" and penetrates through the "opening" of the sky "like an arrow." The vertiginous escape of the soul through the *brahmanandra* is described like that of an arrow of light, similar to a shooting star. Similar images are found in all of central Asia, and even elsewhere.

"But then what's to be done?" asks G.G., whose disappointment is visible.

I suggest that he orient his research towards the morphology and history of the image of the ascension of the soul compared to the flight of the arrow in classical literatures among the church fathers and in Christian folklore of the Middle Ages. Very ill-at-ease, G.G. then admits that the subject no longer interests him. He had only latched onto it when he had believed he possessed proof that Dante had been influenced by Moslem eschatology . . .

This is how I wasted almost an hour of my time, without counting the fifteen minutes it took me to write this entry. But it is not a useless task, for it will henceforth remind me of how *one must not* proceed with students in search of subjects for their term papers. And I will gain serenity from it.

15 December

Christinel left yesterday for New York. It's unusually cold out.
I walk over to Regenstein Library, and for several hours I go from one
floor to another, then go back down several times to the main floor to
use the card catalogue, only to go back upstairs to look for the reference
I'm interested in. Tired, a bit weary, I get ready to leave when I realize
I've mislaid my fur hat. I must have forgotten it somewhere, in some
corner of the stacks, while going through a book—but which one? The
library has five floors, and there are in all a good dozen kilometers of
stacks. I had stopped in front of at least fifty of them to look for a book,
verify a citation, etc. . . . Of course, I had all my bibliographical
notecards in my pocket, but I had stuffed them in there at random, out
of order. Yet I remembered having begun my research in the section on
classical archeology. In front of the first set of stacks I suddenly
remembered that I had stopped on the way, in the middle of that
interminable corridor that goes through the entire building, to consult
certain collections of journals, and rather than going directly to the
section on classical archeology, I had let myself be tempted by the
numerous rows that separate the shelves. I went off then a bit
haphazardly, quickening my step and trembling each time I noticed an
empty space between books, hoping to find my hat there.

After having searched the section on classical archeology in vain, I
took the elevator to continue my search on the second floor, aisle by
aisle. But when I got out of the elevator and saw before me a corridor
almost identical to the one I had just gone down a few moments earlier,
I suddenly had the impression of living a waking dream, and that this
dream was going to turn into a nightmare. If there had been a seat within
arm's reach, I would have certainly sat down to try to concentrate on
something else. But I knew that chairs were rare, that one found them
only in certain hidden corners, and that they were in any case almost
always being used. I went back down to the reading room, where I was
able to rest awhile in an armchair in front of the Loeb collection of
classical authors. Then, quickly making up my mind, I headed toward

the exit, not without having wrapped my scarf around my head like a turban, and I went back home.

I didn't have any illusions. Weeks could go by before a library employee finds my fur hat and takes it to the lost and found, sincerely believing that its owner is in the vicinity and will soon be coming to claim it. And to think that the harsh Chicago winter has only just begun!

I had to resign myself to call Christinel in New York to find out where she had bought the hat I had lost, and a half hour later a taxi let me out at Marshall Field's, only a few moments before the store closed for the day. Luckily I saw in the distance that long table, almost endless, on which were what at first glance seemed to be large baskets, filled to the brim with all sorts of fur hats . . .

December

Admirable Edgar L.! For some time a Latin verse was going through my head: *Claudite jam rivos, pueri; sat prata biberunt.* I well knew it was from Virgil, but where exactly was it found? I asked Edgar, and he answered that it was a verse from the Third Bucolic. I went to look for the Bucolics in the library, and started going through the book from beginning to end. Indeed, it was in the Third Bucolic that I was able to find my verse. Whence my great sadness for this memory that I sense is escaping me more each year, and even from day to day.

Celtic myth of sovereignty: In Ireland the king was considered to be the husband of the goddess Medb, and that *hieros gamos* assured the prosperity and independence of the island. Throughout the centuries, poets continued to see in the figure of the legitimate king the partner of the autochthonous goddess. In the eighteenth century the Stuarts, then in exile, were considered to be the true spouses of the goddess, that is, of Ireland, those who were in fact on the throne being only foreign usurpers who had to have used force to bring the goddess Medb to their mercy.

To add to my file on the archaic origins of Irish institutions.

NEW YORK, *24 December*

I must do some research on the life and activities of Olympiodorus of Thebes (Egypt). I only know that he lived in the fifth century and that he was the principal representative of the Byzantine diplomatic service. He was sent on missions just about everywhere—to Rome, Nubia, and on the Dnieper. There is an anecdote about him that I find enchanting: Olympiodorus didn't go anywhere without his parrot, who spoke the purest classical Greek, that of Attica.

I'm writing this little note in Lisette's apartment, and as usual, I remember our first stay here, in September 1956, after the crossing on board the *Ile de France* in the company of Mamy and Christinel. I was supposed to stay a year, nine months to be precise, the time needed to complete the Haskell Lectures at the University of Chicago and to give courses as a visiting professor in the history of religions for three trimesters. And I have never stopped congratulating myself for having accepted, a few weeks later, the chair in the history of religions that was offered me at that admirable university.

3 January 1973

The weather is superb at the beginning of this new year. The sky is unbelievably blue. Not one cloud, but it is quite cold. I spent almost the whole day in my office sorting documents on prehistoric religions, notably those of the Mesolithic era. Then I wrote a good half dozen letters, some of which were four or five pages long. Today, Wednesday, at the time I'm writing these lines, I'm on my fourth.

7 January

I've begun drafting the chapter on the religions of the Meso-lithic, but I don't feel well. As always in these situations I know that I must not stop writing.

12 January

In his book on the BaMbuti, a pygmy tribe of the tropical forest, Turnbull tells of how one evening, seeing the young Kenge, the life of all parties, dancing alone in a clearing, he could not hide his surprise.

"But I'm *not* dancing alone!" exclaimed Kenge. "I am dancing with the forest, dancing with the moon!"

Turnbull adds that Kenge ignored his presence with the "utmost unconcern" and continued unperturbed his dance of love and life (C. Turnbull, *The Forest People*, p. 272).

In his doctoral thesis, Jerry L. devotes several pages to an analysis of the meaning of this communion with the moon and the forest, and the commentary he gives on it deserves consideration. For if Jerry, who is black, experienced the need to explain in detail Kenge's response to Turnbull, one must deduce that such a laborious exegesis was necessary, and it is exactly this that saddens me. This proves that only a *commentary* can communicate to a reader of today a meaning which should, however, be *obvious*.

14 January

To add to the file on a comparative history of the "initiatory trial" of William Tell: According to the nuptial rites of the Lubas, a tribe of the southern Congo, the groom must shoot an arrow from a certain distance, hitting an egg placed on the head of his future wife. Of course, this trial constitutes the ritual anticipation of the deflowering and the guarantee of its accomplishment, the egg being the symbol of the female sexual organs.

16 January

An astonishingly beautiful day, as if made especially to render this city, so rich in contrasts, quite attractive. There are many Americans who adore Chicago and seize the slightest opportunity to sing its praises. When I want to tease them I tell them what Julien Green wrote in his journal in 1942–1943. During a brief visit he had to make to Chicago, he was so disturbed by what he saw on his way from the train station to his hotel that for three days he refused to go out of his room, preferring to read from morning to night.

21–23 January

Sick as a dog. Yesterday and today I had to spend hours at Billings Hospital, where I was given all sorts of tests. As usual, Dr.

Cohen discovers nothing abnormal. Or rather, my affliction is the price I pay for taking six or eight aspirin tablets daily when I have my arthritis attacks.

What is most curious is that I often happen to "forget" my pain even before swallowing the first tablet. It was enough to think intensely about such and such a subject—a memory, an idea that was going through my head, the page I was getting ready to write—for the pain to disappear immediately.

But on these late winter mornings, after barely a few hours of laborious and troubled sleep (because I sometimes read until three o'clock in the morning, and afterwards it takes me a good hour to fall asleep), the only thing that really matters to me is the very hot and very strong coffee Christinel brings me.

25 January

When I read or reread books or studies on the life of Muhammad and the beginnings of Islam, I manage to discover revealing, or sometimes just simply humorous, details. Just today I came across this passage by Ibn Sa'd, which I no longer remembered: Speaking of the beauty of the ten sons of Abd el Muttalib, whose proud bearing and noble features were without equal among Arabs, the chronicler points out "that no one had a more noble profile. They all had noses so big that the noses drank even before the lips had touched the cup . . ."

28 January

Thanks to the flu and fever, it's been two days since I've left my room. As if by design this happens to me when I am slaving away in the hopes of finishing up the final paragraphs on the religions of the Neolithic.

I try to put my memory to work. I think again about the hospital in Albion, and I see myself after I left intensive care, in that other room with the astonishing glass walls. Then I go back farther into the past, a bit at random, and I remember my last encounter with Papini in 1952, or the conversation I had with Ortega y Gasset in 1943 in Lisbon in the course of which I told him that it was possible he was wrong in stating that all Western ontology proceeded from the *gigantesca arbitrariedad* of Parmenides, who claimed that the Becoming could not participate in the Being. When I compared it to Indian ontology, which asserts the contrary: "I'm not familiar with these texts," he politely replied, "and I thus don't have the right to contradict you. All the same, I wonder to what extent one may speak of a systematic Indian philosophy." I promised to send him Shankara's commentary on the *Brahma-Sutra,* which I indeed intended to obtain from the library of the British Institute whence Eugenio Navarro brought me all the books I needed. But it happened that of the fifty volumes of the *Sacred Books of the East,* Shankara's translation was conspicuously absent . . .

5 February

Yesterday I finished the chapter on the religions of the Mesolithic and the Neolithic. During the night I tidied up my office, and this morning I've begun to sort my files on Mesopotamia. I find course outlines from four or five years ago, as well as numerous, copiously annotated texts.

February

I was delighted to read this quote by a first-rate physicist, Louis Kahn (*Time,* 15 January 1973): "We are actually born out of light, you might say. I believe light is the maker of all material. Material is spent light." In English, this final sentence is pleasing to the ear, and very suggestive: *"Matter is spent light."* [1]

This reminds me of archaic beliefs and myths relating to light, and more specifically to the "inner light," a notion of capital importance in Indian spirituality. In fact, the experience of this "inner light"(*antar-jiotih*) is the only possible proof of what the Indians call the "realization of self," through which man becomes fully conscious of his own being (*atman*). The light is consubstantial both with the Being (*atman-Brahman*) and with Immortality. Beginning in the Vedic period one sees the appearance of the Divinity-Sun-Light-Spirit (*atman*) equivalence.

1. The quote from Kahn (who is actually an architect rather than a physicist) is given here as it appeared in *Time* magazine. Eliade gave only the last sentence in English, using the word *matter* rather than *material.*—ED.

And since each one of these epiphanies of the Being is a source of creation on different cosmic levels, the series of equivalences must be crowned with another epiphany: the *semen virile*.

I've devoted an entire study to this question ("Spirit, Light, and Seed").[1] I will therefore not come back to it. But Louis Kahn's assertion—"*matter is spent light*"—makes me ponder those myths according to which the primordial being was created from light, and was sexless. According to certain Gnostic, but also Judeo-Christian, legends, Adam lost the light as soon as he had sinned, thus after having become conscious of the sexual act. According to Tibetan and Mongolian mythologies, the first human beings were made out of light and had no sex, and it was sexual instinct that made genital organs appear. Unions were accomplished through sight alone, and procreation through light: It was sufficient for the light radiating from the man to reach the body of the woman. Afterwards people learned to caress each other, and it is thus that they discovered sexual union. But then the light in them went out, and the sun and the moon appeared in the sky . . .

Thanks to such myths, the concepts and techniques unique to Indian Tantrism and to Gnosticism are more understandable. In Tantrism the *semen virile* is in a certain way "materialized" light, and the rite of sexual union (*maithuna*) must be interpreted from this perspective. This isn't the place to repeat all that I've written on the orgiastic rites of the Ebionites, who, just like the followers of Manichaeanism and of other Gnostic sects, believed in the existence of miniscule particles of divine light inside the seminal fluid.

It is rather interesting to note that, according to physicists today, matter is nothing but "spent" and petrified light, whereas according to the myths I've just mentioned, light—epiphany of the Spirit—is hidden, or rather is held captive in living matter, and more precisely in that which constitutes its very essence and is the source of all life, the *semen virile*. It is only when life itself is "spent," that is, at the time of death, that light is definitively materialized and petrified.

1. This study appears in *Occultism, Witchcraft, and Cultural Fashions,* The University of Chicago Press, 1976.—TRAN.

This is obviously not the place to compare two opposing conceptions of the world. But supposing that one day someone writes a comparative history of ontology, the myths I've just cited will necessarily have to serve as a point of departure. They cannot illustrate more clearly the specific homology of all archaic ontologies, for one discovers in them the same series of equivalences: absolute reality—sacred (divine)—spirit—creativity—life—Eros.

"Notions of virtue and sin exist only in humans. They have no meaning for creatures other than men" (*Mahâbhârata* 12.238.28). This means that the animal world doesn't know of them, no more than do the gods, or even the demons.

The same idea is found in other cultural contexts, but it is in India that it has been considered most and applied in multiple realms, both philosophical and religious. In Indian thought, the *perfection* to which a human being aspires has nothing to do with his own condition. It is only insofar as the human condition can be cancelled, or overcome—among other means, through yoga techniques, mystical experience, philosophy or ascesis, hashish or orgiastic practices—that one can reach that paradoxical state of *absolute freedom* which is the goal of Indian spirituality. But overcoming the human condition also implies that an existential modality is realized where good and evil—"virtue and sin"—lose all meaning or have the same value.

But what is most interesting is that it is only man, and man alone, who can attain absolute freedom, and that he alone can know that state of indescribable beatitude which in texts is called *samadhi, saccidananda, nirvâna,* etc. . . . As for the gods, they benefit from a most agreeable and even very long existence, for they can live up to tens and hundreds of millions of years. They are not for all that immortal, and cannot as such attain freedom. When a god wishes to "free himself," he must first become incarnate, that is, take on the "human condition."

According to the Freudians, as well as to many others, C. G. Jung is a "mystic." They claim that he improvises, imagines, generalizes, etc. I find it offensive to say that about a man who took the trouble to analyze sixty-seven thousand dreams, those of his patients as well as of his collaborators, before proposing his own theory on dreams.

The first example of how Italian populations were seduced by Oriental cults: the sanctuary built by an Etruscan king to the goddess Astarte.

PITTSBURGH, *1 March*

Despite an attack of arthritis, I did have to fly to Pittsburgh, for I had promised a long time ago to give a mini-course at the Catholic University.

Sanda L. came to get us at the airport, and we'll spend the night at her house. Tomorrow, Christinel will leave for New York and I'll go stay with the Holy Ghost Fathers.

PITTSBURGH, *2 March*

First lecture on sacred space and time. (I'm summarizing the course I've already given at Princeton University.) Then debates with students. In the evening, more debates, this time with professors.

My room is located on the uppermost of the twenty floors in this immense building that accommodates restaurants and rooms reserved for men and women students, as well as several lecture halls.

The teaching fathers must live on this same floor. When I came in, at around ten in the evening, I noticed some of them playing poker. Father C., heavy, fat, voluble, very nice, is as it were both the guardian and the manager of my floor, and I have the impression he never leaves it. He is the life of these poker parties that carry on until late into the night. I'm writing these lines at two in the morning, and I can hear his outbursts all the way from his room at the floor's entrance. One of his partners has undoubtedly expressed interest in going to bed . . .

PITTSBURGH, *3 March*

Arthritis attack. Nothing else to do but patiently accept my pain. Today, second session: an hour and a half course first, then discussions with students. After lunch, other debates followed by two mini-courses combined into one hour. We have dinner with Father C. and two other professors in a well-known restaurant built onto the banks overlooking the river.

PITTSBURGH, *4 March*

This afternoon, stroll in the park. I realize that I have as yet hardly seen the city at all.

The taping of my dialogue with Father M. in the studios of the university television station is a true catastrophe, even worse than I would have imagined. Never again will I agree to converse in front of microphones, blinded by projectors, intimidated by technicians who watch me, and especially listen to me, with apparent weariness. They had good reason. I fidgeted around on my chair, chopped my sentences, and pronounced certain words in a faint voice . . .

CHICAGO, *6 March*

To retain: this declaration by Trevelyan, who is considered to be one of the principal English historians of this century. "Let the science and research of the historian find the fact, and let his imagination and art make clear its significance."

10 March

Yesterday we invited around twenty friends, university colleagues for the most part, to come celebrate my sixty-sixth birthday in the apartment Alexandra lent us. I received several gifts. My favorite was a chain from which hung a bizarrely cut stone, the work of Sonia Gilkey. It has disappeared. I had left it with other gifts in Florica's room. When we were getting ready to leave, I couldn't find it again. It was probably the young man who was serving champagne who took it.

I was thirty-three when I left Rumania. Since then, thirty-three more years have gone by. This causes me to reflect, and most particularly on the contents of my *Autobiography*. I do believe I have managed to bring it up to the time of my departure for England. Should I continue it in the same way, year to year? Wouldn't it be preferable to begin the narrative of my life *starting with today,* then go backwards in order to rediscover the Mircea Eliade of my youth, he who bade farewell to his family and friends on the train platform in Bucharest one April afternoon in 1940?

March

Modern art: *All matter,* even the least aesthetic, including waste and excrement, can serve as a basis for artistic expression. Musn't we see in this another way of sacralizing brute matter: the stone considered *as such,* and not by the way in which it has been worked?

Already in Plato's time the Greeks were fascinated by "origins" and genealogies: "They adore being told the genealogy of heroes and (great) men, as well as the history of the origins of their cities. In short [they love] all tales relating to events of the past" (*Hippias major* 285d).

25 March

I'm finishing the chapter on Mesopotamian religions, which I had begun on 6 February. I wonder whether this *History of Religious Ideas* will be easily understood in the way I am writing it. On the one hand, I'd like it to be an easy-to-read manual. But on the other hand, the selection of "creative moments" in different religions is made by the generalist that I am, and not by a specialist, who could reproach me for having insisted too much on . . . or for having omitted . . . etc. Yet, even if my interpretation of essential texts is sometimes the fruit of twenty or thirty years of research and personal reflections, when I'm dealing with religions that I haven't had the opportunity to study in depth, either because they didn't interest me particularly or because I was unable to obtain a large part of the critical bibliography (as was the case for Japanese religions), I also present the interpretations of certain specialists. The fact remains that I have never referred to their interpretations except insofar as they overlapped those of the generalist that I am. I could not under any circumstances accept responsibility for the interpretation or the commentaries of an Orientalist, for example, whether he is a philologist, archeologist, or epigraphist, who, after having read and translated a religious text, would attempt to explain it or to present it from the perspective of notions that were in style eighty years ago, such as animism, fetishism, *mana,* magic, or by using the theories of Frazer, Durkheim, Lévy-Bruhl, etc.

2 April

I had that dream again out of which I always awaken at peace, almost happy: I was in an unknown town that spread out in a circular arc above a gulf. I walked up streets bordered by superb houses and ancient dwellings of a style which I couldn't name. Some were in ruins, but were nevertheless of very great nobility, like preciously preserved museum pieces. One could visit them freely: No guard, no barrier prevented one from entering them, and there was no need to buy a ticket to go in. I kept climbing and climbing, and finally reached the top. The town spread out at my feet around the gulf far, far below me. I don't remember having seen one fishing scow, not one boat on the sea. All the same, the town wasn't dead. I constantly met passersby and numerous children, but they never uttered a word. In last night's dream, smiling children showed me cherry trees in bloom on the side of the road.

5 April

I must one day write an article on these American students who, although extraordinarily talented, suddenly abandon their studies, sometimes definitively, for "existential" reasons. I do believe I have already cited the case of that student who excelled in anthropology, but who nevertheless dropped everything to go live in the middle of a forest in British Columbia. In the History of Religions Department I've witnessed even more remarkable cases: After having taken courses for two years one of my best students, the young P.R., left the University of Chicago to go live with the one she loved, who had found a job in California. The job in question consisted of removing as quickly as possible from racetracks horses that had to be destroyed or had been injured . . .

And what more can be said of the unforgettable Dorothy P.? Christinel and I had met her when she was in her second year of college. She took my courses for a while. She was an extraordinary girl: She succeeded in learning Persian so quickly and so well that she was selected from among ten or fifteen of the best candidates in a competition in Oriental studies, which allowed her to go spend several months in Iran. She was also interested in Bengali, which she had begun to study, and in medieval art and literature. She could play the guitar, draw, paint, etc. . . . When she had graduated from the college, she decided to drop everything, although she had been offered numerous scholarships, and she moved to New York to take care of children from three to six years old.

10 April

Yesterday evening, gathering at the Quadrangle Club in the company of Florica, Alexandra, and Octav Onicescu. I hadn't seen Onicescu since the winter of 1940! Although now more than eighty years old, he remains just as I knew him then. With reserve and conciseness he describes for us, sometimes subtly, the situation in Rumania. It's not possible for me to summarize what he said here.

All evening I felt both moved and melancholy. Too many memories were assailing me, most without importance, in any event. I think of those ten volumes of the complete works of Paul Tannery that Nae Ionescu and Onicescu, both enthralled by the history of sciences, had bought together. I remember having consulted them myself, in 1927 or 1928. I wonder what has become of those magnificent books. Is there at least one of them left?

12 April

I'm reading Charlie Chaplin's autobiography with the greatest interest. If it is truly he who wrote it, and in its entirety, one must consider Chaplin to be an authentic writer, and his account will certainly contribute to a better understanding of America in the 1950s. The most popular artist of the time could do nothing against the intrigues and slander orchestrated so well by the "Establishment." In the end, he had to leave the United States and move to Switzerland.

Ten or fifteen years have gone by since then, and the scandal provoked by the accusations of crypto-communism brought against him has today become unthinkable. If, however, it erupted, it would result very quickly in Chaplin's apotheosis.

13 April

Today I received a visit from the linguist C. Poghirc, the author of an admirable book on B. P. Hasdeu.[1] Then circumstances dictate that I see M. again . . . Forty-three years have gone by since our last meeting. I have the impression of living an unbelievable, false, unreal, and in a certain sense, very tasteless moment.

14 April

Evening spent at Edward Levi's, the president of our university, in honor of John Nef. In the course of our conversation we come to speak about the influence of social, political, and economic realities on religious creation. I would have liked to have drawn the attention of the other guests to the fact that in the past, barely a few centuries ago, wars, politics, and the economy itself *all had a religious significance*. Accordingly, they were tributaries of a certain metaphysics.

Back home, I regretted my reserve. Certain truths seem so obvious to me that I refuse to point them out, for I would feel that I was presenting truisms. I'm probably wrong: Certain things are only obvious to people who, like me, know how to distinguish between behaviors inherent in traditional societies, in which war, for example, is above all a rite, and those that are born and develop in our desacralized societies.

20 April

Lisette has arrived from New York.

1. Bogdan P. Hasdeu (1836–1907): Rumanian historian, encyclopedist, and philologist. His *Magnum Etymologicum Romaniae,* a monument of scholarship, remains the basis for Rumanian linguistics.—C.G.

I won't resist the temptation to tell the anecdote of which the filmmaker Paul Fejos was the hero in 1936, and which goes back to the time when he was not yet one of the directors of the Wenner-Gren Foundation. He was on board a steamboat, off the shore of Denmark, when he took a fancy to a young starlet and journalist by the name of Inge Arvad. She had very much admired his watch, a little marvel of watchmaking, which showed not only the hours, minutes, and seconds, but also the date and the phases of the moon. Paul Fejos stripped it from his wrist and held it out to Inge, saying: "It is yours." Of course, the young woman refused. Upon which Fejos threw the watch overboard.

"What could she do but marry him?" adds John W. Dodds, Paul Fejos's biographer (*The Several Lives of Paul Fejos,* 1973, p. 52).

23 April

The poet Cezar Baltag and his wife came to see us in the late afternoon, and we took them to dinner at the Quadrangle Club. They spent some time in Iowa City as writers in residence, just as Adrian Paunescu, Banulescu, and Marin Sorescu had done before them a few years earlier. I note once again, not without pleasure, that one can survive both as a man and as an artist in a posthistorical society.

26 April

M. has left on a lecture tour of several universities. I thus have one or two weeks of tranquility before me.

I have not yet written anything about her being with us, but I must write in more detail about it in the second volume of my *Autobiography.* I will thus limit myself to underlining here how admirably— "angelically" said Y.—Christinel treated her, accompanying her everywhere, giving her all her time. But there would be too much to say about it.

28 April

I noticed William O'Meara in the distance, immobile on the edge of the sidewalk. I thought he was waiting for the light to turn green to cross the street. But having caught up to him I realized that he was in no way concerned with traffic lights. His head bent slightly to the right, he was simply letting the rays of sunlight bathe his face, and was in no hurry to leave.˙

He jumped when I said hello to him. Then with his usual soft and sad smile he informed me that Jacques Maritain had just died in France, in a monastery, at the age of ninety-one. Had Maritain ever guessed that he would live so long? When in 1957 or 1958 I met him for the first time at John Nef's, several years after his first heart attack, I was impressed by the severity of the regimen he imposed upon himself. One would have thought that he was trying to atone for the sins of his youth. He was sitting, stretched out, his feet on a stool, and he excused himself for greeting me in that position. He was only following his doctor's orders, he said. Having been warned by John Nef that I risked tiring him by asking him too many questions, I hardly dared open my mouth at all. I therefore let him speak and intervened as little as possible. He told me how much he had liked *Myth of the Eternal Return,* which he had used on many occasions and which he had often cited during the Gilford Lectures. He also asked me what had become of one of my former students, Mihaï Sora, whose *Dialogue intérieur* he had liked very much. But our conversation was rather stiff, so much did I fear tiring him, and I jumped from one subject to another. I spoke to him about how *Three Reformers: Luther, Descartes, Rousseau,* the first book I had read by him in 1928, had left an impression on me, and I immediately regretted saying so, for, with an annoyed smile, he admitted that he was no longer satisfied with that work which he had written forty years earlier. And suddenly, perhaps because he had gone back forty years in time, he asked me about Mircea Vulcanescu. At the time, in 1957, I knew nothing specific about him, except that he was still in prison but was believed to be alive.

Since then I've had the opportunity to see Jacques Maritain several times again, but I was always obsessed with the fear of tiring him. I have never met anyone so influenced by a heart ailment. It is true that it occurred when Jacques Maritain was seventy years old. He gave the

impression of fearing terribly another attack, which would then be fatal.
"I have to obey my doctor," he would say as an excuse each time he got
up from the table immediately after dessert to go lie down in his room.

"He suffered a lot in the end," O'Meara told me. "He wanted to die,
but death didn't want him."

Perhaps Jacques Maritain thus atoned for having too rigorously
"obeyed his doctor's orders."

WINSTON-SALEM (NORTH CAROLINA), *3 May*

We arrived yesterday, having been invited by Mary Stevenson.
This is the first time we've been to North Carolina. True spring weather
greets us, weather I had forgotten existed during those long years spent
in Chicago. The house, located on the outskirts of the city, has a flower
garden in front of it. On the other side an orchard extends all the way
to the neighboring woods.

At the end of the day a storm breaks. It lasts throughout the night. My
arthritis makes me suffer terribly. I don't think I slept more than two
hours. During such attacks I well know that aspirin is not enough to help
me, and I opt for other means, those of anamnesis exercises, as I like
to call them. I thus begin to recall my pericarditis of the night of 8–9
March 1971, and I see myself in my office at Albion reading, or rather
rereading, the texts engraved on the gold plates that were discovered in
Petelia and Eleutherae. I had gotten to the famous passage, "Hail to
thee who dost travel by the right-hand road toward the sacred fields and
grove of Persephone," when I felt a brutal, atrocious pain in my neck,
such as I had never felt before. I couldn't even swallow my saliva. I
managed with great difficulty to get up from my desk. Despite the
arthritis attack that had been torturing my knees for more than four
hours, I had decided nevertheless to go take two more aspirin tablets. It
was then that I felt as if my heart was in a vise. Without any doubt,
something I was as yet unaware of was going to happen, but I wasn't
afraid. In just a few hours more I would be sixty-four years old. I
couldn't imagine a lovelier death than to leave this world the very day
of my birth. I was sure, however, that I was not going to experience
physical death. If this heart attack had a meaning (and if it didn't it was

up to me to give it one), I was in the process of undergoing an initiatory trial in the course of which one must suffer terribly, and even "die" in a certain sense, to facilitate one's ability to be reborn. I then began to "visualize" my heart, as I had been taught to do . . .

I have just written this passage in the study that Mary has kindly put at my disposal. I've brought with me several files filled with notes, as well as the chapter I'm currently writing on the religion of the Hittites. I would need several hours to relate in detail the anamnesis exercises which I engaged in last night. Some day I must decide to do so, for these meditation exercises, apart from their cathartic value, are in themselves most instructive, and even "aesthetic" in the sense that they project he who engages in them into a universe of images that is gradually transformed into a sort of dramatic production; everything is part of the performance.

This morning it is still raining. Professor Mac Ricketts, one of my former students, has just arrived from Luisburg. He has learned Rumanian to be able to read my literary writings in their original texts.

During the afternoon the sky finally clears. A long walk on the avenue, past houses half hidden by trees.

WINSTON-SALEM, *4 May*

The weather is glorious. We go by car to Reynolds House to visit that old-time dwelling, at the same time a villa, a palace, and a museum, endowed with a melancholy charm. While looking out the window at the rose bushes that grow bending into flowering arches, I suddenly want to write a short story.

WINSTON-SALEM, *5 May*

A long night of insomnia, which happens to me rarely. I couldn't fall asleep until daybreak. This morning is just as superb as yesterday. Car ride in the neighboring hills. I spend a good part of the afternoon in my office writing note upon note in my yellow notebook.

CHICAGO, *7 May*

We came back in the evening. I reread my notes of the day before yesterday on the *puer eternus*. Jung's interpretation is uniquely of a psychological nature. According to him, every adult conceals within himself an "eternal child" in perpetual development, who never reaches maturity, and who has a permanent need for care and education. Jung is most certainly correct. All the same, one must nevertheless not forget all there is beyond these psychological considerations. The mythology of the *puer eternus* must be completed by a yet insufficiently elucidated "ontology," by a specific modality of existing in the world which would appeal to spontaneity, games, and the need for pure and gratuitous creativity. To complete with my reflections of September 1957.

9 May

Lecture by Jean Filliozat. I hadn't seen him since September 1958 in Japan, at the time of the International Congress of the History of Religions. While listening to him, I remembered our first conversations at the Asiatic Society and at the Institute of Indian Civilization. Not without melancholy, I recall those years when I believed I would be able to return totally and exclusively to my Indian studies. But it is probably not in my nature to confine myself to only one discipline, be it one of the vastest. During the three years I lived in India I believe I learned what I essentially needed to continue my work in the direction in which I had set myself. I always experience the same pleasure in immersing myself again in my "Indian file," even when the subjects of my courses don't necessarily lend themselves to doing so. But after a few weeks—two months at the most—of intense work, I come across other subjects of interest, and I put my Indian file back into a corner of my bookshelves.

12 May

Mateï Calinescu, visiting professor at Indiana University in Bloomington, came to see me the day before yesterday. All evening we discuss at length the current status of culture, and above all, of literature and literary criticism back home in Rumania.

20 May

I speak with R. about the relationships between logic and fantasy. I cite the case of Nicolas Ciarletta, whose doctor had prescribed hydrotherapeutics for him, for he had found his liver rather "tired and lazy." Nicolas diligently followed the treatment that had been prescribed for him. Glass in hand, he waited his turn patiently at the spring, chatted with the other patients about its therapeutic virtues, and conscientiously had his goblet refilled. Then, like everyone else, he took a fifteen-minute walk in the park around the spa so that the miraculous water could take effect. But he never knew the taste of it. After taking a few steps he emptied the contents of his glass onto the ground, and carried on with his walk. It is thus that he underwent "treatment" for three whole weeks, without missing even one day.

22 May

Nietzsche: "When one is who I am, one loses—as Goethe said—the right to be judged by one's peers" (*Werke* 12.337).

30 May

I receive a letter from Vienna from Professor Otto Höfler. He announces that I have just been named—very probably thanks to him—corresponding member of the Austrian Academy of Sciences. It was he who, upon the publication of my *Patterns,* succeeded in persuading Otto Müller to publish it in German. I have a lengthy correspondence with him. As a Germanist and a specialist in Nordic religions, he was delighted that there were still historians of religions concerned with deciphering the meaning of religious creations, and who were not content to simply retrace their history.

Otto Höfler's scholarship is astounding, whether he is dealing with philology, archeology, or historiography. I remember my enthusiasm when I read for the first time, pencil in hand, *Geheimkulte der Germanen.* And once again I think about the unprecedented catastrophe brought on by nazism that affected every realm of existence. Between 1934 and 1940 research in military initiatory rites of diverse Indo-European nations had been considerably developed. During these years several works were published which have since become classics, and which had as authors Höfler, Stig Wikander, Jan de Vries, and Georges

Dumézil. Then the war broke out, and when it ended the extermination camps, the crematoria, Buchenwald, Auschwitz, and so many other horrors were discovered.

Since then, those studies on the military initiatory rites of Indo-European peoples, despite their high scientific level and quality, have become suspect, and their authors risk being considered Nazis, or pro-Nazis.

1 June

T.A. tells me that his wife threw him out of the house. They were to remain separated for two or three years.

5 June

Since I learned how the two great invalids of the century, Franz Rosenzweig and Giovanni Papini, were able to overcome their infirmities and continue their work, although they had both become petrified alive, buried within their own bodies (Papini was in addition almost blind, and during the last months of his life was only able to articulate unintelligible sounds), I've discovered another subject of curiosity. Indeed, I would very much like to know how certain authors of genius have learned to cope with the afflictions inherent in aging. I was quite astonished to read in the correspondence between Goethe and Frédéric Soret a letter dated 16 November 1823, in which Goethe tells of his heart ailment: "This illness," he says, "prevents me from working coherently. I can't even allow myself to read for a long time, and if I want to think, I must do so, so to speak, on the sly, and by surprise in good intervals."

"To think on the sly and by surprise"! What pleasure Nietzsche would have taken in reading that line!

10 June

In writing about his first visit to Italy in 1843, Samuel Butler alludes to those beggars "who followed my father's carriage all day long, and who, when we didn't give them anything, shouted at the top of their lungs: Heretics! Heretics!''

M., to whom I read this excerpt from the *Notebooks,* shakes his head with melancholy.

"What a happy time it was," he tells me, "when insults could still make use of religious vocabulary!''

16 June

Stormy weather. It's hot and stifling. The sky is dark and sinister, like at the approach of a typhoon. The storm finally breaks on two sides at once. Our campus seems to attract all the lightning of the storm.

And it is in such weather that I receive a visit from Sargeant, the music critic for the *New Yorker,* who has come to give me his manuscript of the *Bhagavad-Gita:* text in Devanagari, transliteration, literal translation, grammatical analysis of each verse, literary translation, commentaries, etc. . . . Never before have I seen such a great amount of work on this subject. The manuscript is almost two thousand typewritten pages.

I met Sargeant for the first time in New York a few years ago. He very much admired Ionel Perlea and sang his praises in the long reviews he devoted to this great conductor after each of his concerts. Fascinated with Sanskrit, he admitted to me on our first encounter that he had launched into studying it alone and without a teacher, taking advantage of each moment he had free, before going to a concert, for example, while tying his tie, or in the morning while his wife prepared breakfast. This monumental edition of the *Bhagavad-Gita* took him several years. This morning he went to talk with Hans van Buitenen, who, for his part, is translating the integral text of *Mahâbhârata.* This evening I went to see him at his hotel, and he asked me to write a "little" preface. I joyfully accepted.

17 June

I finally finish and polish up the chapter on the religions of Ugarit. I don't know what the specialists in Semitic religions will think

of it, assuming they take the time to read *A History of Religious Ideas*
. . . All the same, I have the incontestable merit of probably being the
only nonspecialist to have read, and reread—and in four languages—all
the translations of Ugaritic texts that have appeared to date, as well as
all the studies that refer to them.

20 June

At whatever age one loses one's mother, said Paul Tillich, one
remains an orphan forever. This is not the case, he added, with the death
of the father.

22 June

I truly regret not having noted down immediately my conversation with that old gentleman I spoke to at the Windsor airport during the
three hours we spent waiting for the fog to lift. I can't remember how
we came to speak of the "new generation," that of the hippies in
particular, and of the "age limit" which afflicts most office workers
between the ages of sixty and sixty-five. As I was able to notice, the
man had been retired for some time already.

It is a complete waste of time, he told me with a melancholy smile,
for extremely intelligent and cultivated men, philosophers, priests of all
religions, scientists to attempt to give new meaning to the notion of
aging. In a society like that of North America—and all other societies
will end up imitating it sooner or later—aging has lost all meaning.

This situation seems irreversible. A growing number of old people
pretend not to be aware of their "existential situation," a term that
surprised me, coming from this man. They attempt to stop thinking of
it, and with false enthusiasm try to prolong the behavior unique to youth
and younger adults: They are seen "partying," dancing, playing sports,
participating in orgies, etc. . . .

I reminded him that in traditional societies, in Europe as in America,
only two generations ago, old people enjoyed not only a certain respect,
but also had a useful role to play, especially in rural areas and wherever
there were a lot of children, for the good reason that in these societies

each period of life had its specific role and prestige. The man interrupted me abruptly, as if annoyed: "Of course!" he said to me with the same smile as earlier, "but all that has since disappeared and is completely incompatible with current society. It is the price we must pay for having arrived where we are. The pollution of cities, the destruction of nature, the sexual revolution, are nothing compared to this major fact, that is, that old age has lost all meaning. Everything else can be corrected or changed, but not the void that has taken our place, for this is an 'existential transmutation.' "

And since I was looking at him once again with astonishment, and even a bit warily, he added:

"This void can never again be filled."

I did attempt to contradict him. He listened to me politely for a while, then asked me in an ironic tone:

"Do you really believe that one can rediscover innocence once one has lost it?"

27 June

Dinner at Olivier's, the consul general of France. Numerous guests, of all social and intellectual categories.

On the way home the storm breaks again, and we have to travel across a good half of Chicago under thunder and lightning. The storm stops as if by miracle at the precise moment the taxi lets us out in front of our door.

2–7 July

Magnificent summer days, such as one rarely sees in Chicago. I've completed and polished up my chapter on Israel.

July

One sometimes discovers troubling analogies between folkloric creations, which are the expression of popular genius, and certain experiences and conceptions of great modern thinkers. Who would be daring enough to compare Nietzsche, for example, with the shepherd of the *Mioritza?* And yet their respective *existences* are completely comparable. Nietzsche, that great invalid, not only accepted his illness but succeeded in dominating it and in changing its meaning. By assuming it as an integral part of his own destiny, Nietzsche was able to make his illness the unique means of recovering his health. More precisely, he saw in it a *spiritual* means, for, as he writes: "It is through the Spirit that one must help Nature."

But this wasn't all. The suffering, the atrocious migraines, the dizziness, which should have clouded his mind and paralyzed his creative faculties, were on the contrary for him inestimable gifts thanks to which, he recognized himself, he could reach heights which would have otherwise remained inaccessible to him. In truth, Nietzsche succeeded in transfiguring adversity into beatitude, and made it into the tool that would multiply his creative faculties.

The same thing occurs in the popular Rumanian ballad. Learning that he is to be killed, the shepherd does not break down into lamentations and curse his fate. All the same, he does not bow down passively before the *inevitable,* and does not resign himself either to his fate or to the role of victim that destiny assigns him. Quite to the contrary, he sees a privilege in this fatality. For him, death is not that other wedding to which he would be invited by virtue of the ancient symbolism that causes those two radical ruptures in the life of a being to be joined together. It is transfigured into a marriage of cosmic dimensions. In the end the shepherd succeeds in transmuting the event into a "mystery," and in giving new meaning to the world and to existence. His reaction in the face of adversity thus became an example for an entire people.

Gurdjieff hoped that no one would ever speak about or publish anything of his "Teachings." However, in the last ten years, several books by Gurdjieff have been published, not counting all the works that deal with his "Teachings."

This is not an isolated phenomenon. Each day more and more esoteric texts are published which deal with secret initiatory traditions, such as Tantrism, Hermeticism, etc. . . . We are entering into a period that I would be tempted to call *phanic*. We display in broad daylight texts, ideas, beliefs, rites, etc., which normally should have remained hidden, and access to them reserved only to initiates. I don't know whether this phenomenon has been the object of any study dealing with the philosophy of culture. We're dealing, however, with a fact that is as fascinating as it is paradoxical: Secret, that is, "esoteric," doctrines and methods are only unveiled and put within the reach of everyone *because they no longer have any chance of being understood*. They can henceforth only be badly understood and poorly interpreted by non-initiates.

I read several pages from a recently published book (1972), *Social Sciences as Sorcery*. The author, Stanislav Andreski, is professor of sociology at the University of Reading. It's worth citing certain passages from it. For example: ". . . the moral disorientation and fanatic nihilism which afflict modern youth have been stimulated by the popular brands of sociology and psychology with their bias for overlooking the more inspiring achievements and focusing on the dismal average or even the subnormal" [p. 34].

And further: "By interpreting every manifestation of warm feelings between persons of the same sex as latent homosexuality, the psycho-analysts (to give another example) have debased and well-nigh destroyed the concept of friendship. . ." [p. 34].

Or yet: ". . . social and political studies have opened the gates of academic pastures to a large number of aspirants to the status of a scientist who might have been perfectly useful citizens as post-office managers or hospital almoners, but who have been tempted into charlatanry by being faced with a subject utterly beyond their mental powers" [p. 204].

Professor Andreski denounces the accreted importance from which benefits what he calls the "nebulous verbosity which opens a road to the most prestigious academic posts to people of small intelligence whose limitations would stand naked if they had to state what they have to say clearly and succinctly" [p. 82].

Finally, this concise and virulent sentence that deserves to become famous: "Never have so many stayed in school so long to learn so little" [p. 208].

Unfortunately, the situation is irreversible. At least for the moment.

Only for the pleasure of again seeing him fly into a rage against one of his favorite authors, I cite for Felix F. this passage by André Gide: "The social question! . . . If I had encountered that great trap at the beginning of my career, I should never have written anything worthwhile" (*Journal,* 30 May 1940).

It is possible that an esoteric doctrine may be transmitted by someone who doesn't take it at all seriously. This happened to A. W. Howitt when he described in great detail the secret initiatory rites of the tribes of southeastern Australia. Adopted by the Kurnaï as one of their own, he had attended their initiatory ceremonies. But Howitt saw in their doctrine and their initiatory rites only "primitive customs and beliefs," suitable for inspiring the interest of anthropologists, but lacking in any spiritual significance. Shortly after he had described their secret ceremonies the Kurnaï tribes disappeared. It is thus thanks to the curiosity Howitt showed at the time that we know today the essence of one of the most ancient secret doctrines that was still being practiced at the end of the nineteenth century.

This case of "transmission through misunderstanding" of fragments of archaic spiritual doctrines is, moreover, not an isolated one. In earlier times, esoteric doctrines were communicated through successive initiations from one generation to the next. Or rather, mutilated and perverted, they were transmitted by adversaries, as was the case with Hellenistic mysteries, Hermeticism, and Gnosticism. "Transmission through misunderstanding" is characteristic of the present civilization. If the last vestiges of traditional spirituality have been able to be saved *in extremis,* this is owed to men whose concerns and goals were something entirely different: missionaries, anthropologists, explorers, journalists, etc.

1 August

For several days I've been reading—or rather rereading—authors I had liked very much when I was young, and even very young: Papini, Panzini, Goethe. Of Papini's works I remember certain volumes of prose poetry, such as *Giorni di festa,* and the first part of *Un uomo finito.* Alfredo Panzini disappoints me. I had never had the opportunity to reread *Il padrone sono mè*! I must have been around seventeen when, while reading this book for the first time, I felt I was having a true revelation, so new did the writing seem to me. The author let his pen run away at the whim of inspiration, shamelessly using a mixture of dialogues, humor, and scholarship (I had already read his *Xantippe* and *Il diavolo nella mia libreria*), and didn't hesitate to use dialectal expressions and locutions. The title of the book is proof of this, for it would have been more correct to write *Il padrone sono io!*

But Goethe improves with each new reading. I reread in a single sitting *Dichtung und Wahrheit.*

3 August

Appointment at Billings Hospital for a whole series of tests. And as always, Dr. Cohen assures me "that everything is normal." The taste of blood that I sometimes have in my mouth is probably due to an inflammation of the gums.

4 August

It was indeed that. The dentist immediately decides to extract one of my canine teeth. But I will have to take penicillin for three full days. I already foresee the consequences . . .

No date

I always pay close attention to these young people who "practice yoga," and who tell of their experiences during certain meditation exercises in terms wherein I recognize entire phrases from my books . . .

It's been a long time since I've heard from Douglas W., who left almost two years ago for the Middle East. I have only received a postcard from him from Cairo and, several months later, a letter from Teheran, which couldn't have been more banal when one knows his usual style.

His ambition was to write vast and daring syntheses, and one of his numerous projects was to compile a list of "fateful dates" in the history of the West, with appropriate commentary. I recently discovered a little note he had drafted for me to help me understand the general idea of his work. Thus 28 October 1492 was for him one of those "fateful dates." Indeed, on that day Luis de Torres and Rodrigo de Jerez, two of Christopher Columbus' companions, sighted natives of Cuba smoking rolls of dried leaves. They were, of course, tobacco leaves. Six years later, in 1498, Rodrigo de Jerez brought back to Spain entire crates of these leaves, which he, too, began to smoke in the streets of Barcelona.

This was only the presentation of concrete facts. There followed commentaries, albeit barely sketched out in the note he had given me: The first references to tobacco in writings of the time; reactions by the Inquisition; the extension of the use of tobacco across Europe; the first medical observations on the subject, etc. . . . According to Douglas, the day that the two Spaniards discovered "the taste for tobacco" should be marked with a black stone, *because they were not even aware of the ritual value of the act of smoking.* "The taste for tobacco" thus became a *profane* habit. It is I who had told this to Douglas. Tobacco, once introduced into Europe, *was considered to be a drug, and lost all sacramental value.* Four centuries later we can witness the consequences of this, which are sometimes dramatic.

On 23 October 1828, Goethe said to Eckermann that God's disappointment with regard to humanity would become such that He would one day decide to totally destroy it, which would result in a "rejuvenated Creation," *einer verjüngten Schöpfung.*

Who will ever succeed in counting the archaic images, visions, and ideas that can be discovered in Goethe's work! The "renewal of

Creation'' is one of the specific and fundamental concepts of archaic thought. For "primitives," as well as for Oriental civilizations, the universe, life, man, "history," had a unique model: the cosmic cycle such as it appears to us, closed in on itself in the rhythm of the seasons. Humanity follows the same rules as all organic forms that are born, develop, grow, and die: Rich in creative potential and perfect *in its beginnings,* it ends up exhausting its resources due to the simple fact that it endures, that it exists *in time.* In the end, at the end of its strength, it degenerates and must be destroyed to make place for another humanity.

It's not surprising to see Goethe take up this idea, although it was unusual at the time he dared formulate it. For Goethe, Nature was the supreme model. It was obviously not the same nature that nineteenth-century naturalists were beginning to explore and were getting ready to conquer, but the Nature that was conceived of by the alchemists of the Renaissance and their precursors. It was, just like the living and mysterious cosmos, in a perpetual state of renewal. The Mystery of Nature, both an example and a model, indeed consisted of this palingenesis which even authorized—at least this was believed at the time—the regeneration of plants out of their own ashes. The alchemists, whose eschatology was always present in Goethe's mind, pursued no other goals. The quest for the Philosopher's Stone was only the legitimate application of this mysterious palingenesis.

16 August

I'm getting ready to leave. In other words, I undertake first of all to reply to the letters that have accumulated on my blotting pad. There are around thirty of them. It will be impossible for me to reply to all my correspondents, as many French as Rumanian. As usual, I will sacrifice my friends.

NEW YORK, 19 August

I left my briefcase full of manuscripts in the taxi that brought us from the airport. It contained specifically my datebook, my notebook, and files containing the first ten chapters of *A History,* volume 1. Luckily I only realized it two hours later, while getting up from the table to show a journal to Lisette. I didn't have time to weigh the extent of the disaster, for a few minutes later we heard the front doorbell ring. It was our taxi driver, a young Puerto Rican. He had well remembered the address of the building, but obviously didn't know our floor or the apartment number. As soon as he had finished work he returned to where he remembered having let us out, rang at random at several tenants' doors, and ended up getting us. When I saw him holding my briefcase, I almost embraced him. I offered him a five-dollar bill, which he refused, explaining that I had already given him a generous tip. Finally, Lisette managed to slip the bill into his jacket pocket.

NEW YORK, *20 August*

Upset to discover the doors of the Metropolitan Museum closed. It has almost become a ritual: As soon as we arrive in New York we always go there first.

NEW YORK, *21 August*

Upon arriving at Kennedy Airport I realize I've misplaced my reading glasses. I must have left them in the taxi.

I would be tempted to see a "sign" in this, but how to interpret it? In the automobile (= the *Vehicle*) I forget everything I've written of importance in the last three or four years, as well as the instrument (= the *Tool*) that allowed me to write those hundreds of pages, for with my regular glasses I can neither read nor write. The first two interpretations of the symbols that that implies jump out at me. The third troubles me.

PARIS, *22 August*

We arrived tonight. Giza and Dinu were waiting for us at Orly. Sibylle is on vacation until 1 September.

23 August

I get a new pair of glasses. In the evening we have dinner at Giza and Dinu's. I learn from them what is happening in the news, for usually, since I never read newspapers, it is Christinel who communicates current events to me, after having heard them on television.

24 August

I reread *Le Colonel Chabert,* especially because of the memories that are attached to it. It is, I believe, the third book I read by Balzac in Rumanian translation, after *Le Père Goriot* and *Gobseck,* when I was twelve or thirteen years old. I can still see the grey and green cover of that inexpensive edition. I've never forgotten the passage in which one sees the colonel stand up out of the common grave, his head sticking like a mushroom out of the snow that covered the battlefield, and the frightened cries of the peasants upon seeing him, the courage of the woman who first dared to approach him . . .

The next morning I took the book with me to the lycée, and during the recess I summarized the story for several of my friends. My friend Mircea M. was the only one to have already read it. He was to become, just like me, an unconditional "Balzacian." In a serious and anguished voice, I read them the scene in which one sees the colonel's head come out from among the dead bodies. After closing the book, I was aware that I had visibly impressed them. A moment later the bell rang, and we headed back towards the classroom. I walked with my head and shoulders leaning slightly forward, savoring my triumph. A little more, and I would have been taken for the real author . . .

TURKU, *26 August*

We change planes twice, first in Brussels, then in Helsinki, and we arrive in Turku around nine o'clock in the evening. We go to the students' dormitory where the members of the congress are being housed. At the restaurant-bar we find Joe Kitagawa, Werblowski, Hans Penner, and his wife.

Suddenly there is music: The "cabaret" performance is beginning. A girl, completely nude, contorts herself in front of us, gets on her knees, stretches out on the carpet, and, according to what I was told, started to mimic a sexual coupling while practically masturbating. Personally, absorbed by my conversation with Zwi, I had stopped watching her after a few minutes.

Don't forget that we are in a university restaurant-bar in 1973, and in Finland.

TURKU, *27 August*

This morning, first meeting of the members of the Congress of the History of Religions. I can finally meet certain colleagues whose writings I had already admired, Honko, for example.

Lunch in the student cafeteria, barely a few hundred meters from the lecture rooms. I only go to a few of the paper presentations. In the evening, dinner in the company of Joe Kitagawa, Zwi Werblowski, and other friends at an excellent restaurant.

I wandered for a long time around the rooms and halls of the university, lingering in front of the bulletin boards reserved for students. I didn't see one political slogan on them, not the slightest Marxist propaganda. And yet, Finland is in the zone of Soviet influence. By the way, I omitted to point out that at the airport no one inspected our luggage.

What pleasure I used to get from going to international meetings! And not only to those in the history of religions or Orientalism! Besides the fact that they gave me the opportunity to meet or meet again certain scholars whom I admired, the massive presence of so many scholars in the same place was enchanting. Still young, I had quickly realized that the *greater* a scholar was—by virtue of his scholarship, his intelligence, his originality, and the quality of his writings—the more modest he was. There are obviously exceptions . . . But those who intrigued me the most were the unproductive—I daren't say the mediocre—whose scientific prestige rested almost exclusively on the fact that they were university professors, and therefore members of diverse national or international boards. The congresses gave them the opportunity to live their greatest moments, their "existential" moments. For several days, sometimes a week, they lived knowing they would attract general attention, especially if the congress was held in a provincial city or in the capital of a small country. The local press published articles and group photos in their honor, and if in addition they were lucky enough to belong to some international board or another, they found themselves interviewed . . . They came for the most part with their wives, and the happiness that could be read in the latter's eyes was a pleasure to see. It was the only opportunity they had, these spouses of specialists in eccentric disciplines—South-Arabic epigraphy, Oceanian linguistics, Sumarian grammar, etc.—to see the scientific talent and the international prestige of their husbands publicly acknowledged, and with great fanfare.

And what an astonishing spectacle it was to see the extent to which these university figures, most of them of a "certain age," took themselves seriously, strutted about, felt proud of their degrees . . .

TURKU, *28 August*

During the discussion that followed a paper on methodology in the history of religions, I felt like speaking up. I would have wanted to say only this, that is, that every historian of religions, no matter what method he uses, must absolutely have read this passage by William James, a copy of which I just happened to have in my pocket: "A Beethoven string quartet is truly, as someone has said, a scraping of horses' tails on cats' bowels, and may be exhaustively described in such terms; but the application of this description in no way precludes the simultaneous applicability of an entirely different description" (*The Sentiment of Rationality*).

We decided only today to go to the Sibelius Museum. We were looking, not without some amusement, at the hat and cane of the maestro in the case where they were displayed, offered up for the veneration due objects that had become historic, when we heard the first measures of the Third Symphony. The museum in fact doubles as an auditorium. The museum's record collection is very complete, and visitors can come here to listen to any work by Sibelius they wish to hear. We, too, sit down and listen meditatively.

But the time passes, and there are many other relics to view. I remember having one day seen the photograph of the great conductor Yrjö Kilpinen (1892–1959). Admirable face, the very image of a musician of genius. All the same, I knew almost nothing about him, not even his name. We get up and leave on tiptoe to continue looking at the display cases. We see a selection of the maestro's favorite cigars (Havanas, Dutch cigars), then a series of photographs dominated by the one showing Sibelius receiving the diploma of Doctor *honoris causa* from Yale University, not to mention the books in all languages— Hungarian, Chinese, Japanese, etc.—that have been devoted to him. Finally we pass in front of the cases where manuscripts, and most especially those of Sibelius's first scores, are displayed. F. contemplates them at length, scrutinizes them with avidity and a morose delectation. We guess he is somewhat frustrated.

After leaving the museum and sitting down on a bench near the cathedral, I begin to understand what he was feeling. Just like many others, F. would have liked to know the real reasons why Sibelius never composed anything at all during the last twenty years of his life. Why didn't he write that so long-awaited eighth symphony? Did he feel too old? Did he fear not measuring up to the masterpiece he had conceived but which he hesitated to accomplish? These questions continue to torment F. . . . To decipher the origin and causes of the sterility of an artist of genius seems as essential to him as knowing the hermeneutics of his creative power. Neither old age nor exhaustion suffices to explain it.

I admit to him that I had asked myself the same question concerning Brancusi and the indigence of his creativity during the last twenty-five years of his life. I rapidly summarize the diverse hypotheses I've constructed to explain it (cf. *Fragments d'un Journal I,* p. 532 *et seq.* [*Journal II, 1957–1969,* p. 291 *et seq.*]), but I am forced to recognize that there isn't for the moment any way to verify them. I agree with F. in thinking that the disappearance of an artist's creativity is as mysterious a phenomenon as is the epiphany of its first manifestation. But how can we learn about such a process? Sometimes—and this is Brancusi's case—the artist deludes himself by repeating himself over and over again. But sometimes, having arrived at a certain age, he stops creating and maintains an absolute mutism about everything that concerns his "interior laboratory." This is Sibelius's case. We more or less know that he planned to compose an eighth symphony, but we don't know anything about his aborted attempts, nor about the stages he had to go through before giving up on it definitively.

TURKU, *29 August*

We spend the afternoon on a boat: the gulf, the "port" (so tiny that it should really be called a mere landing), the pine forest, sauna baths, and finally the hotel. We walk along the shoreline between the rocks. I linger to watch a little dog playing with a dead fish that it uncovered on the sand next to a large rock. A light mist extends over the water, and the twilight is indescribably melancholy. The splendor of the pines and the birches of the forest.

Van B. and I talk about prehistoric religions. With us is a young student, very blond, who smiles whenever we look at her. She is preparing a doctoral thesis on Siberian shamanism, and will soon be leaving for the USSR to consult I can't remember which archives. I'd like to be twenty years younger and in her shoes . . .

TURKU, *30 August*

The weather has rarely been as beautiful as today. I attend the closing debate, but my attention is often distracted. I needed only to turn my eyes toward the window to feel far, very far away from "methodology" and its concerns.

I would like to know more about contemporary Finnish literature, and especially about the new tendencies in the Finnish school of folklore. I would also like to know what certain of my colleagues, Maarti Haavio among others, are working on. I wasn't able to talk with Honko as much as I would have liked. In some ways, Finnish scholars are in the best position to accomplish what seems to me to be the mission of the new generation of historians of religions, that is, the exploitation of the documents available in ethnography and folklore, and this from the perspective of the history of religions. For this purpose they have at their disposal monumental archives and have every opportunity to observe, in their own country—in Lapland—archaic populations. Besides, in addition to the more common languages, they know Russian and can easily learn Hungarian and the other Finno-Ugrian languages. Some of them have already started on this path, in particular Uno Harva.

In the evening, gala dinner in a superb restaurant in the heart of the forest.

HELSINKI, *31 August*

We leave Turku at twelve-thirty in the company of Anne and Hans Penner. Our train car is full of students, and we soon discover the unusual side of this splendid Finnish youth. We saw each student drink at least two or three bottles of beer, whence the general drunkenness and confusion. But it was a sad, heavy drunkenness.

We checked in at the Hotel Seurahuones, built, it would seem, in 1917. Although it has been renovated since then, it clearly shows its age. It undoubtedly resembles the hotels of St. Petersburg before the revolution.

Then we walk through the city as far as the port, where we watch the departure of the Helsinki-Leningrad steamer. In the evening, at the hotel bar, we are surprised by the ugliness of so many old people, or of those aged before their time. One would say that they don't belong to the same people as do the youth.

HELSINKI, *1 September*

Rain, fog, and cold. It's the first time it's rained since our arrival in Finland. In the company of Hans Penner, I spend over an hour at the Akademska bookstore, undoubtedly the biggest in Europe, where it is possible to obtain books from a good dozen countries. An admirable subject for an essayist! (I hardly dare imagine the enthusiasm of an Ortega y Gasset . . .)

In the evening, with Penner, Rantanen (of the American Cultural Services), and their spouses, we have dinner at the Linnunrata Ravintoh, a magnificent restaurant outside Helsinki, built about ten years ago. The high-priced, exclusive restaurant is on the twelfth floor, whereas the floor above it accommodates the student cafeteria, crammed with hippies. What a scandal when one of them appears, having gotten off the elevator on the wrong floor . . .

We have coffee at Rantanen's. His wife, an actress, made her debut in *La Cantatrice chauve* quite a few years ago. She tells us picturesque anecdotes of the opening night, but can't believe I've known Eugène Ionesco since 1933. For her, still a young woman, the year 1933 belongs almost to prehistory, whereas Ionesco is an avant-garde author *par excellence*.

HELSINKI, *2 September*

Sunday, rainy and depressing. We spent the morning visiting the Temppelcankio, that extraordinary cathedral carved entirely out of rock. The light filters through thick windows, placed with rare joy in the rocky walls.

We then go to the Russian church, where we attend the end of the religious service. I should mention those gentle and melancholy beings that we noticed there.

PARIS, *4 September*

We arrived the day before yesterday, and Sibylle was waiting for us at Le Bourget. All tanned, rejuvenated, rested, she once again looks the way we remember she does when she returns from vacation.

This early Parisian autumn is more beautiful than ever. I spend all day at home cleaning up the notes I brought back from Finland.

PARIS, *5 September*

The weather is still just as superb. In two words one would say it is a glorious day.

Jean Varenne comes for the interview I had promised him for the journal *Question de* . . . But he has brought a tape recorder, and that is enough to make me lose all my faculties. I respond to his questions without the least spontaneity and do nothing but proffer banalities. Our conversation could have otherwise been interesting, for we were both trained as Indianists, having spent several years in India, and are both fascinated by the same issues. For example, regarding the history of religions, the importance of rites.

6 September

The interest people show these days in Asian spirituality has all the characteristics and intensity of a fad. But fads rarely endure. This infatuation with Oriental values does not date from yesterday, and it reappears after a more or less lengthy interval. It is certainly natural that each generation finds *something else* to glean from this fascinating and inexhaustible Orient. All the same, the behavior of our more recent converts differs so radically from that of their predecessors that one has difficulty believing that they all undergo the same "revelation" which an old saying, simplistic but perfectly correct under the circumstances, suffices to define: *ex Oriente lux.* How, for example, do the Anglo-American "Vedantists" of 1920–1930, timid, chlorotic, asexual, resemble the young Americans of today who proclaim themselves to be fervent followers of diverse schools of Zen or yoga, but who in practice devote themselves to perpetual and monotonous orgies and combine in total aberration alcohol, sex, and drugs.

One resists only with great difficulty the "spirit of the times," that famous *Zeitgeist,* and we're in the process of experiencing, as we all know, the most radical revolution ever known in the realm of sexual mores and ethics. This is how spiritual "freedom" or "liberation" obtained through yoga techniques and with Zen meditation has ended up being confused with sexual freedom and license.

The phenomenon isn't new. What is original is that in our time, licentiousness tries to find justification in "spirituality."

PARIS, *10 September*

I come across this passage from Gide's *Journal* which I've intended for some time to show to certain writers and critics to see their reactions: "Oppression cannot debase the best; and as for the others, it matters little. Hurrah for thought held in check! The world can be saved solely by a few. It is in non-liberal epochs that the free mind achieves the highest virtue" (28 September 1940). What would the Rumanian writers of today think of this?

PARIS, *11 September*

A. R. came to see me at the end of the afternoon. His features haven't changed. He takes me aside to congratulate me on the "distinctions conferred on me by three academies," on the Japanese publication of my complete works, etc. . . . Then, resting his elbows on the table, he gives me the news from Rumania, where everything is getting worse and worse. The only ones who escape the common fate are tourists and foreigners. A Rumanian, by the mere fact that he is under the jurisdiction of the State, is of no interest. But if this same Rumanian can produce a foreign passport, everything changes: He finds a hotel room without difficulty and manages to get served in restaurants.

The situation of higher education has become tragic: The graduates of the Faculty of Romance Languages have been appointed professors of physical education . . .

I briefly summarize for him my conversation with M., whose visit I had told him about in my last letter. He is visibly impressed by what I am telling him. Then he asks me if I know anything about a certain Al. Ghica who, in the second half of the nineteenth century, had converted to Buddhism and had gone to India. Having arrived in the Himalayas, he was admitted into an *ashram* and had even become somewhat of a guru. I answer that I never heard of him, either in Calcutta or even in any of the Himalayan *ashrams* where I had occasion to stay. I finally learn the reason for such curiosity: Recently, A. R. received a visit from a certain Sbierea, a young colonel in voluntary retirement who, overcome by a true passion for India, launched himself into the study of Sanskrit and Hindi. He even managed to go and spend several months there. When he returned he told A.R. that he had picked up Ghica's trail, and found out that when Ghica had realized that the monks of the monastery where he had been admitted wanted to "use" him (?), he left, and no one knew what had become of him since. I can't help thinking that A.R. is telling me all this only in the hope of learning more about the mysterious disappearance of "Dr. Zerlendi."[1]

14 September

I've noted in my datebook our visit from the Kitagawas, who stayed in Paris from September 6 to 9 (Cioran had seen to finding them a hotel), as well as all my meetings with French colleagues or Rumanian writers, our evenings at Sibylle's, and even the restaurants where we've dined. This evening we're going to Cioran's. In this way I will more easily be able to reconstruct my schedule during these Parisian weeks. As for the rest, that is, what is most important—reading notes, diverse remarks, certain conversations—I relegate everything to scattered pieces of paper, which allows me to write without a preconceived plan, and when I have the opportunity to do so.

The current popular interest in occult sciences among the Anglo-American public is not limited to the success of certain works, generally of lamentable quality, dealing with astrology, alchemy, yoga, or parapsychology. One can also read other recent books on sorcery or Hermeticism, which are quite honorable and sometimes even excellent. As for parapsychology, it is undergoing a period of renewal. I have been strongly urged to read *The Roots of Coincidence* by Koestler, and especially *Psychic Discoveries beyond the Iron Curtain* by Ostrander and Schroeder. It was from one of my colleagues, a "scientist liberated from scientistic prejudice," as he likes to define himself, that I first heard of the old Russian woman Nelya Nikhaïlova and of the young Israeli Uri Geller. They are, he says, the two greatest parapsychologists of our time. They can both make small objects move a short distance solely through mental concentration. Geller has in addition displayed his gifts in telepathy at the Stanford Research Institute. His chances of success, claim my friend the "scientist," were one in a billion.

I understand his interest in such performances. It is not the extent to which they were "scientifically" controlled that matters, but much

1. The principal character in *The Secret of Dr. Honigberger* (cf. *Nights at Serampre*)— C.G.

rather the fact that the "mind" can manifest an "energy" capable of direct action on matter. Spiritual techniques rise to the rank of physico-chemical experiments and can thus be taken seriously by scholars. In short, my colleague hopes that the success of experiments currently being undertaken in parapsychology will one day allow for the integration of the two universes that are for the time being separated: that of space-time, and that of the world within.

But it is easy to guess how such an integration will be interpreted by those who, unlike my friend, are not yet "free from scientistic prejudice . . ."

15 September

I receive a visit from S.A.G. . . . I had heard a lot about him from Constantin Noïca, from Poghirc, and from Arion Roşu. He had written me several letters, in defiance of the censors, one of which, a very long one, was from Calcutta. He is frank, sincere, direct, free of all inhibition, and his "presence" is such that he immediately wins me over. We spend more than three hours together and make a date for the day after tomorrow.

What can I say about our meeting? In his letters Noïca had already informed me of the great respect S.A.G. had for me. He knew in depth all that I had written. According to him, *The Forbidden Forest* was my most successful work, and perhaps the best novel in all Rumanian literature. It was for having read it in French translation, in 1955–1956, that he was sentenced and had to spend more than five years in prison. It was, moreover, for this same reason that Vladimir Streinu—who had borrowed the book from Cioculescu, although the latter didn't have to suffer the consequences—Nicolas Steinhart, and Dinu Pillat found themselves incriminated in the trial of Constantin Noïca. I will say nothing more about this trial, which will remain in the annals of Rumanian culture as one of the blackest and saddest moments in all our history. I only hope that from among the condemned some of them have taken the trouble to write the story of their ordeal. That at least would be saved. S.A.G. tells me about the disappointment he and his friends felt in me and in Cioran when they discovered that neither he nor I had seen fit to write the least article in the foreign press on that monstrous trial in which they had been implicated for having read our books, and for that alone. I inform him of the reasons for our silence at the time: Any protest on our part—on mine as well as on Cioran's—could only have hurt them, for it would have been interpreted as a confirmation of our profoundly "reactionary" nature.

He was very moved to meet M. in Calcutta in the autumn of 1972. At the time M. was already familiar with my novel, and she complained about not having received a reply to the letters she had been sending me since 1950 (?). I also learn that Veronica Porumbacu, that Stalinist who had told M. that I was "dead" in the eyes of all Rumanians because I had been a "Nazi," subsequently translated her poems for publication in the journal *XXe siècle,* and intends to have them preceded by excerpts from my novel commented on by her. S.A.G. suggests I write to the head of the journal to protest.

He would have very much liked to have brought me photos of Strada Mantuleasa, but in the middle of September, in Bucharest, he was unable to find a roll of film for his Leica . . .[1]

What are the reasons that *Aspects du mythe* has not appeared in Rumanian translation? Because no one there dares take the responsibility for sending the manuscript to the printer. Two or three years ago, the quote I had cited from a work by Norman Cohn, in which nazism and communism were considered to be contemporary messianisms, had "posed a problem" for them. I had resolved it myself, and at my suggestion they had suppressed the litigious citation. And yet the translation remains locked up in a drawer, and no one dares to take it out.

17 September

S.A.G. comes back to see me. He arrives suddenly, a little after four o'clock. In the evening, with Christinel, we have dinner at the Carlos restaurant.

1. Strada Mantuleasa is the setting of Eliade's novel *The Old Man and the Bureaucrats.*—C.G.

I ask him a number of very precise questions: What happened to so and so? How did X or Y behave in prison? etc. . . . It would be useless to mention here what I learn from him. We also speak of India. He displays surprising intuition and understands admirably Indian thought. He gives me gripping details of the research he has undertaken on several occasions in order to discover the true identity of Zerlendi, and to pick up the trail of Dr. Honigberger in Brashov. He has in any event succeeded in tracking down one of his descendants, who let him read some of the doctor's yet unpublished letters.

What energy certain Rumanians put into researching and reading my books! A doctor has even copied *Yoga* by hand in its entirety . . .

The person who pursued and persecuted me between 1945 and 1955, whose name I've forgotten, was informed of all my actions and movements in Paris, and of my desperate efforts not to die of hunger. He was aware of my candidacy at the Centre National de la Recherche Scientifique in 1947 and had even read the letter that I had sent to the director after I had been informed of their refusal. It must have reached Rumania, where they laughed loudly in high places over the arguments I tried to put forth, claiming, for example, that I had been forced to write *Yoga* in English, but that it was in French that the book had been published for the first time . . .

September

Popular demonstration in Milan upon the death of Allende. Some demonstrators notice an English tourist raising his arm. The fascist salute! The demonstrators rush over to him. He is beaten, covered with punches, his body is trampled. It would not have taken much for him to have lost his life there, which would surely have happened if the police hadn't pulled him out at the last minute. While he is being taken by ambulance to the hospital, a nurse is surprised by his thoughtlessness: How could he have displayed the fascist salute at a communist demonstration!

"But I wasn't giving the fascist salute," cried the wounded man, "I was hailing a taxi . . ."

What must such an anecdote make one think of? From which universe, which imagination was it born? That of Charlie Chaplin? Of Ionesco? Or of the concentration camps?

CHICAGO, *6 October*
We returned yesterday afternoon after a short stop in Montreal. In this early autumn we rediscover the warmth and serenity of a Parisian sky.

I leaf through my datebook of the last two weeks. The number of people I was able to see in Paris is unbelievable!

I prepare the review list for *No Souvenirs,* which will soon be published. I included the names and addresses of a good fifteen writers and critics residing in Rumania. I would be curious to know how many of them will receive their copies . . .

13 October
At least two of Zeno's paradoxes have been expressed by Chinese logicians and sophists. Here, for example, is the famous aporia of Achilles and the tortoise: "If a stick one foot long is cut in half every day, it will still have something left after ten thousand generations." And here is the Chinese counterpart of the famous sophism about the arrow that flies and yet does not fly: "There are times when a flying arrow is neither in motion nor at rest." I've taken the two examples above from a list of "paradoxes" which were debated by Chinese philosophers in 320 B.C., according to Joseph Needham (*Science and Civilization in China,* vol. 2, pp. 190–91).

When he was working on the first volume of *Griechische Denker* (*Greek Thinkers*), which was published in parts starting in 1893, Theodor Gomperz knew only of the paradox of Achilles and the tortoise in the version given by Chuang-Tze (*Sacred Books of the East,* vol. 40, p. 320). He recalls it in a note, with this commentary: "Interesting sidelights on the so-called sophisms of the Eristics, and, among them, on Zeno's 'Achilles and the tortoise,' are furnished by the subtle intellect of the Chinese" (*Greek Thinkers,* vol. 1, p. 201, n. 1). That is all he says about it, but it is probable that this simple allusion, despite its brevity, inspired Guthrie to read the remarkable work by Needham. He thus discovered the Chinese version of the paradox of the arrow, a version which Guthrie rightly considers to be more profound and more original than its Greek homologue (*A History of Greek Philosophy*, vol. 2, p. 101).

All the same, I would like to know whether anyone has ever been curious enough to undertake detailed comparative research into the consequences and the implications of these paradoxes on the respective thinking of the two civilizations. How could they both have arrived at quasi-identical formulations? And for what reasons exactly does the Chinese version of the paradox of the arrow open up an unknown "problematics" of Greek thought?

14 October

Today wrote no fewer than nine letters, some of which were several pages long. I don't even dare to think about those I still have left to write.

17 October

Joint seminar with Paul Ricoeur on hermeneutics in philosophy and the history of religions. Ricoeur gives an excellent historic overview, from Aristotle up to Kant.

19 October

I receive a visit from Aurel Martin, the director of Editura Minerva in Bucharest. He asks me to prepare an outline for a Rumanian edition of my complete works. This will be, he says, an "ambitious project" which will not be completed in the immediate future, for it will first be necessary to translate close to four thousand pages from the original texts in English or French. But it is desirable, he continues, for an author to specify himself, and in his lifetime, the criteria according to which his diverse writings should be assembled, and on this I am in complete agreement with him.

All the while we were discussing this project, I had the impression that it was not about myself that we were talking, but about someone else, that unknown person who in twenty or thirty years would enter into the history of Rumanian culture and literature. But who can foresee the future *relevancy* of my works—or that of anyone else's, as far as that goes—around the year 2000?

23 October

First lecture on the religious history of agricultural civilizations. I am once again surprised at the fervor I display in presenting and analyzing that revolution—the discovery of agriculture—that occurred fifteen thousand years ago, and whose consequences have not yet ceased to be felt. Everything became possible from the moment man preferred a sedentary life to the nomadic existence he had led for two million years.

October

Last evening, in the course of a discussion, X. once again brought up the subject that is dear to him, that of "the future of religions," and more specifically, the future of the Christian religion. He thinks that industrial society, because it has rendered obsolete traditional systems of values (patriarchal family, religion considered as a "total" institution, etc. . . . .) has entered into a process of desacralization, henceforth irreversible.

How can one not agree with this? The Hebrews were in the same situation each time "History" temporarily granted them peace and prosperity! They then turned away from Yahweh and established a cult to the divinities of fecundity, Baal and Astarte. It was only when the terror of history once again became unbearable that they returned to Yahweh. In our time industrial society benefits in full from technical progress and its advantages. One might say we are witnessing the triumph of divinities similar to Baal and Astarte, but which are desacralized. However, technical progress demands certain forms of political organization which render the return of terror to History inevitable. In my opinion there is no doubt that new religious creations of considerable importance will be born of this very terror.

Of course, the possibility of a nuclear conflict is a real one. But in this case, as well, we find ourselves confronted with a religious perspective. Indeed, from two things comes the one: Either humanity will find itself reduced to some tens or hundreds of thousands of individuals who, to survive, will possess only a rudimentary technology, in which case the theory of cosmic cycles will be proved confirmed. Or else the species *homo sapiens* will disappear entirely from the face of the earth, and thus the biblical prophesy will be fulfilled, that is, that the fruit of the tree of knowledge is the bearer of death, not only for individuals (which was the traditional interpretation), but *for the entire species.*

1 November

From noon to five o'clock I meet with students in my office in Meadville and spend a half hour with each of them. I ask the newcomers to tell me about their studies, the professors they've had before me, and especially the *personal* reasons that have led them to study the history of religions, as well as the area in which they wish to specialize. I also ask them which Oriental languages they plan to learn. I have not yet dared to tell them that Giuseppe Tucci demanded that every student preparing a doctoral thesis on Buddhism promise to learn the five languages he considered indispensable: Sanskrit, Pali, Tibetan, Chinese, and Japanese . . .

9 November

Yesterday evening at eight o'clock in the immense Red Lacquer Room of the Palmer House I gave a lecture on mythologies of death. More than two thousand people attended, many of whom had to find seats where they could—on the stage, behind me, or right on the floor. I felt I had returned to the good old days of the Criterion group[1] in Bucharest in the 1930s. Applause right from the beginning after Chuck Long had introduced me. Prolonged applause which lasted several minutes when I had finished.

1. See *Autobiography,* vol. 1, part 3.—C.G.

A year ago, when Chuck Long was appointed president of the American Academy of Religions, he had asked me if I would give the opening lecture at the next congress, which was to take place in November 1973. He had, moreover, put a lot of pressure on the governing board "to have me come." I agreed to do it all the more willingly since I knew that Chuck Long would be leaving the University of Chicago that same year.

For a long time I've dreamt of writing a small work on mythologies of death, and I despair of ever having enough time to do it. Taken as a whole, the little text of my lecture wouldn't be useless, despite its gaps; I'm forced to recognize that it covers only part of the material that would be in the book I propose to write. Certain descriptive chapters, notably those relating to the geography of funerary rites, have been purely and simply omitted.

And what if, I asked myself while the room erupted in applause, I were to die tonight from a heart attack, just like Tillich? But he, at least, had finished his work, whereas it will take me five or six more years before seeing the completion of mine.

10 November

Ran into T.A. at the Palmer House. He has grown his beard, which is almost entirely white, and I have difficulty recognizing him. He tells me that Alma has left him for good. Last summer, in June, he still maintained the hope of reconciling with her. According to Tom, their separation is due above all to the role that God plays in his life. But in June, he claimed that their separation was due above all to Alma's adherence to women's lib.

11 November

I've established a new record: ten letters written today! Yesterday I had a visit from Mac Ricketts and Doeing. Both of them participated in the American Academy of Religion meetings, and both have learned Rumanian only to be able to learn more about my "beginnings." Doeing even made the trip to Bucharest twice, and, at the library of the Rumanian Academy, consulted the journals and newspapers to which I had contributed from 1925 to 1939. He copied and summarized hundreds of articles. I don't remember whether I took care to put down in my journal what he told me of his Bucharest experiences, and in particular about that "observer" who always sat down next to him in the reading room, and about those other "observers" whom he had on his heels in the lobby of the hotel, etc. I've read his doctoral thesis, which I find very interesting insofar as it concerns me, given the great number of texts cited.

13 November

Third lecture in the series, "Religious History of Agricultural Civilizations," dealing this time with those mysterious Megalithic civilizations. I must find the time—but when?—to write the long study entitled *Megaliths and History of Religions* for our journal. During the last twenty years I've gathered considerable material, and I've even led a seminar on the subject. And despite that, I'm not very sure I've understood it from every angle.

28 November

Admirable lecture by Mateï Calinescu on the concept of modernity. Literary critics of Eastern Europe essentially differ from those of the West and from the United States in that the information of the latter is limited to a bibliography in two languages, at most three, whereas those from Rumania, Poland, or Hungary master at least four Western languages, and as for some of them, Russian, as well.

But to what end? The most mediocre of monographs published in one of the well-known languages benefits from an audience that extends over three continents, and it is taken into account in all the specialized journals. But even a brilliant work published in one of the Eastern European languages must often wait twenty or thirty years before it is "discovered."

November

Theodore L. has chosen as a subject for his doctoral thesis the religious significance of artistic creations in Japan. He submits to me the chapter he has devoted to the *chado,* the "tea ceremony." During a seminar a few years ago, I had tried to show to what extent the history of religions can clarify the meaning of artistic creations, notably in archaic civilizations and in those of the Orient. Today, while reading this study on the *chado,* I remembered that year long ago, in 1922, when I discovered *The Book of Tea* by Okakura Kakuzo. I had the impression that another world of values was opening up before me, whose existence I hadn't dreamt of. *The Book of Tea* remains even today an excellent introduction to Sino-Japanese spirituality. But as Theodore L. demonstrates, its analysis can be pursued much farther.

A few preliminary remarks are in order. In his book *Zen in Japanese Art,* Hasumi writes that in Japan art is the royal path that leads to the Absolute. However, numerous scholars, and even some Japanese, do not consider the tea ceremony to be, strictly speaking, an "art," and rather see in it an "aesthetic diversion." Such an attitude seems groundless to me. *Do,* which comes from the Chinese *tao,* means "path." The tea ceremony—like all other "paths" (*do*): painting, poetry, floral art, calligraphy, archery, etc.—also constitutes a spiritual technique, for it places he who practices it in a "nirvanic" state in his everyday life. It is fascinating to follow the process by which artistic pastimes are gradually transformed into spiritual techniques. According to pre-Buddhist Japanese tradition, thus prior to 550 A.D., Nature is fundamentally "good and beautiful." In other words, Nature also participates in sacrality. In Shintoism, no rupture exists between the Cosmos, Man, and the Divine, which is manifest by millions of *kami.* Then, under the influence of the Buddhism that came from China, and in particular of the fundamental idea of the *Mahayana,* one came to consider all of reality as inscribed in the "Body of the Law" (Buddhic), the *Dharmakaya.* This means that men are themselves expected to become *Buddhas,* or more exactly, that they must become conscious that they are indeed Buddhas.

Kukay (774–835), the founder of the *Tendaï* school, asserts that all that is "beautiful" shares the essence of Buddha. In this way, therefore, art and religion constitute a unique and same reality. Thanks to Kukay, the traditional Japanese conception of the "sacrality" of Nature takes on a new dimension, and gradually the idea was formed that the entire phenomenal world participates in absolute reality, and thus in the essence of Buddha. It is thus that Nature, from being simply "sacred" as it was previously considered to be, now becomes "soterial." In fact, whereas Buddhist art of southern Asia and China concentrates on the representation of Buddha, Japanese artists, influenced by Shintoist tradition, continue to represent images of Nature almost exclusively.

Under the circumstances, this is another interpretation of Buddhism. Nirvanic "illumination" is declared to be superior to Buddhist *doctrine,* superior to the Buddha himself. Suddenly "illumination" is demythologized and ceases to project the one who experiences it onto a superior level of reality. It involves something else, apparently much simpler: The understanding of the world and of human existence is radically modified following the intuitive experience of the true essence of Buddha. Illumination is obtained spontaneously, without particular effort: "Spiritual culture cannot be cultivated." Artistic activities, such as dance or the tea ceremony, are spontaneous creations of that "nirvanic reality." Life, in its best-known and most commonplace aspects, can thus become an Art.

Rikiu describes the tea ceremony thus:

> The essence of the Tea Ceremony
> Simply consists of boiling the water,
> Preparing the Tea
> and drinking it. Nothing else!
> This must be understood well.

In other words, the most natural and insignificant gestures become soterial actions, indeed insofar as they are a part of everyday life and are carried out serenely and gratuitously. In this way, man belongs to several universes—the cosmic, the aesthetic, the religious—without rupture and without contradiction.

Rikiu's "aesthetics" can be summed up in two words: *sabi* and *wabi,* which can only be translated by paraphrases. The first word signifies "the very great beauty of what is ancient and vigorous." As for *wabi*, it applies to "the nature of that which becomes beautiful by reason of its destitution." Theodore L. cites a poem in which, contrary to the old Japanese cliche of the splendor of cherry trees in bloom, the author evokes the somber beauty of what is rustic and simple:

> As far as the eye can see
> One perceives neither cherry trees in bloom nor
> Maple-tree leaves colored purple.
> There is only the river bank and the thatch-roofed
>   hovels
> In this autumn twilight.

For Rikiu, the *sabi* and the *wabi* authorize the nirvanic experience, which means that one can achieve the condition of Buddha *at any time and in any place,* and even (one would be tempted to say "especially") in the course of the most banal existence. One can undergo the nirvanic experience with the most simple and common-place actions, which is what happens during the tea ceremony. It follows that the soterial message of Buddhism is found implicitly mixed into gestures of daily life, such as "boiling water, preparing tea, and drinking it."

Useless to underline the *contemporary* character of such a concep-tion, and the passion people would show in meditating and commenting on it if it were brought to the attention of certain American and European types—at least to the same degree that they are aware of the doctrine and techniques of Zen. It has never been more essential than it is today to reveal the transhistorical meaning and importance that is hidden in the depths of an existence condemned to be carried out *exclusively* in immanent and opaque banality. Its spiritual and religious significance, and thus the "salvational" message of all experience, is camouflaged in the profane, in the flow of daily activities. To discover a transhistorical significance in them would be to decode them, to decipher the message they conceal.

Obviously, the "sacred" is always hidden behind the mask of "profane" realities or actions. Indeed, the religious experience consists of "tearing off the veil" and of ripping off the mask. But in our time this dialectic of the sacred is difficult to get underway. It involves an enormous problem which I will not broach here. I will limit myself to recalling that the majority of contemporary religious currents insist on the necessity of accepting Nature, Life, and History such as we find them, and thus of looking for our own accomplishment—or our salvation, or our deliverance, or our beatitude—*in this world*. This is just exactly the role that has fallen to the tea ceremony, and to other Japanese "arts."

19 December

Since yesterday the snow has been falling endlessly. It accumulates in drifts, like it used to do in Bucharest in the winter. Memories surge up in me: I think of my childhood, of the attic on Strada Melodiei, of the little windows that sometimes disappeared under the snow and frost. I'd like to immerse myself in one of my favorite "winter reading materials," *Gösta Berling,* for example, or *Le problème des Centaures* by Georges Dumézil. Luckily, a molar I had believed for a long time was condemned begins to torment me again. I go back to work, and gradually the pain subsides, and with it my memories and my melancholy.

20 December

Morning appointment with the dentist to have my molar extracted. One of the roots had penetrated into a sinus, and Dr. W. fills the space with a sort of plug made out of plastic. He warns me, however, that the plug in question risks coming loose. I must therefore avoid sneezing or blowing my nose for at least a week. When I tell him that we will be leaving in a few days for Palm Beach, he gives me the addresses and telephone numbers of several dentists he knows there, advising me to go see one of them on his referral and to specify that I have a perforation of the sinus, and to do so "at the first sign of trouble." I can't ask for more, but what "sign" is he referring to exactly? And to think that this happens on the eve of our departure, on the eve of our first winter vacation in fifteen years . . .

PALM BEACH, *24 December*

We arrived yesterday afternoon. Mihaï Marinescu succeeded in finding us a little two-room suite, surprisingly inexpensive, at the Ocean View. How many years it has taken us to finally decide to visit Florida! As soon as we leave our plane, we are amazed by what we see. First, the weather: true spring. Then all those flowering trees, those unknown birds, those orange butterflies that slowly flap their wings around a Coca-Cola truck. After depositing our luggage, we go walking on the ocean front, less than a hundred meters from our hotel.

This morning we went to explore the city. Its charm, even its elegance, have something artificial about them. It reminds one of a Hollywood set from the 1930s. Even though it's very mild and there is no breeze, I keep my beret firmly on my head, fearing I might sneeze.

In the afternoon the Marinescus take us by car to see the greenhouses where their orchids come from, about twenty kilometers from Palm Beach. On a bunch of poinsettia I discover a good dozen species of hymenoptera yet unknown to me: large wasps with blue wings; others, smaller but also blue; still others, diversely colored, which resemble tiny bees. I try to imagine what the first entomologists who landed in Florida a century and a half ago must have felt having encountered such a spectacle, and their dithyrambic articles destined for European scientific journals. Brehm cited them and summed them up in his exhaustive work, *Die Insekten.*

PALM BEACH, *25 December*

It is quite simply superb out; the temperature is 26°C. We walk around all morning. Then we are surprised to learn that restaurants are closed until the evening. We must then content ourselves with eating some nuts and apples in our hotel room.

In the evening we invite the Marinescus to a restaurant, La Marmite. Mihaï admits that he feels a bit guilty for earning so much money, much more, in any case, than many ''true creators.'' I try to persuade him that an engineer in aeronautics, such as he, is in his own way just as much a creator.

PALM BEACH, *26 December*

We are awakened at nine o'clock by the noise made by workers who have come to repair and repaint the wall of the corridor, right in front of our door. We hurry to take refuge on the beach.

I realize with a puerile joy that as of tomorrow I will be able to sneeze without fear . . .

PALM BEACH, *December*

I wasn't able to find at the public library the book by Alexander von Humboldt, *Examen critique de l'histoire et de la géographie du nouveau continent* (Paris, 1837). I had read it in Lisbon some thirty years ago, and I vaguely remembered that in volume 3 Humboldt recalled the legend of a "Fountain of Youth" which Spanish navigators had learned of through the tales of Cuban natives. More probably, the Spaniards were only transposing into the New World the old myth of an earthly paradise that they had known since their childhood. In 1512, when Juan Ponce de León discovered the Bimini Islands in the Bahamian archipelago, he was persuaded that he would find the famous Fountain of Youth there.

I can't remember the circumstances following which he began to doubt the existence of the famous fountain, but what is certain is that on Bimini he heard for the first time about a paradisiacal land located somewhere in the northwest. He went in search of it, and it is thus that Juan Ponce de León discovered Florida.

It was not, moreover, the first time explorers, having gone in search of an earthly paradise, discovered lands that were up until then unknown, and Florida was not the first such land described in paradisiacal terms, the author picking up old literary cliches inherited from the Orient and from Greek antiquity. I still remember the amazing monograph by Leonardo Olschki, *Storia letteraria delle scoperte geografiche* (1937), that shows the extent to which navigators were conditioned by their youthful readings and by traditional images of a nature prodigious in beauties and in joys of all kinds. All the accounts tell of Christopher Columbus's ecstasy when, having landed in the New World, he heard the song of the nightingales. Yet there are no nightingales in America . . .

I wonder what I will really retain of the very contradictory impressions I was left with after that entire day spent in Miami. What can I say about the depressing banality of the "popular" neighborhoods—that is, where native Miamians live, those who aren't poor, but yet are not millionaires? Then, without even noticing, we are on an endless bridge, on the edge of the ocean. We are able to pass by true palaces, or catch sight of villas hidden among immense gardens of tropical plants, not to mention the multitude of all types and sizes of cars we see that move and pass each other in all directions on all the roads.

This is because, as Marinescu tells me, in the middle of winter this Atlantic coast of Florida, from Miami to Jacksonville, enjoys an almost ideal climate. I say "almost" because it can't be compared to that which is found on the other side of the peninsula, on the Gulf of Mexico, in St. Petersburg, for example. In winter one would believe one was in paradise. All the same, one begins to regret that this little city is inhabited only by old people, obviously very rich, but also very old. Its fame is owed to the fact that it has the highest mortality rate in all the United States, and perhaps in the entire world. Statisticians maintain that the mortality rate here is equal to that which occurred at the time of the Spanish-flu epidemic. This is all the more curious for the transient traveler, as he notices nothing abnormal; rather, to the contrary. Certain people even claim never to have seen even one funeral procession in St. Petersburg. However, if one pursues the point as far as a cemetery, one can only be astonished by the abundance of sprays and wreaths that are still very fresh. In such abundance, in fact, that one would think one was at a horticulturist's . . .

I reread the pages I've written these last few days. I should have said more about Miami, about that restaurant, for example, where Marinescu had invited us, and where I was astonished to notice how strongly one experiences, everywhere in the United States, the sensation of always entering the same establishment.

I try in vain to remember that chapter in Alexander von Humboldt's *Examen critique,* and I regret—once again—being deprived of the "photographic memory" of a Berthold Laufer or a Paul Pelliot. I've known for at least thirty years that if I had been endowed with one, my life would have taken a completely different course. For in my youth I couldn't have resisted the desire to learn a quantity of Asian languages. The fact remains that I had and still do have endless admiration for Paul Pelliot's photographic memory. An anecdote, almost forgotten today, is, however, quite telling: When the twenty thousand manuscripts from the caves of Tun-Houang were discovered, it was decided that the unearthed treasure would be shared by France, Great Britain, and China. It was Pelliot who had the honor of examining before anyone else the documents that were discovered, and of choosing the portion that would go to France. Since the great Orientalist had read everything, absolutely everything, that was known of at the time in the way of publications or manuscripts, not only in Chinese but also in other Oriental languages, he had only to glance at the first lines of each of the Tun-Houang manuscripts to ascertain immediately whether it was a yet unknown, and thus unpublished, document. And this is why today the most important texts are found in Paris . . .

Today we went to Safari Land. It is an immense park, scattered with clearings, around which winds a road where cars travel slowly, all windows rolled up. I can't even imagine how they were able to achieve this sample of an African landscape, more natural than nature, to such a degree that the lions, languidly resting on rocks, or the giraffes, busy nibbling the last leaves at the top of a stunted and dried-up tree, are no longer even startling. A bit farther, a herd of zebra; then some hippopotami drowsing in their swamp.

I don't really know what to think of it. In all appearances it is not a zoological park in the strict sense. The animals here are free to a certain extent to come and go as they please. If one thinks of other zoos and their cages, under the circumstances these animals enjoy relative freedom. The fact remains that they are still in a "forced environment." For them, it could be worse. I can't help thinking of the tens and hundreds of thousands of inmates in the prisons and camps of Eastern Europe. How happy they would be if they, too, found themselves simply "confined to quarters"!

When I first met him in London in 1940 Theodor Besterman was working on a project of great importance. He intended to show, in four volumes, all aspects of North America at the time of its discovery, and before its colonization by Europeans. The first volume was to be devoted to the fauna and flora, and the following three to the indigenous population: tribes, institutions, religions, customs, arts, etc. . . . Having discovered an unexpected passion for Voltaire, whose complete works (and especially the correspondence) he intended to translate into English, Besterman abandoned his original project.

But in Paris, around 1947, he lent me the manuscript of the first volume of his work. How I regret not being able to dive back into it again after this trip over a large part of Florida! I could then have an idea of the flora and fauna that reigned here almost five centuries ago . . . The flora was probably less varied than it is today. Quantities of new species have been imported since then, either from Pacific islands (bougainvillaea, for example), or from Australia (eucalyptus), or even from Europe (among other things, all the ornamental flowers and numerous varieties of trees).

PALM BEACH, *2 January 1974*

Since this morning the sky is grey and it's raining.

Through a letter from Georges Dumézil, forwarded from Chicago, I learn of the death of Father Jean de Menasce. I knew that for several years already he had been unable to speak. He expressed himself only with guttural sounds and by the few words he managed to type out, using only one finger of his left hand. When I saw him for the last time in 1970 his right arm was paralyzed, he had trouble walking, but he could still speak without difficulty.

I've often thought of the ordeal he must have gone through since his first attack of hemiplegia in the spring of 1959, which was followed by several others.

Born of a very rich Jewish family from Alexandria, Jean de Menasce had been, I was told, a true arbiter of elegance, and doubled as a poet. He was one of the first to translate T. S. Eliot, then he launched himself into the study of Hebrew, Kabala, and Christian mystical theology. Shortly after converting, he decided to become a monk. His faith remained unshaken to his final day, but no one would ever know how he was able to maintain it intact. Anyone else but he would have seen in his afflictions a manifestation of the anger of Yahweh, the one of the Old Testament, the true and only God.

CHICAGO, *January*

When I immerse myself in my files from the first ten years of my stay in Chicago, in which I've put notes, letters, course outlines, and a quantity of remarks and diverse reflections, I have the impression of excavating my own "history." But I try to contain myself in order not to let the hopes and emotions experienced at the time resurface.

A mysterious instinct seems to deflect me to certain facts of major importance. A detail that might seem trivial, but is so in appearance only: It is a fact that in the United States people throw into the garbage *a billion* glass or plastic bottles daily. A good portion of them end up in the sea, making it sicker than it already is (a few years ago an international congress took place on the theme: "The Mediterranean—A Sick Sea"). What doesn't reach the ocean is thrown here and there, in gutters, garbage dumps, work sites, lakes. But what will happen fifteen or twenty years from now? What will become of these millions of bottles, not to mention the millions of diverse containers that are incinerated every day, at the same time as the thousands of tons of printed paper?

Upon awakening this morning, I asked myself a little riddle: When one has known the Orient at twenty-one years old, the West at thirty-three, the New World at forty-nine, what more is there left to know? Quite clever, whoever can answer . . .

3 February

I've learned that in the course of these last few years around three hundred Rumanian doctors have asked to take advantage of the right to political asylum and have moved to the United States. Most took advantage when they were granted a passport to participate in a congress, and never went back (this is a wide-ranging phenomenon which involves all levels of society: workers, athletes, musicians, architects, writers, and scientists). If they were sure to obtain a passport each time they are invited to a congress or, concerning students, each time they obtain a foreign scholarship, the number of defections would be much lower, especially among doctors, scientists, historians, and philosophers.

But all of this is well known, and I wouldn't feel the need to point it out if I hadn't happened to learn that in the past five or six years a good twenty Rumanian doctors had in fact moved to Chicago. No one has ever seen them at the Rumanian church, the natural meeting place of all exiles. None of them has tried to meet those of their countrymen who have preceded them to the United States by ten or twenty years. They are content to attend to their affairs in the hospitals or the institutions where they've been able to find work. Just like other Americans they seem to have only one goal in life: To own the latest-model car and an apartment in a luxury building, with a pool if possible.

The refugees I knew in Paris between 1945 and 1956, whatever their age or their profession, had, if one may say so, another ideal: They had fled Rumania above all to bear witness in the West to the situation that reigned back there, and to fight for the liberation of the country. Among the recent refugees, there are very few who still believe that raising the consciousness of "international public opinion," or the "battle for the reconquest of liberties," will have concrete results. In a great majority, those who don't believe in miracles no longer believe in anything. What they aim for is much more modest: Too happy to have finally discovered freedom, they are content to borrow from the host country its own "ideals," that is, a car, a single-family house, etc. . . .

5 February

I've just reread what I wrote the day before yesterday, and I fear I've been a bit too severe. The voluntary isolation of the doctors in Chicago, like that of so many other Rumanian intellectuals in exile, in the United States as elsewhere, is perhaps only a defense mechanism against all the "politico-social activities" in which they found themselves forced to participate in Rumania, those "discussion meetings," draining and endless, all those litanies of worn-out cliches, of stereotypical speeches and forced applause. The newcomers will need a lot of time before they agree to join up with other Rumanians, to go to their gatherings, their committees, and in a word, to "participate" in all the social activities this implies.

13 February

Oral examination of Sandy S., one of my students, who is writing a thesis on the "revival" in the United States. It is a captivating subject richly instructive for the new generation of scholars. Sandy analyzes the phenomenon of the American revival not in the light of the history—or the sociology—of Protestantism, but in that of the history of religions. One has trouble imagining what is left to discover in an area that has already been abundantly explored by historians and sociologists, unless one considers it from another angle. What then becomes obvious is the structural identity of this ancestral and universal heritage formed by initiatory scenarios which is discovered in those used by so very many preachers and visionaries of all the sects issued from the Reformation!

For several years already I've said over and over to myself and to my colleagues and students that a true *universal* history of religions will only be possible when the enormous mass of documents in the possession, on the one hand, of ethnologists and folklorists, and on the other, of historians of diverse faiths and Christian sects, are interpreted by historians of religions and are incorporated into their own reference systems.

14 February

Had dinner yesterday with Charles and Alice Long at the Quadrangle Club. I feel somewhat sad at the idea that Chuck will be leaving the University of Chicago this summer to assume the chair in the history of religions at Chapel Hill in North Carolina. But he's been in Chicago now almost thirty years. He had been a student of Joachim Wach. At the time of my arrival he was an instructor. After completing his doctoral degree he became associate professor and dean of students, and finally full professor. He feels the need to know other university settings, even though he recognizes that the best department in the history of religions is here in Chicago. He undoubtedly has his reasons, but I am crushed. Our friendship goes back to when I first arrived in the United States. Rare are those who know as well as he my views on the history of religions, and share them. In addition, he's an excellent professor, even though he publishes too little, for, like many American scholars, he is afflicted with "perfectionitis." Being fascinated by primitive religions, helped in this by his training as a theologian and by the experience acquired as a black North American, he is in my opinion one of the rare people capable of conceiving a systematic and historical theology of archaic populations, and above all of those of pre-Christian Africa.

19 February

This need to anticipate the arrival of the Messiah through rites carried out at regular intervals, or even through a specific behavior, is truly touching! I have just reread the text of the manuscripts of Qumran. For the Essenes, the meals they took together reproduced through anticipation the "eschatological banquet" they hoped to be able to celebrate in the near future. It was the same for the first Christians. The ceremony of "breaking bread" was meant above all to commemorate the Last Supper, but its goal was also to anticipate the feast that was to take place at the End of Time. In the Hellenistic period this practice was rather common, as is seen in the initiatory banquets of the Mysteries of Dionysus.

These same beliefs, and the hope that certain gestures and certain rites can anticipate and especially hasten the coming of the messianic era, are still found in our time. Berdiaev never consummated his marriage with his wife, so sure was he that in acting thus he was already putting himself into that third age announced by Joachim of Fiore, that of spiritual freedom and of the supremacy of the Holy Spirit, when everyone will be as brothers and sisters, and consequently where sexual relationships will be abolished. With a few variants, this same concept is found in a number of other civilizations, from India to Tibet, from Mongolia to the Middle East.

Another example: Although he no longer believed in the literal interpretation of the dogma, Teilhard de Chardin nevertheless did not renounce the priesthood, for by the simple fact of celebrating mass every morning, he had the sensation of anticipating the transmutation of the cosmic substance in the flesh and blood of Christ.

24 February

The boy and girl clutching each other, leaning against a wall, were simulating copulation. One had only to notice their look or their smiles to realize that their only goal was to scandalize passersby, who in their eyes represented the Establishment in all its horror and hypocrisy.

True copulation in public is not an innovation. The Cynics didn't behave in any other way: like animals they urinated, defecated, masturbated, and had intercourse in front of everyone. They went around dressed in rags and intentionally employed obscene, provocative, and aggressive language. Yelling like beasts, they in addition gesticulated like madmen. But their behavior was sheltered behind a certain philosophy, and the goal they pursued was of a parareligious nature. By imitating animals, the Cynics—like the Taoists, moreover—were attempting to rediscover the natural spontaneity and "wisdom" that civilization had suppressed. Some among them even insisted on eating their meat raw, even though that diet of "savages," according to Diogenes Laërtius (4.22), gave them colic . . .

During Dionysiac orgies, meat was also torn apart and devoured raw, but that was a sort of omophagia through which one was believed to mystically assimilate the body of Dionysus, and thus rediscover primordial joy and freedom. I've analyzed this phenomenon in *A History of Religious Ideas* (§ 124). Besides, by becoming objects of scandal, the Cynics gave proof of their total emancipation from the values imposed by society. Their model was Heracles, in his lifetime "the most shameful and despicable of men," but who, after his death, was divinized: It was to him that mortals addressed their prayers to protect them from misery and from moral decay (Dio Chrysostom *Orationes* 8.29).

25 February

Returning to public copulation, of which the contortions of my young friends of yesterday naively simulated the spectacle, let's add that it was attested to, between the second century B.C. and the seventh century A.D., in theory as in practice, among the followers of the Sivaist sect, Pāsupata. Repulsively dirty, they tried to appear as abject, obscene, aggressive, and demented as possible. The follower imitates the animal (*pāsu*) in the hope of being transformed into Siva, the lord of the beasts (*pāsupata*). The object of scorn and humiliated by all his contemporaries, considered by them to be an abject, disgusting, injurious, and beaten brute, he thus acquires a superhuman personality, and in time reaches absolute freedom (*moksha*). Through this return to animality, the *pāsupata* finally achieves the divine condition of Siva: *everything becomes permissible.*

By simulating coitus in public, the young couple of yesterday was attempting, with the paltry means offered by our desacralized society, to prove that for them, too, *all is permitted.* But I can imagine their reaction if someone had told them that by "imitating animals" they were only carrying out a ritual act destined in the end to identify them with Heracles or Siva . . .

27 February

I reread the preceding pages. There is so much to say on this subject! This parody of copulation in public constitutes only one of the aspects, uniquely negative and polemical (down with the Establishment!), of a much vaster and otherwise important phenomenon, that is, the rediscovery by certain young people—and not only hippies—of cosmic religiosity. Ritual nudity, free and spontaneous sexual union, belong to a syndrome in which one guesses the yearning for lost Paradise, for a return to the state before original sin, before the knowledge of good and evil.

In addition, one musn't forget that sexuality, and especially sexual imagination and symbolics, have played a significant role throughout all of the *spiritual* history of humanity. I will give only one example of this, that of the ambiguity of sexual symbolism and vocabulary. All terms can be understood simultaneously in their concrete sense and in their spiritual, "mystical" sense. For certain Tantric schools, the *Sahajiya,* among others, the vocabulary, which is both paradoxical and enigmatic, aims to surprise and shock the noninitiated. Extremely arduous exercises of yoga meditation are presented in erotic terms: "coupling with an outcast prostitute" means in fact "a state of nirvanic joy" and "absolute liberty." For the initiates, this confusion in terms, permanent and omnipresent, aims to hasten the passing from a profane condition. The *coincidentia oppositorum* succeeds, on all levels, in revealing that ultimate and mysterious reality that is as inaccessible to understanding as is religious faith. It is quite obvious that there are circumstances in which, taking into account the disciple's level of preparation, the sexual techniques of yoga must be carried out concretely. Even in this case, the sexual experience finds itself in some way transfigured, and ceases to be of a uniquely physiological nature.

This deliberate will to provoke public disgrace and collective indignation is found in other cultural contexts. Thus, to better consecrate their definitive rupture with the "world," in other words, with the existing society of the Roman Empire, the Christian nuns of the first centuries intentionally wore the clothes of courtesans. Certain monks got themselves up in pieced-together costumes of diverse colors, true harlequin coats, and behaved as the "mentally ill," etc. . . . .

7 March

The meaning of Isaac's sacrifice was not evident to Abraham. In appearance it was an infanticide, and for Abraham it was unthinkable that Yahweh could ask him to make such a gesture. The "sacrality" of Isaac's sacrifice was camouflaged, not in the "profane," but in a "crime." To compare with the current situation: In our time religious experience has become unrecognizable, for it is camouflaged in its contrary—in materialism, antireligion, etc. . . . .

16 March

While leafing through my datebook I notice that the story I've just finished today, *Incognito à Buchenwald,* was started on 11 March. On 13 March I received *Manuscriptum,* the journal at the end of which Mircea Handoca presented *Iphigenia,* a play I wrote in 1939, the only one of mine to have been performed (at the National Theatre of Bucharest during the winter of 1941). But I never saw it, for in April 1940 I had been named cultural attaché of our legation in London. Strange coincidence: I received this copy of *Iphigenia* while I was writing a story whose characters were young actors rehearsing a play entitled *Incognito à Buchenwald,* a rather enigmatic play, by the way, whose subject and genre are difficult for the reader to discern, but which, through the eyes of the characters, and especially of those of Ieronim Tanase (the director in my story *Uniformes de général*), aimed above all for the magico-spiritual transformation of the whole audience.

20 March

Last seminar of the year. I am free until October, which doesn't prevent me from breaking out in cold sweats when I think about the work that awaits me, and which is urgent. Most important, my lecture for the John Nuveen Lectures. I've chosen a subject that is particularly dear to me: witchcraft from the perspective of the history of religions. It is a singularly arduous subject, which I intend to limit to the relationships between witchcraft and magico-religious beliefs in Europe. I will, moreover, deal only with certain aspects of it.

22 March

I have just reread *Incognito à Buchenwald*. I feared I would be disappointed, but nothing of the kind happened, which is rather rare when I reread one of my texts so soon after having written it. It remains to be seen, of course, if it will please the reader, all the more since the last sentence opens up a "mystery," or an enigma, and I will undoubtedly have to write another story to resolve it. But my story pleases me, for it picks up certain characters from *The Old Man and the Bureaucrats, Uniformes de général,* and, to a lesser degree, *La Demeure de Dionis.*

23 March

I find it curious, for someone who does not really feel a vocation as a playwright—with the exception of *Iphigenia,* but that was a work of youth—not to have hesitated to deal with theatrical issues in three of my stories: *Adio!, Uniformes de général,* and *Incognito à Buchenwald.* But it always involves reconsidering the dramatic presentation, although I never specify what exactly this reconsideration consists of.

In the last few days, I had a conversation with one of my students, Marjorie Y., and since we were talking about the transmutation of time and space through dramatic performance, she asked if I had ever attended a performance of a play by Robert Wilson. I replied that I hadn't, and it happens that today I have in hand articles on and reviews of Robert Wilson's latest work, *The Life and Times of Joseph Stalin,* performed last December in New York. The play goes on for twelve hours, from seven in the morning to seven in the evening. A critic, Martin Gottfried, gives the reasons for this: "The length is partly because that is simply how long it takes, but mainly to take the time to slow down your pace of life, draw you into its rhythm, and make you susceptible to hypnotism, trance, and perhaps, pull your brain waves into an alpha state. To put it very plainly, Wilson can draw you toward the most exciting aspect of drugs—freedom of consciousness and imagination—without feeding chemicals into your system.''

And further: ''If you are willing to be enfolded and then set really free—to let go of the moorings that have made your life seem logical and 'real'—Wilson can show you a world of inner vision and outer dreams, his and then yours.''

Another critic, Mel Gussow, writes: ''Instead of trying to condense time as in traditional theater, Mr. Wilson expands time. One minute becomes an hour. As a key to his method, he described a favorite image: a mother picking up a crying baby, a scene filled with tenderness—until it is witnessed in slow motion. Then, said Mr. Wilson, the mother lunges at the child, and the child rears back in fright. Mr. Wilson, as slow-motion camera, sees such a flash of reality as a series of complex emotions. Actually, by Mr. Wilson's own standards, *Stalin* is medium-length. *Deafman Glance,* his last major work to be seen in New York, ran three hours. His KA MOUNTAIN AND GUARD*enia Terrace* which was staged last year on a mountain in Iran, ran 168 hours.''

Naturally, the dramatic production I allude to in my story, or more precisely, the one the director mentions, but never explicitly, was not going to occupy the stage for 168 hours, nor even 12. But the secret of the production resides in the methods used to project both actors and audience into a space-time that is inaccessible in everyday experience. For Ieronim, the director, it is by calling upon diverse dramaturgical techniques, such as gymnastics, choreography, yoga, ecstasy, etc. . . . that one can succeed in going beyond the human condition, even in annulling it.

1 April

I begin writing the text of my lecture. I've intentionally chosen an enigmatic and aggressive title: ''The Professor and the Witches.''

14 April

Magnificently cold weather. It is surely going to snow. I write two pages of my lecture. Usually, after having drafted about half of a text that will be read out loud, I end up regretting the chosen subject, which always seems to be too important to be presented out loud, before a necessarily disparate audience. This inhibits all my desire to push the analysis as far as I should. I do remember, however, that Heidegger read *Was ist Metaphysik?* in an auditorium filled with people, and where his students were in the minority.

18 April

This afternoon I attended Zwi Werblowski's lecture. In the evening, dinner at the Quadrangle Club in the company of Zwi and Kitagawa. We finish the evening at our house, where other friends join us. Long discussions. I give Zwi copies of *No Souvenirs* and *The Old Man and the Bureaucrats* in German translation. Zwi is one of the rare scholars who can be interested in books other than those in his speciality.

April

Impossible to remember the name of that student who always came without warning, and always in torrential rain. After three or four fruitless attempts on his part I was finally able to see him and speak with him.

Since we were looking out the window at the water falling in torrents, I told him, just for fun, but also because I felt exasperated, this anecdote taken from the works of the great Chinese historian Sse-ma Kuang: For an entire summer the T'ang empire had been ravaged by catastrophic floods. The emperor, known after his death by the name of Hsien-tsong, was convinced that the floods were due to an excess of *yin,* that is, of the feminine force, which was causing an imbalance in cosmic harmony. And since, as Son of the Sky, he knew he was capable of reestablishing equilibrium, Hsien-tsong had two hundred carriages filled with women leave his palace . . . Woman indeed incarnated the *yin* force, and thus that of water.

"That explains everything!" exclaimed my student, who had listened to me attentively, almost with rapture. "This deluge must be the fault of women's lib . . . ! For weeks the militants have been agitating like hornets . . . ''

He was quiet a moment, looked at me quizzically, then added with the greatest seriousness:

"But we can't do anything about it. There is no way of expelling *them* . . . ''

29 April

Certain days deserve to be marked with a white stone. For example, when one makes a little discovery without having wanted or expected to. While reading *Wittgenstein's Vienna,* I came upon this little passage: "Wittgenstein was unwilling to discuss technical points in philosophy with the members of the Vienna Circle, and he insisted rather on reading poetry to them, especially the poems of Rabindranath Tagore."

15 May

I have no sooner finished "The Professor and the Witches" than I must write the text of another lecture on the current popular interest in occult sciences, which I must soon give in Philadelphia as part of the Freud Lectures. A vast subject! It may seem ironical, but how significant, to point out that at the beginning of the century Freud confided in Jung his fears of soon seeing occultism and spiritism enjoying a revival in popularity. Around 1950 Jung himself told me how worried Freud was at the idea that ghosts might really exist! Only, he said, psychoanalytic theory and practice, or more precisely, the generalization and popularization of psychoanalysis as a global discipline, were in a position to thwart this new peril.

Nevertheless, within the last ten years there has been a renewal of interest in the occult sciences, especially in the United States, that is, in the very place where Freud and psychoanalysis have taken root most firmly, not only in scientific circles, but also among the most general public.

Must one see here a link of cause and effect? This isn't inconceivable. The two vogues, that of psychoanalysis and that of the occult sciences, have in common their opposition to the ideology and the way of life transmitted by the "bourgeois society of consumption," in other words, by the Establishment. Both translate a profound disappointment in the Christian churches, as well as in the crass ignorance of the true content of Judeo-Christian tradition. They express, each in its own way, the yearning of modern man, and his hope for a spiritual *renovatio* that would finally give a meaning to and a justification for his own existence.

7 May

Another word concerning my Freud Lecture: In the course of the last thirty years, two collections of esoteric texts have been discovered: the manuscripts of Qumran, of Essenian origin, and the Egyptian Gnostic library of Nag Hamâdi. Within the same period of time, thus still in the course of the last thirty years, there have been published, in translation or in their original languages, a considerable number of texts of esoteric origin and structure. These are texts that until then were only transmitted or commented on orally, and only for the benefit of "initiates." I'm thinking under the circumstances especially of the Tantra, of Taoist texts, and of those belonging to Iranian esoteric tradition. But I'm also thinking of the authoritative studies by Gershom Sholem, Henry Corbin, G. Tucci, Frances Yates, etc. In short, texts once considered to be "secret" are today considerably well known due to the publication abilities at our disposal.

This process of "de-occulting" esoteric and initiatory traditions deserves to be brought up again. It could be the object of a very instructive study in the history of ideas, for it lends itself to comparisons with similar situations already encountered in the past; for example, the "rediscovery" of texts that had disappeared for millennia, and which served as themes for very popular legends in the Hellenistic period, in medieval India, in the Renaissance, etc. But the significance of this phenomenon is only fully understood if one interprets it from the angle of tradition. Indeed, esoteric texts are only brought to light, and only become accessible to the public, to all publics, on the eve of great historical cataclysms, when the "end of the world" is near, the end of *our* world, of course.

13 May

Today I gave my lecture, "The Professor and the Witches." It will be the subject of a publication whose title will be clearly less aggressive: "Remarks on Witchcraft in Europe." It was Edward Levi who introduced me to the audience in Swift Hall. The room was full to bursting. I wonder all the same whether the audience followed me all the way through. I went on much too long: Indeed, I spoke for almost an hour and a half.

In the evening, a big dinner at the Quadrangle Club given by Joe Kitagawa. Mrs. Nuveen, the Levis, and a good dozen professors were there. I'm noting all this to remind myself of a small regret: As my lecture was letting out, a young Sinologist who was passing through Chicago came up to talk to me. I was much too tired, and could only give him a few minutes. But what he managed to say in so little time turned out to be fascinating. I very much hoped to continue our conversation during dinner, or at least during cocktails, but he hadn't been invited and had disappeared. I've forgotten his name and don't even know at what university he is preparing his doctorate.

19 May

I had a visit today from S.T., whom I had had as a student several years ago. I thought he had given up his doctorate, and that drugs were the reason. I had vaguely heard that he had found work unrelated to the history of religions. We chat for almost fifteen minutes without my being able to make him reconsider his decision: He's preparing a thesis on different types of "spiritual bodies," and especially on those referred to in Indian tradition, and which I have myself analyzed in *Yoga* and during a seminar on mysticism and subtle physiology. I had discussed bodies issued from "spiritual substance," which Buddha speaks of, the "spiritual" or "divine body," the *cinmaya divya deha* of the yogis, the "mature body," or *pakva*, of the alchemists, etc. Since he had done a seminar project on this subject he was perfectly familiar with the literature relating to the "mysterious embryo," that immortal being issued from the exemplary fusion of the *yin* and *yang* forces and which, formed in the very body of the Taoist alchemist, escapes at the time of death through the occiput and ascends to Heaven.

But my student wanted to remain there. I made him see that all of that was already well known, and that it would be in his interest to enlarge the scope of his research. Even if he abstained from broaching the notion of "pneumatic body" unique to Christianity and Gnosticism, he would certainly need to speak of the "celestial bodies" of Iranian tradition which Henry Corbin has dealt with so competently. He would also have to discover analogous ideas and beliefs in Christian alchemy and theology, and especially see what happened subsequent to Boehme and Swedenborg.

To my great surprise, for I knew he was taken with esoterism, although he was only interested in the Orient, he replied that he would never let himself get dragged into "the jungle of Christian theosophy." Before the thousands and thousands of pages he would have to read if he ever hazarded it, most without great philosophical interest, he gave up. I pointed out that Schelling had also arrived at the notion of "spiritual body" (*Geistleibichkeit*) after having explored only a part of that "jungle."

"There's too much!" he exclaimed. "It would take me at least ten years to finish with it!"

I did indeed have to admit he was right.

PHILADELPHIA, *24 May*

Very bad night, awake at eight o'clock, then hasty departure for the airport. When we arrive in Philadelphia the heat is a shock, and a thunderstorm is threatening. We're staying at the Barclay Hotel. It is a "historic" hotel, it would seem, whose front faces a superb public square which was once the upper class's favorite place to stroll, and which is today predominately black. I lie down and have an hour's rest before rereading the text of my lecture for the Freud Memorial Lectures this evening. Why the devil did I accept a year ago this invitation of the Philadelphia Society of Psychoanalysis? I was undoubtedly enticed by the very fact of having been invited, I who for thirty or forty years have continued to denounce Freud's theories concerning religion. From two things, one, I told myself: either they've read nothing I've written, or in the opposite case, they want me to present my own theories, which means they've stopped stiffening on dogmatic and intransigent positions and are opening up, in principle, to criticism of the Freudian dogma. My lecture is entitled "The Vogue of Occultism." I must mention that the cycle of lectures, which has been going on for twenty-one years, was inaugurated by Anna Freud. It was she, too, who last year delivered the twentieth memorial lecture.

While the storm is erupting I reread my manuscript. At six o'clock the editor-in-chief of the journal of psychoanalysis that will publish the text of my lecture comes to pick us up at the hotel. We have dinner at the museum restaurant, where I find Dr. Eckart, the president of the society, whom I already know, as well as about ten other men and their wives. Christinel's great success: When Dr. Eckart stepped up to the rostrum to introduce me to the audience, he begins his little talk with "Mrs. Eliade, ladies and gentlemen . . . " The room, which can hold close to five hundred people, is almost full. Then I start speaking, with some spirit, it seems, for the audience listens to me attentively for close to an hour and a quarter. The lecture is followed by a "champagne reception" where there are close to two hundred people. Those who have paid to be there, of course . . . I find myself inundated with questions, to which I try to respond as intelligently as possible.

Return to the hotel around midnight.

PHILADELPHIA, *25 May*

After breakfast we go by taxi to the Barnes Foundation in Merion, a few kilometers from Philadelphia. As Dr. Eckart was unable to get tickets for us, we try our luck. Indeed, the museum is only open a few days a week, and they only let two hundred visitors in at a time. A hundred or so tickets are reserved months in advance. The other hundred are distributed at the door to visitors who wait on line at the entrance at least a half hour before the doors open.

The two hours spent at the Barnes Foundation have left an extraordinary impression on us. We are amazed, almost dumbfounded, by this profusion of masterpieces: three hundred Renoirs, seventy Matisses, not to mention the Manets, Degas, Seurats, Picassos, etc. . . . If I could, and if I had the time, I would trace the career of that great industrialist, a manufacturer of pharmaceutical products who made his fortune by putting on the market a medicine against coughs and the flu. Around 1910 he began collecting the works of French masters of impression-ism, although at least in the beginning he didn't feel especially attracted to them. He mostly bought paintings by Renoir and Matisse, his favorite painters.

I will not attempt to describe how one feels crushed in the presence of several hundred canvases by the same artist. That had never happened to me before, not even during the most beautiful retrospec-tives I had the opportunity to see; that of Van Gogh at the Orangerie, for example, ten or fifteen years ago. Words are powerless before such a sensation, which is not, moreover, of a purely aesthetic nature, but is due above all to the "effect of mass" which comes out of viewing the complete works—or almost complete—of one artist. To mention only Renoir, I do believe that close to two-thirds of his canvases are collected here.

NEW YORK, *26 May*

I will not soon forget my day yesterday, especially those few hours spent visiting the museum and the park of the Barnes Foundation. I will need several weeks to assimilate all that I've just discovered and learned. How sad I am, too, to know that I will never have the time to do it! After having seen the originals, I would, however, have liked to linger and leaf through the catalogs of reproductions, and read the most recent studies on impressionism, on contemporary painting. But when will I find the time?

We had lunch at Dr. Eckart's; he had come to pick us up at the museum exit. What a host! And what a beautiful house he has, nestled between trees and flowers! What is remarkable about Dr. Eckart is that despite his being a specialist in cerebral physiology—and he is also a very strict disciple of the Freudian school—he remains no less a fervent Christian, a Catholic, no less. I would have liked to talk with him longer. But it was already three o'clock, and we had to go back to the hotel as quickly as possible, pack our bags, and hurry to the station if we didn't want to miss the train to New York.

I had almost forgotten what a train trip in the United States is like. Comfortable, of course, but how melancholy! The steward brings you your order, then retires into his corner with slow and muted footsteps. One would think one had gone back several generations, to a world that is no longer ours. The age of railroad travel is in the process of dying out, if it hasn't happened already, and without anyone even noticing.

Lisette is waiting for us at home, more relaxed than usual. This time she didn't need to call the airport to find out if our plane had arrived on time! She has invited B. and T. Coste to see us.

CHICAGO, *June*

There would be so much to say in the preface to *A History of Religious Ideas!* I would first of all like to specify that I have never experienced an inferiority complex, as was the case with a good number of my Western colleagues. I have never been a seminarian like the Sinologist, Creel, and so many others. I have never had to defend myself against the too-great influence of the church, unlike many Italian scholars. Crises of conscience or revolts, incited, exacerbated by an education in a Jesuit environment, the anguish of the confessional, a too-rigorous indoctrination, have always remained foreign to me. In Rumania, the children and youths of my generation were unburdened with these shackles. Religion was one of the components of the culture to which I belonged, and I couldn't have accepted it more naturally. Christianity in its Oriental form, Orthodoxy, was intimately linked to the very history of the Rumanian people, which allowed me to judge without a complex both what it meant and what it had contributed as much on a spiritual level as on a historical one. I could make my own judgments, have my own criticisms, my own refusals, freely and without risk.

It is to this full and total freedom that I owe the objectivity I've been able to have, and the sympathy I've shown toward the religious phenomenon. It is to that freedom that I owe having become a historian of religions without prejudice of any sort. All of this would deserve to be commented on at greater length. To compare with E. de Martino's situation, for example, etc. . . .

12 June

Farewell dinner in honor of Chuck and Alice Long. I'm beginning to get used to the idea that soon he will no longer be with us. All the same, I'm curious to know what he'll show he can do in his new position at Chapel Hill.

In these last few days I've drafted the notes for "Witchcraft" and prepared the text for the printer. I am grateful to Joe Kitagawa for having insisted so strongly that I give him as early as possible the text of this John Nuveen Lecture. Otherwise I would have been tempted to develop certain passages, or to add some, and this essay would have remained in a drawer awaiting just the right moment. And I have so much to do these days . . .

22 June

Besides the notes for "Witchcraft" and some letters to write, nothing in particular to note. I sort through files, manuscripts, and books, etc. . . . that I will bring with me to Paris.

24 June

Dinner at Olivier's, the consul general of France. For a few hours I immerse myself once again in the "diplomatic" atmosphere I knew so well between 1941 and 1945. Return home in the storm.

PARIS, 26 June

We took off last night at eight o'clock. I didn't close my eyes all night. Dinu and Giza were waiting for us at the new Roissy airport.

PARIS, 8 July

I've relegated to my datebook my appointments, visits, what I've read. It's taken me until today to adapt to my new Parisian rhythm. I spent a week drowsing during the day, and was unable to sleep at night.

Useless to say with what pleasure I've reread seven complete volumes of Balzac, in the Marcel Bouteron edition.

12 July

We go with Sibylle and Marie-France Ionesco to spend the day at Eugène's and Rodica's "mill" to celebrate their thirty-eight years of marriage.

Among other things we recall our memories of the Paris of 1945–1950, and of our poverty then. Curiously, certain details of that time remain engraved in our memories, whereas others have completely disappeared. Without Rodica's help, I would never have remembered our reunion upon my arrival in Paris. She had put Marie-France into my arms, at the time barely a year old, and couldn't keep from laughing at my distress. I held the baby like a package, at arm's length, and didn't dare hold it next to me. While listening to Rodica, I suddenly remember what had caused me to behave so awkwardly. I had just read an article that dealt with the risks a baby faced when it was put into arms "foreign to the familial environment" or into others "having just arrived," from the provinces or elsewhere. And I had in fact just arrived from Portugal.

July

Today I learn of the death of Julius Evola. Our last meeting goes back about ten years, even though I have passed through Rome several times since then. Memories surge up in me, those of my years at university, the books we had discovered together, the letters I received from him in Calcutta in which he instantly begged me not to speak to him of yoga, or of "magical powers," except to report precise facts to which I had personally been a witness. In India I also received several publications from him, but I only remember a few issues of the journal *Krur.*

I had met him for the first time in 1937 at Nae Ionescu's. Besides the three of us, Octave Onicescu and our professor's current girlfriend were also there. That very morning Evola had had the opportunity to talk with Codreanu, and that meeting had impressed him greatly. Since Evola had asked him about the political tactics he expected to employ and the Legion's chances during the coming elections, Codreanu had spoken to him about the effects of incarceration on the individual, of the ascesis it provokes, the contemplative virtues that can arise there, in solitude, a silence and a darkness which are just so many means by which an individual is revealed to himself. Evola was still dazzled by him. I vaguely remember the remarks he made then on the disappearance of contemplative disciplines in the political battle of the West.

Then the war came, and I heard nothing more of Evola until the day when I received his letter from Rome at the Hôtel de Suède. He had obtained my address through René Guénon, who must have gotten it himself from Valsan. He let me know that he was henceforth "immo-bilized for the rest of his days," but that he would be happy to see me at his home, in the event that I should pass through Rome.

That is what I did in August 1949, after having notified him by phone of my visit. Having arrived at his home, I was taken into the drawing room where his father and a nurse asked me to wait while they helped him get up from his chair. He greeted me standing up and shook my hands for a long time. Then his father and the nurse helped him to sit down again, which he couldn't have done himself without collapsing. We talked for over an hour. He told me that since from then on he had all the time in the world, he took advantage of it by translating French and German authors. He also spoke about *Metaphysics of Sex,* a book he was planning to write. We were at that point in our conversation when he took a little key out of his pocket, showed me an ivory elephant, and told me how to open it. The elephant contained a miniature bar, with numerous flasks and little glasses all made of crystal. He asked me what I'd like to drink, but the afternoon was steamy, and I didn't want any alcohol. He insisted, however, under the pretext that we were carrying out a rite and I had to submit to it. I had to give in, and we both raised our glasses before ceremoniously drinking the contents.

I was to see Evola only once more, in 1952 or 1953, but we corresponded regularly. One day I received a rather bitter letter from him in which he reproached me for never citing him, no more than did Guénon. I answered him as best I could, and I must one day give the reasons and explanations that that response called for. My argument couldn't have been simpler. The books I write are intended for today's audience, and not for initiates. Unlike Guénon and his emulators, I believe I have nothing to write that would be intended especially for them.

BRUGES, *18 July*

Departure from Paris at one o'clock. The sky is grey and menacing, and we waste no time driving in a downpour. In places the road is flooded and Sibylle's car advances with difficulty. Finally the sky clears, and around four-thirty we arrive in Bruges under a summer sky that seems to belong to another world and another century. I have trouble grasping that such a city can still exist, that it is inhabited, and that it is located less than three hundred kilometers from Paris. And as usual, I regret that it's taken me so many years before deciding to visit it.

We leave our luggage at the Hôtel du Duc de Bourgogne, and go walking along the canals. At the end of the day, a ride in a barge. "The Venice of the North," Bruges is called, but it is something else entirely! I can't exactly describe what I'm experiencing. I feel outside time, outside that which was mine just this morning in Paris. I am moved, but also calm, as if something unknown were suddenly going to be revealed to me. Back at the hotel, at dinner time, I finally begin to understand what I'm feeling. I am writing these lines in all haste, and I don't know whether, when I reread them, I will still remember all the minute facts, all these revelations in their present freshness. I do believe I have rediscovered, with an intensity close to paroxysm, the creative function of scenery. I had only to enter a city that technological progress has spared, that so-called modern architecture and its "living machines" haven't disfigured, I had only to escape everyday tedium, its routine, and to feel as free as at the dawn of a new life, to recover the spontaneity and joys of the imagination.

I have long experience with this sort of feeling. I even knew that special circumstances, such as a "change of scene," aren't necessary to cause it. Nevertheless, it is in Bruges that I have discovered to what extent the *imagination* can become creative when it is stimulated by "scenery" (as well as by any work of art), and from then on can pave the way for a true "renaissance," or in other words, a regeneration of the whole self.

BRUGES, *19 July*

     Superb morning. We visit the Memling Museum, then the Beaux-Arts Museum. Useless to say anything about it here, except to mention the astonishing beauty of the buildings and the palaces that house the works of art, the Hospital of St. John, among others, its "Apothicarium" of meticulous cleanliness which doesn't smell like a pharmacy. We lunch on sandwiches at an outdoor cafe in full sunlight.

Memling, of course—but any other great painter would have done the same, for there is no need to be a great connoisseur to experience that feeling of resurrection I recalled yesterday. All that is needed is to know how to look. The world one discovers belongs to another universe, with its own finality and values. The contemplation of works of art indeed liberates all the forces of the imagination that up until then have been held prisoner, chained up, oppressed. The same is true for certain discoveries, for certain "revelations," rather, that can be of a musical or poetic nature, or that occur before certain natural sites, they, too, of monumental beauty. Under such circumstances, the "change of scenery" equals the discovery of a "new world," engendered by the dialectics of the creative imagination. All of this should be developed.

AMSTERDAM

     We arrive at four o'clock in the afternoon, and we stop at the Polen Hotel, on the Rokin. It is the very model of the hotel-caravanserai. It's very hot. Behind the hotel there is a street reserved exclusively for pedestrians. It is literally covered with garbage, old newspapers, dirty papers rolled up in balls, beer and Coca-Cola bottles, empty cans, and greasy boxes. The slums in the large cities of the Orient don't offer such a revolting sight. This spreading of rubbish is most certainly intentional and deliberate, undoubtedly out of revolt against the Establishment.

We meet Liliane for the first time. Then Sorin arrives and takes us to the boat where they both live. We go have dinner together in a Turkish restaurant, and we chat until midnight.

AMSTERDAM, *20 July*

The weather is still just as beautiful. We have lunch on board the boat. I remember my first stay in Amsterdam, in September 1950, on the occasion of a congress in the history of religions. I didn't have a dime. Maurice Leenhardt invited me to a restaurant one day only to be able to put something else in my mouth besides those never-ending sandwiches which I usually ate. A good number of scholars, teachers, professors, friends I met then have today disappeared: Leenhardt, Massignon, Pettazzoni, Van der Leeuw, Pincherle . . .

I remember, too, that at the time *La Nuit bengali* was being published. Since the German translation had been rather successful, I imagined that the French version would make me as famous vis-à-vis the public and the critics, as the original Rumanian edition had done in 1933. Gone would be the poverty with which I struggled, all the more since the success I so hoped for would allow me to have other of my novels translated while awaiting the publication of the one I was then working on, *Forbidden Forest.* If it had happened thus, I would have devoted almost all my time to literature and relegated the history of religions to second place, even though *Shamanism* was at the time almost entirely drafted, and I had already begun work on the second edition, considerably revised and enlarged, of my book on yoga.

But *La Nuit bengali* was not as successful as I had expected it to be, nor was, five years later, *Forbidden Forest;* so that insofar as literature was concerned, for a long time I had to be content with writing simple stories and little "fantastic" novels such as *The Old Man and the Bureaucrats,* which I wrote, by the way, mainly for my personal pleasure, or for Christinel's or for a few Rumanian friends.

We spend the afternoon at the Van Gogh museum.

After having dined in a French restaurant, we return to the boat to listen to records. Then Sorin shows us an amateur film he shot in Bucharest, and I am greatly surprised to see my sister and mother in front of their little house. It's been thirty-two years since I've seen them *move!* I've had to be content with seeing them in photos and speaking to them on the telephone.

BRUSSELS, *22 July*

The weather is more and more beautiful.

Sorin and Liliane accompany us by car as far as Breda, and we say goodbye at four o'clock in the afternoon. At the end of the day we arrive in Brussels, where Marie-Louise and Christian Dehollain have reserved two rooms for us in a charming and delightful hotel, the Mayflower. We have dinner at the Dehollains'. From the windows of their apartment, the surrounding gardens seem to be grouped in an immense park from which emerges, strangely, the bell tower of a church.

PUERTO DE ANDRAITX, *7 August*

We arrived a week ago in this little fishing village located about thirty kilometers from Palma. Sibylle and Jacqueline had come to meet us at the airport. It's hot, but we can easily breathe. Sibylle takes us across Palma in a rented car. The city is inundated with tourists. It would seem there are more than a million of them . . . We move into two rooms on the top floor of the Villa Italia Hotel. Immense, majestic, antiquated, melancholy; we were taken with it on first sight. The architect who built it must have read D'Annunzio. White marble spiral staircases climb as far as the third balcony, which extends like an orchestra pit across the hotel's facade. The building, with its debauchery of marble and its old pink walls, is the image of Italian villas of the 1900s. One can imagine Duse's pleasure in performing *La città morta* on this immense terrace, under the pink stone balconies with the Mediterranean at her feet and, in the background, that hill looking out over the hotel upon which olive trees and umbrella pines are scattered.

I turned one of our two rooms into an office, even though the table in it hardly lends itself to any sort of work. It is a chess table that threatens to collapse at any movement of my arms.

9 August

I have seldom spent such a beautiful summer vacation. The same intensely blue sky greets us upon our awakening, and the sea breeze makes the heat easy to bear.

Our schedule is the same each day. Around ten o'clock I go with Christinel to the port, where we have found a little café that serves excellent espresso. Then we walk along a road shaded by large trees that follows walls overgrown with lush vines, to the villa where Sibylle has rented an apartment. In Majorca sand beaches are rare, and it is at the foot of rocks, equipped and provided with iron ladders, that we swim. We have lunch at the villa, and I return to the hotel to work for a few hours, if I have the will to do so. Sometimes, the sun-baked road and its clouds of dust raised by passing cars remind me of Rumania.

11 August

In the beginning of the afternoon, an impromptu visit from Stig Wikander, whom I hadn't seen for at least two years. Our conversation goes on until eleven o'clock at night. Stig talks at length about the work of the principal Swedish romantic poet, and of the influence Hermetic symbolism had on him.

13 August

Superb weather. I work energetically until five-thirty, then Sibylle comes to get us to drive us to Palma. There, a café welcomes Stig and me, and we chat in the shadows until eight o'clock. We talk about our favorite subjects: the Vikings and the Arabs, occult traditions whose influence can be detected in the literature of the seventeenth and eighteenth centuries, the latest ideas in vogue in the history of religions, etc. . . .

Sibylle and Christinel return from the airport.

They went to pick up Marie-France Ionesco, who's arrived from Dubrovnik, where she spent her vacation with her parents. Small detail: It seems that every day Eugène, whose indifference to, not to mention negligence in, clothing matters is well known, would appear dressed in the most fashionably elegant attire, wearing a jacket, a tie, and even a hat, all this just to walk along the beach . . . We go have dinner together at the El Tunel restaurant in the old city, where we afterwards stroll around until about midnight. When the time comes to say goodbye, I ironically mention to Stig that we have spoken of everything and everyone today except Raymond Lull, whose statue, however, stands right in the middle of the public square where we were this evening.

15 August

We have learned that our Villa Italia was once a casino. Through a little dormer window, grey with dust, I could indeed perceive the former gambling rooms, today transformed into storerooms and clutter. The manager of the hotel, Jaan, a young German of Baltic origin, is the very image of the Villa Italia, both mysterious and anachronistic. Tall, blond, a rather handsome fellow, he is full of good will, but terribly inefficient. Our hotel is for the most part occupied by young Germans who have come to participate in a workshop at the sailing school of the nautical club, whose buildings can be seen on the other side of the bay. Their instructor is another German, stocky, nervous, with a beard like a Viking. Courses in theory take place each afternoon on the terrace right under the windows of the room where I try to work. Once, late at night, I saw him throw beer bottles, empty ones, of course, but also full ones, at full force against the edge of the patio, where they broke with a lot of noise. "It is a tradition," Jaan told me the next morning. "For centuries all the old salts have done the same thing. I can't do anything about it . . ."

21 August

In the last few days, we went by car to Valldemosa, where we of course visited the house where George Sand and Chopin lived, its melancholy garden still carefully maintained, and the rooms where Chopin suffered so much from the cold.

On the way back, while we were driving on the little winding road that cut into the mountains, Sibylle, probably blinded by the rays of the setting sun, ran off the road into a ditch, but succeeded in stopping the car almost at the edge of a cliff. The accident could have proven fatal. In any event, the motor was seriously damaged. Drivers stopped and asked if they could help us. We asked one of them to call Rousseau, the owner of the villa, to ask him to tell the garage owner from whom Sibylle had rented the car.

We waited until nightfall, but no one came (we learned the next day that Rousseau wasn't home and could not be reached). We then decided to start walking towards the sea, and while admiring the moonlight we forced ourselves to appear in a good mood in order to keep Sibylle from having a "road-hog complex." At eleven o'clock we finally arrived in a tiny, unknown village where, to our great surprise, we were lucky enough to find a taxi whose driver agreed to take us to Puerto. The trip was made at a speed that made our hair stand on end. No one protested: We had dragged the driver out of bed . . .

29 August

My mother is no longer alive. I learned of her death from a telegram I received on 18 August. Sorin then wrote me from Bucharest that when he had arrived at her bedside, she was already dead.

Despite her ninety years, she was still in good health, except in these last months, and still had all her energy. But she could see almost nothing, and was thus no longer able to read. She died quietly, without suffering, just like my father.

I remember our first phone conversation from Paris in the autumn of 1967. In this same year the Rumanian authorities had "reconsidered" me, and my name could henceforth be cited in the press. I had not heard her voice since 1942. She seemed less emotional than I, and told me that it was better I didn't return to Rumania right away, that she could be patient and would wait for me. Never since then, neither in her letters nor by telephone, did she ask me to come see her, not once. One can guess why when one knows that because of me for twenty-five years she and my sister Corina lived in constant terror of the political police. Indeed, I was living in Paris, beyond reach; I could write books and be published. Later, I was appointed professor at the University of Chicago, me, the obscurantist, the retrograde, who had been the assistant to Nae Ionescu and, in addition, a journalist with *Cuvântul*,[1] in short, the very model of the "enemy of the working people."

I think that my mother never forgot that long period of anguish that was marked for my whole family by continual questioning and harassment by the police. My mother could never forget that, even when that situation had ceased, at least in appearance. She fully expected that she would die without seeing me again, but she consoled herself by knowing that I would not give in to the official solicitations of which I began to be the object.

PARIS, *6 September*

We returned from the Balearic Islands on 1 September. The Palma airport was jammed with people. Although the planes took off at intervals of a few minutes for all the big European cities, the mass of departing tourists always seemed just as dense. I counted as many as six summer-camp groups in the airport lobby! It must have been a bit like this in train stations in many European cities during the "decisive days" of the war, as Churchill called them.

In the evening, we go with Sibylle and Jacqueline to have dinner at Giza and Dinu's. While returning from Parly II the deluge that accompanied us all the way home reminded me of the beginning of a monsoon in Bengal. There lacked only that immense electrical unleashing, those flames of blue lightning that endlessly streaked the sky.

12 September

I spent four hours the day before yesterday in the company of R.S., a young Italian scholar who has just received his doctorate with

1. *Cuvântul* (*The Word*). Bucharest daily where Mircea Eliade made his debut as a journalist.—C.G.

a thesis on my works. He speaks Rumanian astonishingly well after only a two-year stay in the country. We met again today and spent a large part of the afternoon discussing his thesis. I admit from the start that I am usually rather reticent at the idea of having to read this type of text, no matter what the author's position regarding me might be, whether he agrees or disagrees with me. But it is their very subject, whether it concerns my literary or academic works, that I find less and less interesting, not that I don't attach any significance to what I've written (at least in part), but much rather because the subject is only too familiar to me. When I manage to make myself well understood, I have nothing else to add. In the opposite case, what more could I say?

13 September

People come to visit all afternoon. I try to note down the names of my guests as they arrive. Last night we found a tramp asleep on the doormat in front of the door to our apartment. It's the little old man whom we often notice on a bench at place Charles-Dullin, next to his bottle of red wine and some scraps of bread. He doesn't beg, but gladly accepts the money Christinel gives him to buy some Gauloises.

He was shocked by our surprise: "But Madame, I'm watching your apartment!" He took the staircase to go down, and it was then that I saw he limped.

14 September

I see Cloclo again for the first time in thirty-two years. And to think that I had known her in elementary school . . .

Late in the evening we phone my sister in Bucharest. I can't get used to the idea that I will never again hear my mother's voice.

16 September

Dinner with Ioan Culianu in a Chinese restaurant. We then chat until midnight in my office.

I've known for a very long time that Dumézil is quite right in affirming that the same is true of the history of religions as of all other disciplines: What is essential is to have that vital enthusiasm.

20 September

A Dutch film maker planned to make a film on the sexual life of Christ. The French authorities prohibited him from making it in France. Some newspapers used this prohibition as a pretext to maintain that there is no more freedom in France, etc. . . . Obviously such a ban has no other effect than to make the object of it famous.

This artist is very lucky. I must learn his name and find out what exactly he expected to do. When I find out I will be quite popular in Chicago, New York, and Santa Barbara, among all those young people who ask me what they must do "to succeed in Paris . . ."

PARIS, *September.*

X., who has read *Fragments d'un Journal* with much interest, asks me why I didn't include material that might relate to the elaboration of my works, or why I only made brief allusions to such material. He undoubtedly imagines that I keep in my possession entire pages where I've noted down massive observations and otherwise more precise remarks on the problems I come across, the difficulties I must resolve, the authors I agree or disagree with, etc. . . . I had told him that in the course of the last four months I had reread several times Deuteronomy, Psalms, and the Prophets, all in the three annotated translations that I usually use. And right after having finished a book (Psalms, for example), I read or consulted certain of the principal critical works that referred to it, as well as the most recent monographs and articles on the subject. X. wanted to know to what extent I noted in my journal all these diverse readings and reflections. Knowing that I was currently drafting chapter 14 of *A History of Religious Ideas,* entitled "The Religion of Israel in the Period of the Kings and the Prophets," he would have liked me to show him my working methods.

His curiosity was only partly legitimate. Of course, it would have been better if I told how, etc. . . . All the same, it has been close to fifty years that I've been working in the history of religions. My reading notes, at least what remains of them, are assembled in innumerable notebooks and files. Some of them, where I wrote summaries and personal reflections, were written more than thirty years ago. Others, on the contrary, are very recent. What more could I say about the way in which I prepared chapter 14? If I tried to do so, such an entry in this "laboratory journal" would take up two or three times as much space as the chapter itself, whichever one it might be. For what and to whom would that be of any use? With very rare exceptions, I am content to note in my datebook the subject and the number of pages written each day, in order to remember later my periods of greatest activity, interrupted by more or less long periods of "sterility" due to courses, travel, illness, or quite simply weariness.

30 September

We have dinner with Madeleine and Georges Dumézil in a restaurant near their home. Dumézil tells me that he has collected recordings of dozens of diverse tales, legends, fables, proverbs, and stories in Tchetchentsish, Ubykh, and other Caucasian languages. He has not yet been able to transcribe them, and there is enough material to fill several thousands of pages. It won't be until he thinks he no longer has much left to say about Indo-European religions and mythologies— assuming that that will happen one day—that he will devote himself to transcribing, translating, and commenting on all that immense Caucasian folkloric material. Dumézil knows a good thirty languages and dialects, but since his youth he has always preferred the Caucasian languages.

3 October

Last night Christinel dreamt that she was all alone in an immense, brilliantly lit ballroom. An invisible band plays a dance tune in which Christinel recognizes, more and more distinctly, a famous waltz. She then begins to dance, alone at first, then she is almost immediately joined by a handsome young man, elegantly dressed, who wraps his arms around her and waltzes with her. Suddenly the band stops, and Christinel asks her partner: "But who are you? I don't know you!" The latter bows respectfully before her and tells her with a smile:

"I am your tramp, Madame." "But how is it that only yesterday you could hardly walk, whereas today you dance so well?" "But it is for you, Madame!" replies the young man, bowing once again.

It's been several weeks since our tramp disappeared. I asked one of his companions today what had become of him. He replied that he had to be taken to the hospital some time ago.

CHICAGO, *8 October*

We returned this afternoon, in precocious autumn weather. Faced with the number of letters and packages of books that have arrived in our absence, as many at home as at my office in Meadville, I already feel exhausted.

16 October

Yesterday I began my course on mythical thought. To my great surprise the room was jammed, and I even noticed in the hall about thirty students who were unable to get in. We had to change rooms, going first to the second floor, then to the ground floor.

During the afternoon, seminar. I recognized some of my favorite students in the group, and that was enough to calm me down. Our discussions promise to be as fascinating as they were two years ago.

October

In a letter to Saint-Martin (*The Unknown Philosophers*) of 25 October 1794, Kirchberger gives a detailed account of the mystical marriage that united Johann-Georg Gichtel and Sophia. He had, by the way, obtained his information from Ueberfeld's preface to the *Works* of Gichtel. The passage we're going to read seems very significant to me: "Sophia, his dear, his divine Sophia whom he loved so much and whom he had never seen, came on Christmas Day 1673 to pay him a first visit. He says in this connection that he saw and heard in the third principle that Virgin who was of an amazing and celestial beauty. She accepted him as her husband upon this first meeting, and the marriage was consummated in inexpressible delights. She distinctly promised him conjugal fidelity: never to abandon him, neither in adversity nor in poverty, neither in sickness nor in death; and that she would always live with him in the interior luminous depths; she assured him she would compensate him amply for all he had sacrificed for her in giving up alliances with rich women who had pursued him. She gave him hope for a spiritual progeny, and as a dowry she brought faith, hope, and essential and substantial charity in her heart. The wedding lasted until the beginning of 1674. He then found more comfortable lodging in a spacious house in Amsterdam whose rent was quite expensive. However, he didn't possess a sou, and he didn't work at all to acquire money and asked nothing of anyone either for himself or for others, and yet he extended hospitality to many friends who came from far away to see him." (Cf. the text of the letter in Antoine Faivre, *Kirchberger et l'Illuminisme du XVIIIe siècle*, 1966, pp. 174–175.)

The theme of the marriage of the soul with the divinity—or with the hypostasis that takes its place—is encountered rather often in the history of the mystical. All the same, Gichtel's marriage shows certain particularities that are unique to it, among other things, the promise Sophia makes to have a "spiritual progeny" and to compensate him materially for all that he had to sacrifice "in giving up alliances with rich women who had pursued him." For Kirchberger, this explains the spacious house in Amsterdam and Gichtel's large fortune.

These same specific elements are found in a curious fashion in the shamanist practices of Siberia and in those of the aborigines of India. I will only give a few examples of them here (cf. *Shamanism*, 1964, pp. 72 *et seq.* and 421 *et seq.*).

Thus a *goldi* shaman tells that when he was young and while he was ill, a very beautiful woman appeared to him, no larger than a little girl, who told him that she was the tutelary spirit (*ayami*) of his shaman ancestors. She added that she loved him and wanted to be his wife. She would make him a shaman and would teach him to cure the sick. "Food will come to us," she said, "from the people." The young man agreed to marry her. He was cured and became a shaman: "She has been coming to me ever since, and I sleep with her as with my own wife, but we have no children."

But what is told of shamanism among the Savara (Saora), an aboriginal Orissan tribe, is even more significant. A feminine tutelary spirit comes to a young man while he is asleep to ask him to marry her. If he refuses, his spirit leaves him, and he dies. A Savara shaman declares that his wife-spirit gave him a boy and two girls. Five years later he married a woman from his village with whom he had three children. The day of the wedding the wife-spirit spoke, through the shaman, to the new bride: "Now you are going to live with my husband. You will fetch his water, husk his rice, cook his food: You will do everything, I can do nothing. All I can do is to help when trouble comes . . ."

Just like Sophia did for Gichtel, the wife-spirit causes a true metamorphosis in her husband. The shaman differs essentially from the other members of his community: He is at the same time a healer, a protector, a visionary poet, and above all the "sage" of his tribe.

25–26 October

Having caught cold, I don't go out of the house. I have to force myself to get to the end of Yeats's fantastico-occultist prose, so unbearable do I find the banality of his esoteric "message." I feel the same about him as I do about Gustav Meyrinck, whom I always enjoy reading—and even rereading—for the pleasure of his talents as a narrator, but not for the allegedly "esoteric" content of his writings.

9 November

The last of these three days of "dialogues with theologians." The day before yesterday, lunch at the Jesuit House in the company of B. Lonergan and Karl Rahner. Yesterday, at Mandel Hall, I was responsible for introducing Cardinal Franz König to the audience, which was easy to do, the cardinal also being a historian of religions and, in addition, the editor of the admirable *Wörterbuch d. Religiongeschichte*. In the evening, a dinner hosted by our faculty in honor of Cardinal König, Rahner, Lonergan, and other theologians. Finally this evening, reception at Edward Levi's in honor of the cardinal. Present were theologians of all the Christian denominations as well as Rabbi Bronstein, my former student, and his wife. It is he who gave the blessing at the beginning of the meal.

SANTA BARBARA, *13 November*
        When our plane took off from Chicago, the city was blanketed in fog. We left behind us a glacial drizzle mixed with flakes of snow made grey and dirty by the ambient pollution. In Santa Barbara, where we arrive at the end of the afternoon, Capps, Bradford, and Michaelson meet us at the airport, and the former two drive us to Montecito, to the Casa de Maria, the sumptuous and melancholy residence which I knew from the exterior, for I had often passed in front of it while I was staying at the San Ysidro Inn. Of all the participants in our symposium, only Mary Stevenson has already arrived. We leave our luggage in room 27, or rather in the little suite we've been assigned, and go as a group to chat in the bar of the San Ysidro.
        It is there that I learn of the death of Thomas O'Dea, which occurred that very morning. Too many memories tie me to him for me to speak of him here. After a phone call from Capps, Raimondo Pannikar comes to join us around nine-thirty, to my very great delight. I had seen him again in Chicago last October for the first time in eighteen years.

SANTA BARBARA, *14 November*
        I am awakened both by the chirping of an unknown bird and by the noise of a jackhammer, which reminds me of the time we stayed at the San Ysidro Inn. After drinking the coffee Sister Bernadette prepares for us, we go to the mission to attend the service in honor of Tom O'Dea. It is R. Pannikar who officiates. Michaelson, with much emotion and conviction, sketches the portrait of the deceased.
        At three-thirty the "Colloquium on Mircea Eliade" begins. In the meantime Zwi Werblowski and certain other friends from the center came to join us. The attendance is rather dense and composed for the most part of professors and "scholars." Mac L. Ricketts opens the

session with a long, very evocative study: "The Image of Death in the Work of Mircea Eliade." Then, short allocutions by C. Larson from the University of Santa Barbara, and by Francis P. Sullivan, S.J., from Loyola University in New Orleans, who states that it was while reading *The Sacred and the Profane* that he was finally able to become himself, that is, a poet! In the evening Dennis Doeing reads a paper called "Mircea Eliade's Spiritual Itinerary from 1926–1928," and he cites numerous passages from my articles of the *Itineraire spirituel* series, which appeared at the time in *Cuvântul*.

Then Th. Jacobson, Pannikar, and Zwi Werblowski come in turn to make their contributions and to share their remembrances. Werblowski proves very warm, without, however, losing his causticity. All the while discussing my "proverbial modesty," he declares that in the realm of the history of religions, we are living in an "Eliade era." At the end of the colloquium I find myself in the company of Kees Bolle, David Rasmunsen, and a few others. But I am too tired to continue.

15 November

I didn't fall asleep until six in the morning! In addition, my arthritis is torturing my wrist. I get up, however, and attend the first paper presentation at nine o'clock. In the afternoon others are given until five o'clock, some of which are excellent. Dinner at five-thirty, then at eight o'clock in the University's big Lehmann Hall auditorium, full to bursting, I read my lecture, "The Vogue of Occultism," and I am frankly a success. Capps points out to me that no one since Paul Tillich has had such an audience. The lecture is followed by a reception that keeps us until eleven-thirty. I speak, I listen, I answer questions, I am exhausted.

Back at the Casa de Maria, I quickly jot down a few notes for my lecture the next day.

SANTA BARBARA, *16 November*

I was finally able to sleep five or six hours straight, much too little to suit me. The fog that blankets the city when we awaken will only let up at the end of the morning.

Today's session opens with critical papers relating to my methodology. J. Waardenbord from Utrecht, Jonathan Smith, and Jacob Needleman from the University of San Francisco speak. At eleven o'clock I, too, speak, to talk about the reflections my books inspire in me. This is the subject of the lecture that I should have given last night at the university, if I had kept to what had been announced. But considering that it wasn't advisable, in front of an audience of five or six hundred people, to broach the subjects that had been dealt with in the course of the colloquium, I abstained from doing so. Useless to summarize these self-reflections on my work. In this lecture, or rather this fifty-minute chat, I outlined my own spiritual itinerary. It is in my belonging to a minor culture that one must seek the reasons for my aversion to all "cultural provincialism." I also brought up the essential element in my development that was formed by my discovery, *not* of the Italian Renaissance, but of the *example* of the "integral humanism" of a Pico della Mirandola. I tell of all that I owed in my training to my Indian experience, the benefit that I had derived from it and how it had helped me later to discover what was concealed in Rumanian folklore. Finally, I stressed a point that was dear to me and which I insisted that all my colleagues and students be made aware of, that is, that in a teacher what he does is infinitely more important than the way in which he does it. Thus, in my case, I consider myself to be among the disciples of Pettazzoni, although I have refused to adopt his methods. But his *example,* insofar as Pettazzoni has attempted to construct a truly *universal* history of religions, has never ceased to inspire me.

I expect to explain myself more clearly on this in the text that will accompany the collection of papers from the colloquium. Capps's remarks on the "Myth of Mircea Eliade" amused me a lot, and I found them interesting, as well.

LOS ANGELES, *17 November*

We left Santa Barbara yesterday afternoon by car. We spend the evening in the company of Dr. Nicolas Costea and his wife. I noticed a little hare that was going through the garden.

CHICAGO, *19 November*

This evening we receive a visit from Ioan Cusa, passing through (Chicago) to attend the Congress of Graphic Arts. The sight of our campus has positively enraptured him, and I quickly understand why: The taxi that brought him went down the Midway, lit at that hour by the golden and orange light of the new streetlamps. "One would think it a forest of copper . . ." he exclaimed.

28 November

Thanksgiving Day. We invited Joe and Evelyn Kitagawa, Mateï Calinescu, Reszeley, etc., to dinner. Animated conversation, as usual. There would be too much to note . . .

1 December

The cold is brisk, and it has begun to snow. I spend the whole day, or almost, working on chapter 17 of *A History*.

2 December

Dinner at Nathan Scott's. Mrs. R. Niebuhr thanks me again for the "great favor" I had done for her a few years ago in sending her, at her request, a dozen or so reprints of my article "History of Religions in Retrospect: 1912–1962."

I understand the reasons for such gratitude: The article, which was purely didactic, includes a very useful critical bibliography. But listening to her talk about this article, and of it *alone,* I suddenly remember that comedy my friend N.D. wanted to write fifty years ago: During one of his voyages, Balzac is approached by an Italian nobleman who, having recognized him, can't stop telling him all the good things he thinks of the articles the famous novelist had written in the collected work, *Les Français peints par eux-mêmes*. He goes on like this for a half hour. This is how the comedy began, but I will never know the end of it, as N.D., having succeeded in getting into the fifth year of medical school, abandoned the theatre.

December

I receive a visit from R., whom I had had as a student six or seven years ago. She is now married, even has a child, and no longer wears glasses. She still remembers her success with her fellow students the day she read her seminar paper on Greek sources in the history of the Celts. In fact, and at my suggestion, she had studied in depth only one work, but the most important one on the subject, *The Celtic Ethnography of Posidonius* by J. J. Tierney. She tells me that when she is with friends, and especially when she invites them over, she sometimes cites certain passages of Posidonius, for example, the one in which he recognizes that in the beginning he had been very impressed by the sight of heads attached to the entrances of the dwellings of Celtic chieftains, but that he had finally gotten used to it, and could later contemplate them without apprehension. Or yet the description of the Celts by Euphorus around 350 B.C., which she found in Strabo: "They are young, plump, well disposed towards the Greeks, and refuse to abandon their homes, even when water has taken them over."

"You can't imagine the success I have among my friends!" she adds. "There are those who ask me to repeat the quotes and write them in their notebook. But it is very different when I talk to them about the Druids. The subject is much too serious, especially when we start talking about metempsychosis. And my husband hates conversations that are too serious. They threaten to go on until well past midnight . . ."

12 December

What a magnificent day! Despite the cold air and the snow on the edge of the sidewalks, the sky is as clear and blue as in the middle of summer.

But what a wind! It blew into my back while I was heading toward Swift Hall. While keeping my head bent, I tried to quicken my step, and the person who was following me must have done the same, judging by the sound of his steps, which I heard coming closer to me. It was a curious sound. It sounded as if the person were trying to catch up to me by skating on the ground. When I thought he had reached me, I turned my head. What I had taken for a man was in fact a little branch with yellowed leaves, miraculously preserved, which the wind had pushed along for some fifteen meters, at the same speed as my own steps.

29 December

We had promised Sibylle to go to Paris to celebrate our twenty-fifth wedding anniversary. I prepare certain files, all the while being almost certain that I will never find the time to work on them.

NEW YORK, 30 December

Arrival at midnight.

NEW YORK, 31 December

We spend New Year's Eve at Lisette's, with Peggy and Burton Feldman, G. Duca, and Sanda.

PARIS, 3 January 1975

We left New York yesterday evening. The flight was very disturbing. For two hours our plane didn't stop pitching and rolling. Shaken like leaves in the winter wind, we sometimes had the impression that the flight was going to turn out badly.

Arrival at eight-thirty in the morning. Sibylle was waiting for us at the airport. Liliane is already at our place, but Sorin is still in Bucharest, awaiting a problematic exit visa.

5 January

Sleepiness. I feel I could sleep all day long, even if it means not closing my eyes all night long. Fortunately I can read: I've brought all my files on Egypt, and in addition, I have on hand the inexhaustible Balzac.

6 January

From three to nine o'clock in the morning, impossible to fall asleep. The sky is grey and the day is depressing.

"I'm going to tell you a big secret, my dear. Don't wait for Judgment Day; it happens daily" (*La Chute,* p. 129). I'd give a lot to know whether Camus understood all that these two lines represent from a *theological* point of view, and more precisely insofar as mystical theology is concerned. I think that he was not aware of it. Camus was above all a moralist, profoundly affected by the terror and the demons of his time. But from a certain theological point of view, the crises and the hopes that characterize man's condition develop above and beyond time and temporality.

7 January

Long bout of insomnia. I take advantage of it to reread the texts of Tell-el-Amarna, and as always, that of the prayer discovered in the sarcophagus of Akhenaton profoundly moves me. Nothing can compare to the religious fervor of this strange pharaoh, nor to the love and the veneration he nourished for Aton, the sun god: "I will breathe in the sweet breath from your mouth. Every day I will contemplate your beauty . . . Give me your hands, charged with your spirit, so that I receive you and live by your spirit. Call my name throughout all eternity; it will never fail to answer your call!"

8 January

I like to remember those nights in Capri, noisy with the song of the crickets, when I tried to work on *Forbidden Forest.* And also that summer night when we got lost in our own neighborhood. We wandered around for more than an hour before finding our Hôtel de Suède . . .

Twenty-five years have gone by, and I still regret not having dared to wake Christinel during that night when, in the train to Rome, having stopped in a wood not far from the border, nightingales started to sing in chorus.

We were very poor then. In 1950 Delia and René LaForgue had lent us their very beautiful apartment on the rue de la Tour, only on the condition that we keep Anna, the housekeeper. How many times did we leave her money for her lunch, only to go ourselves to eat a sandwich in the Luxembourg Gardens, pretending that we had been invited to some friends' home . . .

I have only once forgotten the traditional bouquet of nine flowers. We were at Pennsylvania State University, and I had mistaken the date, thinking it was 8 May. I had agreed to the appointment that two of my colleagues had made, and consequently Christinel went alone to walk in the magnificent park that surrounded the university. She wasn't there more than a quarter of an hour when a storm broke in full force. The tempest had, however, been forecast, but at the hotel no one had warned her. The wind was such that she quickly found herself without an umbrella. She had the sensation not of advancing by her own volition, but rather of being carried along by the tempest. She succeeded in reaching the hotel, but slipped and sprained her ankle.

The explanation for such an accident would be very clear, and my responsibility for it would appear to be quite obvious, if it were considered in the light of Chinese thought.

10 January

Yesterday we celebrated our twenty-fifth wedding anniversary at the Rumanian restaurant La Flûte de Pan, on Ile Saint-Louis. Sibylle and Siegfried had ordered the menu and decorated the room. All our Rumanian and French friends were there, and some of them had even attended our wedding; among others, Madeleine and Georges Dumézil, Stig Wikander, Cioran, and Jacqueline.

Then the *lautari* came for the event. Of course, they played a *hora*[1] for us, and everyone joined in the dance, including Paul Ricoeur, to Simone's great surprise: It was the first time she had ever seen him dance . . .

11 January

Liliane left to go back to Amsterdam. In the evening I phone Corina in Rumania and promise to do the impossible so that we will be

1. *Lautar* (from the Latin *laudator*): Musician specializing in the melodies of Rumanian folklore. *Hora:* Rumanian folk dance.—C.G.

able to see each other this summer. But will she be able to obtain her exit visa?

I immerse myself once again in my Egyptian texts. This time I add brief commentaries. But the most difficult task awaits me in Chicago, when I will have to take up all that I've written in the last few years, cut, prune the text, put it together . . . In the outline I set out for myself for *A History,* volume 1, the manuscript of the chapter on Egyptian religions must be at the very most around sixty typewritten pages.

13 January

In an article by Zwi Werblowski, I learn of a letter from Saint Bernard de Clairvaux (*Patrologia Latina* 182, cols. 169–70). In 1129, an English monk from the diocese of Lincoln, by the name of Philippe, left on a pilgrimage to the Holy Land. En route towards Jerusalem, he stopped in Clairvaux. Some time later the bishop of Lincoln received a letter from Bernard, the abbot of Clairvaux, letting him know that Philippe had arrived at his destination and that he had decided to live there for the rest of his days: "He reached the Holy City, and he has chosen to share the fate [of the elect]. . . . He is no longer a curious spectator, but is a pious inhabitant and rightful citizen of Jerusalem." And Bernard adds: "Clairvaux is this Jerusalem. Our monastery is the (earthly) Jerusalem that the ties of profound faith, the aspiration to perfection, and spiritual kinship unite to [celestial Jerusalem]."

CHICAGO, *16 January*

Routine flight to Boston. To our great disappointment we learn that the plane to Chicago won't leave for three hours. We finally reach our destination, but at night, and exhausted.

19 January

Since our return I've spent my time unwrapping packages of books and reading my mail (once again I am aware of the enormous loss of time caused by traveling, for each time I take a trip it takes me longer and longer before picking up the rhythm of my routine). I read a few books haphazardly, most without interest.

Fortunately, I've finally finished correcting the new edition of *Techniques du Yoga*.

20 January

First lecture in a series on the beginnings of high religions. The room is packed. I believe I notice quite a few freshmen, students who are taking my courses for the first time. To my great regret, when I came to speak about prehistoric religions, I didn't have time to comment in as great length as I had done the preceding year on that annoyed reflection by Teilhard de Chardin, according to whom God still appears to us "as a Neolithic proprietor." This remark, if one judges it in the light of the history of religions, is doubly erroneous. First of all, the image of this "Neolithic proprietor" is relatively recent, going back only twelve or fifteen thousand years. It was preceded by other images, even more archaic: That of God "master of the sky," or those divinities of prehistoric hunters, the "lords of the beasts." Even more serious: For humanity, it is not with such images that the history of religions began, but with the experience of the sacred, with the multiple hierophanies that structure the world and infuse it with meanings. In the end, it is religious symbolism that created man—that is, that differentiated him from the other primates. To realize this, it suffices to compare the behavior of primates in their "familiar space" with the *orientatio*, that rite that establishes the world of men.

22 January

Second lecture on the beginnings of high religions. Q. is surprised to see me persevere in my work, insofar as to him it implies what is most fastidious—scholarship and rigorous research—even though I am perfectly aware of the existence of thermonuclear bombs and other just as threatening dangers. I am obviously aware that *everything* can disappear from one day to the next. But whatever ontology he may adhere to rationally, every man also knows another ontology, born of his own experience, and which is of epiphanic structure. The beauty and perfume of a rose, despite their ephemeral character, exist nonetheless, and this type of existence, "epiphanic and effulgent," can sometimes change the world (many examples of this are known, on which I will not dwell).

In the last analysis, whatever fate the future may hold for our world, or even for our Western civilization alone, and whether or not I succeed in completing my *History of Religious Ideas,* insofar as my research succeeds in revealing long-forgotten ideas, beliefs, and meanings, and in revealing them *just like the rose reveals itself to me,* my work will henceforth find its justification in that.

25 January

Final revision of the manuscript of *Occultism, Witchcraft, and Cultural Fashions* for the University of Chicago Press. I draft a short three-page preface.

Evening spent at Jonathan Smith's, with all my friends and colleagues to celebrate our twenty-five years of marriage. Jerry Brauer proposes a toast to us that is very well phrased and quite humorous. I should have stood up, answered him, thanked him, but a sudden surge of timidity held me glued to my chair . . .

29 January

Today, after my last lecture on the *Bhagavad-Gita,* I decided to throw my notebooks and files on India and Iran into the fire. I have several dozen, some of which date from 1948 or 1950, from the time of the Hôtel de Suède and my Paris years. I must at all costs rid myself of this baggage, which has become useless ever since the respective chapters of the *magnum opus* were drafted.

I can't do it without melancholy. While reading certain notecards which I pick up at random, I remember the notebooks and files kept in India which I had to leave behind me in Rumania. I *know* I had written down ideas, projects, and reflections in them that I planned to develop later. But what's the use of losing oneself in useless regrets!

I do, however, keep the files containing certain course outlines, in case I'll need them next winter.

5 February

The day before yesterday I turned my manuscript over to the university press. Today I begin my seminar on Indo-European religions. I've only admitted a very few students into it, chosen from among the most qualified.

10 February

Ioan Culianu has been with us for the last few days, but he was unable to arrive in time to attend even the final lectures of *The Beginnings of High Religions* series. We have dinner with him this evening at the Quadrangle Club.

14 February

When I maintain a constant and friendly relationship with a Christian priest, whatever his denomination, it often happens that he asks me to call him by his first name as early as our third or fourth encounter. In general these priests find it preferable that I stop calling them *Père, Father, Padre,* or *Parinte.* I give in to their wishes quite unwillingly; I already find it rather troublesome not to be able to act otherwise towards my colleagues on the faculty. It's very difficult for me to explain to them that what I appreciate *in the first place* in them is precisely their religious involvement, and their having known how to follow their vocation. The very fact that they are priests is, moreover, what is most interesting and most remarkable about the majority of them.

16 February

Marghescu and Culianu are with us this evening. Christinel promised them a meal "à la Rumanian." We chat until midnight. Culianu would ask for nothing more than to sit in on my courses, but for the moment I only have the seminar on the Indo-Europeans, itself limited to a dozen students, only two or three of whom show signs of any real ability.

20 February

According to Teilhard, "it is enough for truth to appear only once, in one spirit, so that nothing can ever again keep it from invading and igniting everything."

This "chemical" vision of truth seems rather questionable to me.

28 February

Due to work being done in our apartment, we had to spend four days at the Quadrangle Club, where I continued to revise the chapters on Canaan and Israel.

Last night at the Quadrangle Club I tried in vain to read Tolkien's *The Lord of the Rings*. I don't understand at all how this book has been so successful—several million copies of it have been sold in paperback: Its "fantastic" universe is only a pile of medieval legends that have been laboriously disguised.

Tomorrow we will move back home, despite the smell of fresh paint.

5 March

We're horribly worried to learn that Sibylle has just been operated on for breast cancer.

10 March

The weather is cold and snowy. Yesterday evening we invited around fifteen friends to the Quadrangle Club, and the evening ended at our house. Juliana, Marghescu, and Ioan Culianu were among the youngest.

14 March

Cioran would be very interested to learn that in the Greek Massilia, the place where Marseille would later arise, those wishing to commit suicide first had to ask permission of the senate, and to explain the reasons that induced them to resort to such an act. If those reasons were deemed valid, the candidate was given free of charge the necessary quantity of hemlock.

24 March

I've lost three days in drafting an essay, using my earlier writings, on the structure and function of myth. It will serve as the introduction to a book that McGraw will publish in a high-quality edition.

29 March

Evening spent at Commandant Bumbacescu's, with Ioan Culianu and Marghescu. Also invited were a professor from a university in Transylvania and his wife and son. "What is left for Rumanians to hope for?" I asked him. He didn't reply directly, and was content to point to his son, a little boy of eight or nine. "I only hope," he finally said, "that when he is our age, it will be possible for him to answer that . . ."

4 April

It's been snowing for four days as if it were the middle of winter.

I've revised and polished chapters 1 and 4. I've managed to condense the texts already written and to reduce by a good third the chapter dealing with Egyptian religions.

9 April

An attack of arthritis kept me awake all night. It has nothing to do with the snow and the cold, I told myself, but much rather with the fact that I pushed the "reduction" of the text too far: In doing this I destroyed with my own hands dozens of pages which had taken, however, so much effort over these last few years . . .

10 April

I cannot go beyond the completed past but by destroying massive amounts of material—files, notecards, diverse reflections—

without attempting to make even a meager selection. I must preserve only letters, and a few files relating to certain courses which have now become "classics," and which I will most certainly have to give again in the course of the school year: *From Rig-Veda to Bhagavad-Gita* and *The Beginnings of High Religions,* for example.

11 April

Culianu helps me put some order in my bookshelves. I am forced to admit that certain books, which I believed were buried under files or hidden behind other books in the back of a shelf, are truly gone. Their loss would have once affected me much more than it does today. They are, however, important books which have not been reprinted. But I've learned to separate myself from my books, even from those which I am most attached to. I've already made a gift of many of them to the Meadville library, and of several others to Bruce Lincoln.

But a problem remains: What will I do with the files and all the material relating to the chapters already written for *A History?* Those dealing with India and Iran were already burned, little by little, last winter. I still have two cardboard cartons full of notes and excerpts from texts on prehistoric religions, and a good number of files on Mesopotamia, Syria, Israel, etc. . . .

21 April

I try to share with Paul Ricoeur, he being, like us all, a great admirer of Aristotle, my feelings on the *greatness* of Alexander in the most modern—that is, "Christian"—sense of the term, by referring to the lofty idea he had of the human person. For Aristotle, slaves fully deserved their condition as slaves, because they were "barbaric" by nature. In Susa, however, Alexander married two Achaemenid princesses, and the same day he united in marriage *according to the Persian rite* ninety of his most intimate companions with the daughters of dignitaries from the country, and ten thousand Macedonians with Iranian women. And when at Opis the Macedonians rebelled, reproaching him "for having made Persians his relatives," Alexander replied: "But I have made you *all* my relatives!"

30 April

They have finally decided to open the crates that belonged to Berthold Laufer which have been stacked in the basement of the Field Museum for about forty years. Zelda Hauser, one of the museum volunteers, gives me a wealth of details on Laufer and his life. His wife had a true passion for the movies, and he accompanied her each time she went to see a film, that is, almost every evening. When he had to go to the hospital for tests and learned he had cancer, he jumped out the window of the hospital without even waiting to go home, etc. . . .

I still remember those days I spent at the Imperial Library in Calcutta where I first read books by Laufer, my heated discussions about him with Van Manen at the library of the Asiatic Society, my enthusiasm for the *Sino-Iranica,* which Van Manen had lent me and which I literally devoured until late at night at Mrs. Perris's boarding house. It seemed unbelievable to me that such scholarship could be that of a man who was barely thirty years old! Compared to his, my own readings seemed only too elementary. I couldn't believe that a man could know so much, and in so many areas, and had learned it at the very sources, that is, by reading entire libraries of texts in Chinese, Tibetan, Mongolian, Japanese, etc. . . . My admiration for Laufer and for Paul Pelliot only grew when in the following years I was able to consult the collections of periodicals in the Stadtbibliothek in Berlin.

I recognize I have an immense debt to these two giants in Orientalism. It is to them that I owe not letting myself get involved in comparative research, as I had envisioned doing between 1930 and 1934. I had to realize that I didn't have that "photographic memory" with which they were endowed. What was the use of studying Tibetan, Chinese, or Japanese, when I would have had to spend ten or fifteen years of my life doing it? I therefore gave that up, and limited myself to Sanskrit, the history of religions, ethnology, and folklore. The example of Berthold Laufer taught me to remain faithful to myself, and such a lesson is never forgotten.

2 *May*

Yesterday I began chapter 5. The first part deals with megaliths. I have an enormous amount of documents, assembled over ten or fifteen years, as well as files I had put together for the preparation of my article "Megaliths and the History of Religions." Will I ever see the end of it? Assuming I delay my departure from Chicago this summer, it is not impossible.

But I must write it as quickly as possible, if only to be able to rid myself of the documentation that weighs me down: three bags of papers filled to capacity; files; photocopies of articles, not to mention the books, the books . . . For several years this need I have to burn my papers, to empty out my bookshelves, my drawers, and my library, has become a real obsession. I wonder why.

4 *May*

Last evening we had invited James Barr and his wife, Alexandra and Saul Bellow, Paul Ricoeur, and Dr. Horner to dinner.

Saul hadn't yet read Eugène Ionesco's *Un Solitaire*. I tell him that I would like to be able to retain forever only this one passage from it: "It all checks out. One does what one wants. 'They,' not I. *I* am not part of the battle." (p. 80).

10 *May*

True spring weather, for the first time this year (only two days ago the radiators were still scorching). At one o'clock Culianu is already in the living room in the midst of a fan of files that he has spread out, God knows how, all over the carpet. He has undertaken to file part of my correspondence. I'll see him again in three or four hours, and I hope we'll have time to have a chat. He has come to Chicago intending to work with me. We have already gotten together several times, but have not yet had the opportunity to talk seriously.

Yesterday I immersed myself until late at night in the book by Bazil Gruia, *Blaga inédit,*[1] which made me forget to go to sleep, as always happens to me in such cases, until the approach of dawn. Upon awakening I promised myself to write to Dorli Blaga, who had sent me two volumes of the *Poetry* last year.

I must, of course, but I must do so many things! For some time I've been leading a hectic life, especially since I've decided to divide the first volume of *A History* into two. I still have to draft chapter 5, which will be long and difficult, finish the chapter dealing with Greek gods and heroes, and write either a preface or an introduction, depending on what I decide at the last minute. Most of the chapters of the second volume are now drafted. If I had maintained a chronological order, the first volume would have not only been finished long ago, but would have been printed, as well. And yet, I have to have it all finished before the tenth or twelfth of June, before we leave for Paris.

20 May

For several days the heat has been unbearable. During dinner last night with Alexandra and Saul we spoke of Rudolph Steiner, whom Saul admires very much for the importance he accords to the "active imagination."

Today the heat is even worse than yesterday. At the end of the day the storm broke. One would have thought it was the approach of a cyclone. Despite all my efforts, it's impossible to work.

25 May

When one of my students shows excessive admiration for me, my first concern is to moderate his effusion: I am aware of what will happen later if this "admiration" is not reduced to a reasonable level. Indeed, despite myself, I risk becoming a "father figure" to him. Inevitably, when in time he will have acquired some experience from his personal work and from his own responsibilities, he will find himself

1. Lucian Blaga (1895–1961): Rumanian poet and philosopher, one of the greatest of his generation; left his mark on all Rumanian literature in the period between the two world wars.—C.G.

obliged to "kill his father," if only to be able to prove to himself that he is finally capable of flying with his own wings. I have some experience with this sort of situation, which is most often rather funny, but is sometimes difficult to put up with, and which usually occurs with particularly brilliant students. Now I am careful, and take the necessary precautions as soon as the first symptoms appear.

May 1975

Last evening Brauer invited us to the Court House Restaurant along with Hannah Tillich. I would have given a lot to avoid this encounter, if I had been able to do so.

Hannah got out of the taxi on Harold Rosenberg's arm. She has aged considerably, but has lost nothing of her drive. We greeted each other as if we had parted only the day before, whereas in fact I had not seen her for seven or eight years. But what really stood between us, like an invisible wall, were the years of paralyzing silence due to the publication of her last book. I hadn't immediately thanked her for the copy she had sent me, and after having read it, it was impossible for me to write to her. Since that time, that is, for close to two years, I no longer made any contact with her, so stricken, furious, indignant was I at the way in which she had avenged herself on Paulus, whose celebrity had apparently become unbearable to her. Tillich was rightly considered to be one of the greatest theologians of this century, the most "contemporary" of Christians, etc. . . . In her hatred and contempt for Christianity Hannah was unable to understand how Paulus could be considered a true Christian. In addition, he had been a Lutheran minister. Henceforth she persisted in revealing everything about her husband, absolutely everything, only to be able to destroy Paulus's prestige as a Christian existentialist theologian.

Useless to say any more, for I prefer to finish this entry by talking about our meeting of last evening. Hannah was returning from the Center of New Harmony where, almost ten years ago, the ashes of Paulus Tillich had been scattered. We came quite naturally to talk about this prestigious center, which unfortunately I have never seen. I took care to avoid any reference to her book, although it was impossible for any of us not to think of it, and we all expected to hear Hannah cry out at any moment: ''Well? What do you have to say about it?'' I learned that she had another book in preparation, in which she would talk about all the places where she and Paulus had stayed: New Harmony, Jerusalem, Greece, etc. . . . It is indeed her last chance to express what she still has in her heart and to finally know the glory of which she has dreamt since her youth.

5 *June*

I'm writing a short preface to the Japanese edition of a collection of papers and essays that have never yet been published—and will probably never be—in any of the European languages. This volume is part of the Japanese edition of my complete works in the history of religions and the philosophy of culture. I'm furnishing this precision, which isn't lacking in irony, for my future bibliographers. Another precision, which also isn't lacking in irony, but which is rather bitter this time: In the bibliography of translations of my books and diverse studies there is not one Rumanian edition . . .

9 *June*

Arrival of Burton Feldman, to whom we are abandoning our apartment for the summer. Burton has come to stay here because of the famous Regenstein Library and the resources it provides. He hopes to soon complete the book, or rather, one of the books, that he has had in the works for several years now, and I hope with all my heart that he does so. He's one of the most competent American scholars I know, a true living encyclopedia! The few studies he's published are admirably written, and above all particularly original. But Burton is stricken, he too, with ''perfectionitis,'' an affliction for which a remedy has not yet been found.

NEW YORK, *11 June*

Yesterday, upon arriving on a splendid summer day, I went to spend a few hours at the Metropolitan Museum. This time I limited myself to the rooms devoted to the ancient Orient, Etruria, and Greece. What joy to rediscover my favorite works, the memory of which had almost faded from my mind. Yet I've known them for years.

While going down the stairs I pass a group of young people, Italians and Japanese, who are trying to communicate in a more than approximate English. I retrace my steps and follow them for a few minutes. They're talking about Marco Polo and Giuseppe Tucci.

PARIS, *13 June*

Arrival at ten o'clock in the evening. Sibylle was waiting for us at the airport. What joy to see by the way she looks that the operation she underwent three months ago has not affected her too greatly. She drives us to place Charles-Dullin, and we stay up chatting until late into the night.

The next day I regretfully awaken very late. The weather is superb. I try with great difficulty to apply myself to the definitive revision of my manuscript. I give it up after an hour.

15 June

I haven't yet noted anything on the reception of *Fragments d'un journal I* among American critics and literary historians. Among the letters I've received, certain ones deserve to be pointed out. In one a professor of comparative literature assures me that thanks to the *Journal* he was finally able to ''see the man hidden behind the author of so many scholarly works'' and to recognize in him ''a writer and an artist.'' Another of my readers claims that my *Journal* ''has convinced him of the existential value of the hermeneutics of religious symbolism . . .''

17 June

I complete the revision of the first three chapters.

There is a problem I did not tackle in *A History:* To the occultation of the sacred (the Grail, for example) sometimes corresponds the occultation of salvation techniques which become ''secret.'' But in certain periods, such as the one in which we are living, it is the opposite that takes place. What was "secret" is deciphered and published in tens of thousands of copies, whereas the "sacred," initiatory content remains inaccessible.

20 June

Eugène and Rodica have invited us to dinner at the restaurant on the top floor of the Tour Montparnasse, the fifty-ninth, I believe. This in order not to forget Chicago, Marie-France specifies . . . Then we go to their house with Cioran. Eugène seems to be more and more interested in certain mystical writings. I would have thought that Cioran would have proven just as interested, if only out of loyalty for certain things he read in his youth, the things, among others, relating to those male and female saints he knew so well. But, as he recently admitted to me, simply reading newspapers and weeklies is enough to maintain his "perspective of Greek tragedy and the Apocalypse." Truly, the only problem of the present, he specifies . . .

25 June

The bad weather has persisted for several days, and it is unusually cold. I continue the revision of my manuscript.

Yesterday evening we went to have dinner at the Ritz with John and Evelyn Nef. As usual we recalled our encounters with Jacques Maritain and Chagall in Chicago and Washington, as well as that dinner at which Jean Hippolyte had been the guest of the Committee on Social Thought, and where von Blankenhagen had not opened his mouth the whole evening, since French, he said, "is the only language that a foreigner hasn't the right to mutilate . . ."

This evening we were invited to the Ricoeurs' along with Mme. Mounier and the Marrous. Professor Marrou informs me that *Patterns in Comparative Religion* disappears regularly from the library of the Sorbonne, and that almost every year they have to buy more copies of it. And he adds with a smile: "I would have never believed that one could experience such pleasure in finding out that books had been stolen . . ."

Then we come to talk about memory and the tricks it can play on us. It is possible for us to keep an exact and precise recollection of insignificant details, when we can't retain what is important. I admit to Marrou that it is impossible for me to cite any other sentence from his nevertheless admirable book on history than this one: "the cumbersome work of Benedetto Croce . . ."

June

It sometimes happens that I feel "foreign to myself," and at such times I feel completely happy. This "other" whom I discover in myself seems to have come from elsewhere. I then "listen to myself" with emotion, and with the badly-contained impatience to discover this unknown life of "another" who is, however, myself, a "new life," perhaps.

The more time that passes, the sadder I become at the idea that in all probability certain books that I've dreamt of writing since my youth will never see the light of day. I'm thinking in particular of that *Introduction aux géographies mythiques* that I had begun when I was living at the Hôtel de Suède. I had drafted twelve or fifteen pages of it, which were thrown into the fire by mistake at the same time as other notebooks and manuscripts, both mine and those of collaborators on our journal. From time to time, while looking for something else, I happen to come across papers from long ago, and I reread them with nostalgia. I then swear I will assemble them into a special file, *Géographies mythiques,* but I always put off rearranging my files until later.

Just today I've discovered my notes on the image of the Roman Empire (*Ta Ch'in*) such as it appears in Chinese sources from the Han dynasty, in the second century A.D., which is just as mythical and fabulous as the one that the Romans themselves had of China. In fact, as Rolf Stein writes, the *Ta Ch'in* was in large part "the projection of the Chinese utopian vision of the perfect State." That "Roman Empire" was described in terms that recall the *T'ai P'ing,* the utopian kingdom that the revolutionary movements of the time were seeking to establish, movements that were inspired by Taoism, and at the highest level of which was found the half-secret society of the "Yellow Turbans." These politico-mystical movements sought to resuscitate the Golden Age, and thus the perfect State and universal peace—in a word, the *T'ai P'ing*, or primordial paradise. What is remarkable about this utopia is the "mythologization" of the Far West, the transfiguration of the Roman Empire into a perfect State, the paradise of origins. The phenomenon is attested to, moreover, in many other cultures regardless of their level: After Marco Polo, Europeans also saw in China another "Terrestrial Paradise."

2 July

I have just learned that the most exact definition of the electron is that which was given by Sir Arthur Eddington: "Something unknown that is doing we don't know what." My admiration for men of science truly worthy of that name no longer knows any bounds . . .

6 July

Dinner at Marianne and Francois Parlier's with Cioran and the Lupascos.

Although I didn't mention it, it reminded me of another dinner in the autumn of 1943, but at Benjamin Fondane's, again with Cioran and Lupasco, but in addition, Lica Cracanera. That was for me the one and only opportunity I had to meet Benjamin Fondane. He lived in seclusion with his sister, and saw only a few intimate friends. I told him of my admiration, shared equally by many others, for his book written in Rumanian, *Images et livres de France* [*Images and Books of France*], and told him of the legend about him that was circulating around 1926–1928 among young people of my generation, that is, that he had been called to Paris to oversee the direction of the Imprimerie Gourmontienne. Thanks to him, Remy de Gourmont was to be brought back into the reigning fashion . . .

In the course of our conversation we came to talk about the peoples that history favors, and those, to the contrary, to whom it is unjust. In this respect it wasn't so much *historic reality* I had in mind, nor the ordeals that small nations must endure because of their geographic situation—whether they are stuck between great empires or located on the path of great invasions—but much rather the presence or absence of historical documents. Based on my studies, I maintained that if Herodotus hadn't heard, thanks to the Greeks of the Hellespont, of the myth of Zalmoxis, we would know nothing today about that Geto-Dacian divinity, save his *name*.

Fondane did not entirely agree. According to him, the myth of Zalmoxis, at least such as it is transmitted to us by Herodotus, doesn't teach us very much. It still must be deciphered and interpreted, and it is to this task that contemporary Rumanian historians, poets, and philosophers must apply themselves. It is only in doing so that Zalmoxis can become the equal, as a figure or symbol, of the Greek divinities, and thus contribute to the enrichment of European culture. According to Fondane, historical "bad luck" should be attributed above all to the lack of creative imagination among the representatives of the culture in question. I am not very sure he was right.

8 July

Yesterday Sibylle left for Puerto de Andraitx, where we will join her in a week.

In the evening we have dinner at Corbin's. Henry is completely satisfied with the outcome of the lecture series that took place at University of Saint John of Jerusalem. Although I am one of the founding members, it was impossible for me to go to that colloquium, but I share his joy in finally seeing one of his greatest desires take shape: to bring together a group of scholars, theologians, and philosophers belonging to the three traditions dealing with the Bible, to form them into a sort of Hermeticist circle, and to have them address an audience, restricted of course, but of the elite.

Henry insists that I bring my contribution to the next Eranos lectures. I can only tell him what I've already told Ritsema, that is, that I can't possibly envision a project of that magnitude until I have completed *A History*. Each Eranos lecture requires two or three months of my time to prepare and to write. For Henry it is completely different, for he prepares his lectures from the courses he gives at the Ecole des Hautes Etudes.

11 July

I've finally turned my manuscript over to Jean-Luc Pidoux-Payot. It is close to seven hundred pages, and I must still add a few paragraphs (about twenty pages) and finish the bibliography.

What can I say about this first volume? I have come to doubt that one can make a judgment before the completion of the work, which will take at least several years. In the immediate future its faults will jump to one's eyes to the point of covering up its qualities. Too few readers, I fear, will take the trouble to read the book *from cover to cover,* and to make a strict rule of not skipping over the chapters they consider less interesting.

12 July

While walking on the rue de Rivoli I notice in the distance at an outdoor café two young women who are laughing out loud, both of them very beautiful and elegantly dressed. I see them laughing hysterically and gesticulating. When I reach them I slow down, and their exuberance appears to me in a completely different light: What I had thought at a distance were sounds of voices are now imperceptible, and neither of the two women is uttering a word. In fact, the women are deaf-mutes who are telling each other apparently very funny stories. My reaction is only that much greater, and I feel reinforced in my conviction that the love of life, knowing oneself to be beautiful, young, and rich—which the two young women obviously are—can win out over all infirmities.

PUERTO DE ANDRAITX, *14 July*

Impossible to sleep all night. On place Charles-Dullin the loudspeakers from the restaurant across the street drowned us with waves of pop music until four o'clock in the morning.

Sibylle and Jacqueline were waiting for us at the airport. We are delighted to return to our Villa Italia.

15 July

The weather is superb. I swim for a half hour, then go back to the room determined to write the text Pidoux-Payot is still waiting for. But my heart isn't really in the task, and in addition, the heat is beginning to make itself felt.

19 July

These last few days I've been able to advance in my work. But since last evening the desire to write a story pursues me to the point of obsession. I have as yet only thought of its beginning. The story occurs in present-day Bucharest: A rather ordinary man, dressed in a patched, threadbare cape, stops passersby and asks them: "Excuse me. Could you tell me what year this is?"

21 July

Yesterday I interrupted all work to devote myself to my story. By the end of the day I had written the first ten pages of it in a practically illegible script. Today, I've written ten more pages, all just as illegible. It's been a long time since I've been so "inspired."

26 July

A day doesn't go by without my drafting from ten to twenty pages. I've thought of a title for my story: "La Pèlerine" [the cape]. The action is defined as I advance in my writing.

28 July

I finished my story today, but it's impossible for me to judge it since it is so difficult to reread. I must first decipher my own text word by word.

31 July

I've finished correcting and transcribing *La Pèlerine*. I had to sacrifice passages that were too illegible. There remain ninety-five pages, which I read to our little group consisting of Christinel, Sibylle, Siegfried, and Cella. They liked it.

2 August

It has been said of Bertrand Russell that he was a "man courageous in everything," equally as a man of science, a man of politics, a thinker, and even a "libertine." The three volumes of his *Autobiography* are proof of this. All the same, he always refused to publish in his lifetime stories and tales he had written, and they had to be published in a posthumous edition. One of the most "revolutionary" thinkers of his time, he never dared to oppose Anglo-American academic conceptions or, in particular, to disregard the most venerable of taboos, which specified that one could not simultaneously engage in two activities as contradictory as being both a novelist and a scholar or an intellectual worthy of the name.

10 August

I have finally, laboriously, completed the final paragraphs of *A History,* volume 1. Christinel will still have to type them when we return to Paris.

11 August

I must one day devote a whole essay to something that seems obvious to me, that is, that cosmic rhythms, although ignored or considered negligible by men who want to be "modern," end up reappearing by way of the imagination.

15 August

In Calvin's opinion, and in that of so many other theologians, man is "disgusting, soiled with original sin," etc. . . . All the same, "the weaker you appear to be, the more willingly God will receive thee." *Felix culpa!* Saint Augustine had already exclaimed. And Luther adds: *Pecca fortiter.*

One can affirm that this paradox has its equivalent in Indian thought, and more specifically in Samkhya-Yoga: The more that suffering due to metaphysical ignorance becomes intolerable, the greater chance one has of obtaining deliverance (*moksha, mukti,* etc.). From the perspective of Christianity one can translate: Our chances of redemption become even greater as we commit more sins, or as the consequences of original sin become harder to bear. But whereas in India, with the exception of diverse currents of mystical devotion, deliverance is the crowning achievement of a metaphysical apprenticeship, or of the practice of yoga, for Calvin, Luther, and many other Christian theologians, "Grace is a free gift from God, received only under the condition of 'having faith in Him.' "

PARIS, *17 August*

To our great surprise Corina, Sorin, and Liliane have arrived in Paris and are waiting for us at home. We press them with questions, and our conversation goes on until very late into the night.

20 August

Papini loved to write imaginary biographies. If I had the time, and especially the necessary documentation, I, too, would like to write the biographies of certain intellectuals who were mistaken and were unable to recognize genius when it was standing in front of them. For example, that German professor whose name I've forgotten who had tried to deprecate as much as possible *L'Origine de la tragédie* (on this subject I will recall the blunder committed by the great von Willamowitz); or that other person, the American art critic who, at the time of the proceedings brought against Brancusi by the American customs officials, declared that Brancusi's sculptures were in no way works of art, but were simple blocks of stone or pieces of raw metal.

23 August

We've just learned of the death of Mircea Popescu following a cardiac arrest. Too many memories tie me to him, which I will not recall here. Without him, Rome will never be the same for me.

September

Received a letter from Alphonse Dupront, president of the Université de Paris-Sorbonne. He informs me that next February I will be conferred the title of Doctor *honoris causa*. I've rarely felt such joy. To respect tradition, the news must be kept secret until the eve of the ceremony. Sibylle is all the more delighted since she will now have the opportunity to see us again this winter.

O., who was learned only today of my correspondence with V. Bologa, published in the journal *Steaua* in December 1969, is amazed at the interest I show (an interest that is essentially indestructible since it dates from my student days) in the history of medicine. I try to explain to him, rapidly since it is late, that with the exception of the positivist era (during which there was never unanimity of opinion in this regard), the theories and methods that served as bases for medicine—and this throughout the world—considered man above all in his relationship with the cosmos on the one hand, and with the "Spiritual Universe" on the other. This latter expression covers both divinities and forces of a divine or demonic order, as well as the psycho-mental activity of each individual taken separately. In other words, medical theories and therapeutics prolonged or complemented the theology, mythology, and religious experiences of respective civilizations and historical periods. Thus medicine still referred, in theory and in practice (as was the case during the Renaissance or in the romantic era), to the traditional relationships between Man and the Cosmos, whereas these same relationships were ostracized by official theologies.

As we were parting, I pointed out that traditional therapeutics all aim to restore man to "normalcy," that is, to reestablish the equilibrium that the appearance of pathological syndromes had upset. At a certain moment in the history of the spirit, religions declared themselves alone entitled to be able to reestablish the primordial state, in other words, to return man to his condition before the Fall ("sin"), or before the eruption of Evil in the world. The comparison of the different conceptions of "man in the world" which have come to light in the last five or six thousand years, with the different currents of religious thought and their respective therapeutic systems, could be the object of a fascinating study!

In his polemic against Celsus, Origen evidently proves to be very far from the theses of his adversary. He is, however, also of the opinion (*Contra Celsum* 6.75) that Jesus was ugly (*dyseidēs*). But where did he get this idea? Certainly Origen vehemently proclaimed the historicity of Jesus and the reality of the Passion, Jesus having been crucified to the certain knowledge of the whole population, the earthquake and the night that ensued having been confirmed in the account given by Phlegon of Tralles, etc. . . . But to which "tradition" can the alleged ugliness of Jesus be attributed?

28 September

Last evening I read *La Pèlerine* to our "club," which had gathered at L.M.'s. Since my story belongs to the fantastic genre, I didn't consider myself obligated to take into account entirely the "realities of a socialist country," even though the action takes place in present-day Bucharest. The fact that I may have perhaps committed oversights doesn't trouble me unduly. What surprises me, however, is to note that after all it is with some sympathy that I sketched the portrait of some of my characters who, however, belong to the *Securitate*[1] and to other organizations in charge of repression. As in *The Old Man and the Bureaucrats,* the policeman is not always a brute, and can even display compassion, understanding, and tolerance, even though the reader has the feeling the whole city is living in terror.

I even come to wonder whether this "sympathy" doesn't hide something deeper, whether it is not the translation, in the universe of literary creation, of what I've said over and over since 1938–1939 (cf. *Mitul Reîntegrării* [The Myth of Reintegration]) regarding man's natural propensity towards *coincidentia oppositorum,* and which I've developed in *The Two and the One.*

1. Political police of the Rumanian Socialist Republic.—C.G.

CHICAGO, *13 October*

Truly superb weather greets us on our return. I read in my datebook that on 7 October we had dinner at Yves Bonnefoy's with Henri Michaux, whom I hadn't seen for several years and who seemed unchanged to me. On 9 October Pidoux-Payot sent me the first proofs of my book. On 11 October we were in New York.

14 October

I'm going to have to get back to work on the *Autobiography*.[1] This morning, after having reread the last chapters, I realized the extent to which I had been unfair to myself, on the one hand by minimizing the gifts I had received from nature, and on the other by forcing myself to be as sincere as possible. Pierre Emmanuel is quite right in saying: "Nothing is as partial as sincerity: It is but an angle of vision, a distorting perspective. Anything that doesn't enter into the picture, or only enters by force, is systematically ignored or misjudged."

31 October

The annual meeting of the American Association for the Study of Religions (around five thousand members!), which is currently being held at the Palmer House, gave me the opportunity last evening of seeing Tom Altizer again. In the course of our conversation he informs me that in the session on Judaica three papers were read which related to my own research on the symbolism of the center and of sacred space, and in general on cosmic religiosity. Tom was unable to attend all of the presentations, and he is thus not in a position to give me an exact summary of them. He thinks, however, that this renewal of interest is due above all to the desire many young Judaists are experiencing to go deeper into and to give new value to certain religious creations of cosmological structure which, although witnessed in the Old Testament,

1. The first part of the *Autobiographie* was published in English under the title *Autobiography, Volume 1, 1907–1937: Journey East, Journey West,* Harper & Row, 1981.—C.G.

were contested or even rejected by the Prophets on the one hand, and by the exaltation of the Torah on the other. Actually, these religious creations of cosmological structure, which are thus archetypical and universal, or more exactly, "universalist," whose presence and importance are affirmed in all cultures starting with the Neolithic, have been a permanent source of temptation throughout Jewish history. Proof of this is in the frequency of apostasies and innumerable returns to ancient cults of fertility, to Baal and Belit. The absolute monotheism proclaimed by the Prophets and by the Torah, the faith in a history conceived as a Holy History decided upon and controlled by Yahweh, the certainty that this history had a beginning and would have an end; such a theology couldn't tolerate the "cosmic religiosity" practiced in the *oikoumenē* before Abraham and Moses.

Tom is undoubtedly right. Indeed, R. Rubinstein, who is both a theologian and a rabbi, is attempting to revaluate the actual Judaic ritual system, but also its cosmological aspects, its "archetypes."

8 November

I finish correcting the proofs of *A History,* volume 1. Since 1 November I've had a sore throat. On 5 November Dr. Emil Popescu comes to examine me, accompanied by Dr. Miereanu, who has recently arrived from Rumania to see one of his children. He's one of the great specialists in phlegmon surgery, and he tells me he has operated on several thousand, especially those of children. He opens an instrument bag which must easily date from the beginning of the century—"a true museum piece," affirms Dr. Popescu—chooses a lancet, and undertakes the procedure. It is completed without my truly realizing that it had begun . . .

Then we speak of the friends he had in the Rumania of old, among them several writers, some of whom have long since disappeared. He recites a good dozen epigrams by Pastorel Teodoreanu, to make me laugh, certainly, but also to keep me from talking. I am deeply moved to finally find myself in the company of one of my authentic peers, a witness of that Rumania that I knew and where I, too, lived until the spring of 1940.

13 November

The day before yesterday I delivered my first lecture in the series *Shamanism and Hallucinogens.* I gave the second today, before an even bigger audience. Quite probably, the news of it had spread throughout the campus. What other subject could elicit the interest of this admirable American youth culture?

18 November

More and more I feel the need to keep a secret journal, just as Tolstoy did, for example, a journal destined for me alone, and which would be burned right after my death, or as soon as it is discovered among my papers. In any event, apart from myself it would interest no one. But for me it would be of considerable use: It would permit me, while leafing through it, to remember my attacks of arthritis or of melancholy, my sudden bursts of anger or exaltation, my moments of inspiration, my premonitions, too, not to mention minute everyday details. A sort of *De senectute,* in short, seen under a microscope.

20 November

During my first lecture of the *Shamanism and Hallucinogens* series I had attempted to analyze the reasons for the renewal of interest in shamanism, an interest which grows more and more each day. I stress certain motives: the curiosity of young people, but also of scholars, both in history and in sociology or psychology, about "mysticism" and "occultism;" the sacramental value accorded by the "youth culture" to hallucinogenic drugs, LSD in this respect being able to unleash a mystical experience; the attention given to specifically shamanic creations, bone and wood sculptures, ecstatic dances, shows, etc. . . . . The discovery, still too recent to be well understood, of the spiritual, "religious," function of illnesses. I must one day look deeper into this last point and specify the way in which problems linked to illness, such as psychic crises, but also pains of a physiological nature (fever, migraines, rheumatic pains) can be assumed to be just so many initiatory trials. Uncovering the religious significance of illness and physical pain constitutes in effect shamanism's essential contribution to the history of the spirit.

The hundreds of pages I've devoted to shamanism authorize me, I hope, to be concise. I will thus limit myself to recalling that the shamanic vocation is announced by psychosomatic crises that can be very serious and mistaken for madness. But the suffering is understood and taken to be an initiatory trial comparable to the symbolic death of the neophyte, followed by his resurrection. Complete recovery marks the end of the initiation. The shaman cannot, however, be compared to a sick person who has been cured; he is a new man, endowed with a perfectly integrated personality, and henceforth clearly superior to the rest of his peers. In sum, the illness is the point of departure for the process of personality integration and for a radical spiritual transformation.

A comparable phenomenon can be observed in certain areas of contemporary medicine. More or less consciously, numerous doctors and psychiatrists, especially younger ones, see in psychosomatic afflictions a means of accomplishment, of self-realization. Deep down, and without their being aware of it, they compare them to an "initiation." This fact is all the more significant as initiatory tradition had disappeared, at least in Europe, several centuries ago. In our present-day world the different initiatory scenarios only survive occulted in imaginary universes: fantastico-oneiric activities, literary and artistic creations, etc. But in these circumstances we are dealing with an experience on a completely different level, one which involves contemporary man in his totality: Psychosomatic illness becomes one with the very *existence* of the patient. Insofar as he takes on his illness as an initiatory trial, the patient truly succeeds in *achieving* a spiritual alteration that is in all respects comparable to the process of shamanic initiation.

This should be pursued by comparing shamanic, psychoanalytic, and psychiatric healing techniques, the role of hallucinogens in treatments prescribed by shamans, and the use of LSD in contemporary psychiatry, etc.

December

While looking in my file cabinets and in the boxes stacked on a chair in the corner of my office I come across a file labeled "Story Project." Upon opening it, I see several hastily written pages of notebook paper. The story begins with a young man entering a room: "Excuse me," he says, "I don't want to disturb you, but I saw the door was open . . ." He is then quiet, considers at length the person he is speaking to, then asks him in a timid voice: "You are indeed Mr. X., aren't you? Yes. Well, I'm your son." He then takes a piece of paper out of his pocket and begins to read a poem out loud. "It was a bit obscure," he says after finishing. "It's about the life of my mother, and thus about your own life." Then he disappears for a moment and returns with a suitcase. A young girl appears behind him, hesitant, apparently frightened. "I'd like you to meet my fiancée," he continues. "We have come to ask for your consent, for we will be married in a few hours . . ."

There are other rather disjointed descriptive indications in this file. Impossible to remember the rest of my story, or its conclusion, and I regret this. I do believe I wrote these pages seven or eight years ago in Santa Barbara, upon returning from one of my habitual walks along the beach. I had written them in great haste, for I was waiting for the student who was coming to pick me up to drive me to the university, located about fifteen kilometers from where I was, on the other side of the city.

For a very long time Frank has enjoyed writing down what he calls "significant encounters" between two important people, real or imaginary. In the latter case, they would, of course, be literary characters. He has a whole file of them from which he hopes later to construct a book. He asked me to help him with his task, and today, while rereading volume 10 of *Dichtung und Wahrheit,* I came across this scene which delighted him, and which made him exclaim: "This is the significant encounter *par excellence!*" Shortly after having learned of Herder's arrival in Strasbourg, the young Goethe went to Geist Tavern, where he had arranged to meet a friend passing through town. At the foot of the stairs he noticed a man dressed in black, looking exactly like a Protestant pastor. Goethe recognized Herder and introduced himself to him. They then both climbed the stairs, stopping at each step to better pursue their discussion.

This "dual ascension" and the warmth of their conversation all the way up the stairs prefigures and sums up all that followed, all that Goethe learned from Herder, but also all he would later reject of his teachings.

31 December

It was on 20 December that I fell ill: an intestinal flu that slowed me down in my work. The next day I get back to work, but I feel more and more drowsy. On 23 December I sleep for a good part of the afternoon. In the evening I already feel better, but rather than going to Meadville I reread the *Conversations de Goethe avec Eckermann*, a book which is always able to stimulate and calm me. On 24 December arrival of Uca and Mateï Calinescu, as well as of Sanda L. In the evening, at dinner, we come to talk of preverbal systems of expression. I recall that rite of feminine initiation, still found in Australia thirty or forty years ago (cf. *Birth and Rebirth*), in the course of which *not one word is spoken*. In front of the whole clan, which has come together as for an important ceremony, several women *silently indicate* the recently initiated young girl (that is, she who has been instructed in the mysteries of femininity and maternity during the three days of seclusion which follow the appearance of her first menstrual period). Those in attendance then acclaim her and applaud her loudly. This rite is a new epiphany of the mystery of fertility through which the action of procreating is designated and indicated, not proffered.

We spend Christmas evening at the Kitagawas', and we speak of the symbolism of the winter solstice and of the survival of its celebration, although camouflaged, on the occasion of the Christmas holidays.

I spend this last day of the year completing—a true imposition—the index to my little book *Occultism, Witchcraft, and Cultural Fashions*.

6 January 1976

I have just spent the whole morning at Billings Hospital undergoing all sorts of tests. Back at home, I start working without interruption.

Catullus, talking about the work of his rival Apollonius of Rhodes: "A thick book is as bad as it is thick." This tirade sums up all of Alexandrian poetics.

10 January

I went to Billings Hospital to get the results of my tests. "Nothing in particular to note," Dr. Cohen assures me.

I find in Scholem a text of the *Sanhedrin* (98a) which should be meditated on by all those who take Christianity seriously. One reads here that the Messiah is at the doors of Rome, among the lepers and the beggars. Scholem specifies that this rabbinical legend dates from the second century B.C., in other words, well before Rome, whose legions had destroyed the Temple in A.D. 69 and forced the Jews into the Diaspora, became the seat of the Vicar of Christ and the center of a church that proclaimed itself the accomplishment of biblical messianism.

A splendid image, but how troubling! For the Jews, the "true" Messiah awaits his hour, lost amidst the lepers, and at the doors of Rome, at the very place whence the legions who had destroyed their state, their temple, and Jerusalem, their Holy City, had started out. And it is there that the Messiah continues to wait, even though the Roman Empire has disappeared since then and Rome has become the fief of he who presides over the destinies of Western Christianity.

11 January

It is snowing, and the campus has never been so beautiful. I've begun a seminar on alchemy. I regret noting that not one of my students has seen fit to inform himself on Chinese and Indian alchemies. It is true that I had announced that this seminar would deal only with Hermetic traditions of the Renaissance, the Counter-Reformation, and the Age of Enlightenment. I would have liked, however, for some of my students to have taken the trouble of looking into the concepts and methods of different Asian alchemies. They would have only better grasped what distinguishes them from Western alchemies or, on the contrary, what connects them. I thus found myself obliged to summarize my "Asian file," and thus to complement what I had already said in *The Forge and the Crucible,* a book they have all read and which they now use as a reference, stressing the most recent publications on the subject, those of Sivin, Joseph Needham, etc.

14 January

First seminar on the high gods of Australia and South America. As usual, I began with a summary overview of the subject, which took me a good hour. Then three of my students inquire about "the best way to study primitive religions." I reply that I will cover that during the third or fourth session. They must first familiarize themselves with the *texts* and do as much preliminary research as possible (after all, I've already furnished them with a complete annotated bibliography).

I note once again to what extent American students are anxious to know, as early as the first lesson, the "best methods," no doubt from fear of wasting their time in using outdated methodologies.

15 January

If I had an afternoon to waste, I would write a long and heartfelt "meditation on the incineration of notes and manuscripts." Just yesterday evening I gathered up all my files of notes and excerpts relating to the Mediterranean, Greece, and Egypt, and carried them into the courtyard, where I filled two whole trash cans with them. This morning I undertook the same operation, thus condemning to destruction manuscripts of five chapters: Megaliths, Greece 1 and 2, Egypt, and Mesopotamia. I had kept them until the last minute in the event that I would have to consult them in correcting the printer's proofs. Having completed my corrections, I had nothing more pressing to do than finally rid myself of these piles of paper, some of which go back more than twenty-five years, to the time when I lived on rue de la Tour or in the Val d'Or.

And yet, I can't help feeling somewhat melancholy at separating myself from certain files, especially from those concerning the religions of Greece and the Mediterranean. They contained, transcribed in my own hand, entire passages from my favorite authors: Homer, Hesiod, Herodotus, Pausanias, as well as "personal reflections" drafted in haste while I was reading or transcribing a text; I was so convinced at the time of their profound originality, but when reread several months or several years later they seemed unintelligible to me (so great had been my haste to commit them to paper), or quite simply devoid of interest.

Whatever the case may be, I suddenly realize that this destruction by fire of more than three thousand pages, in the course of only the last few months, is accompanied by a feeling of *impoverishment* without my knowing very well why.

January

That evening meeting was really much too gloomy and insipid, and I was getting angry for having come when, I can't remember in what context, L.L. cited this phrase from Thoreau: "Beware of all enterprises that require new clothes." As if by a miracle, students and professors seemed suddenly to be resuscitated, only by the "shock" provoked by L.L., who saw in this phrase by Thoreau the reflection of all the "obscurantist" and "primitivist" ideology of its author, his resistance before the implications of civilization, industry, technology, and his yearning for original paradise, the simple joys of days gone by, etc. . . . In turn, F. commented on what must be understood by "new clothes," and the ritual function with which they are invested. It was near midnight when I left the room. They were still discussing nudity and the archaic symbolism of clothing . . .

PARIS, *9 February*

We arrived yesterday at midnight. Sibylle had come to get us at the airport. At place Charles-Dullin we are disagreeably surprised by the cold.

Before leaving Chicago I had taken great care to keep the reason for my trip "secret," that is, the doctorate *honoris causa* that awaited me at the Sorbonne. Only Joe Kitagawa knew about it. Several days wasted, as usual, in preparing for the trip. My only activity consisted of writing letters, around thirty in three days.

11 February

Giza and Dinu took us to see *Godspell* at Versailles. I left disappointed. In fact, I left the theatre before the beginning of the second part. This attempt at recreating the Gospel according to Saint Matthew is daring in appearance only. Even if the text of the parables is respected in its entirety, the behavior of those to whom it is addressed clash with it: They sing, yell, roll on the ground, hurl abuse, clutch at each other, etc. . . .

The author's initial mistake is to have made Jesus appear on stage in the guise of a more or less roughhewn hippie who wants to be "charismatic." One has trouble imagining a Jesus dancing to rock music, kissing girls, etc. This view, according to which the reenactment of the evangelical *illud tempus* can only be accomplished by losing Christ in the crowd of sinners such as they appear in our time, is altogether too gratuitous, and even revels in great naivete. No matter what the historical context may be, it is essential that on the contrary Jesus stand out among his contemporaries, not only through the expression and content of his parables, but also through his presence alone. The same scenario would have been otherwise convincing if an unknown person, an anonymous "magister," had preached the Gospel before a group of our contemporaries, both sinners and innocents, being content to *play* the role of Jesus.

13 February

Lunch at Meslin's, titular of the chair in the history of religions at the Sorbonne, who will introduce me at the ceremony tomorrow in the Richelieu Auditorium. He is a young man, very competent, and in addition, very nice.

I have trouble truly grasping the meaning of the title of Doctor *honoris causa* which the Sorbonne is conferring on a refugee who teaches in Chicago, a man without any academic ties to Paris or anywhere else, a historian of religions who is neither Marxist nor a structuralist, and this in 1976 at a time when Marxism, Freudianism, and leftism bear down with all their weight on French culture.

What impresses me most is that before me the only Rumanian on whom this title was conferred was Nicolas Iorga, whom I truly venerated in my youth.

14 February

Moving ceremony at the Richelieu Auditorium. A student choir and orchestra, remarkable for their sobriety, were standing to the left of the podium where Alphonse Dupront presided, surrounded by the five professors in charge of introductions, and the five new recipients. Among the latter, Yehudi Menuhin and Edward Heath, the former prime minister of Great Britain. Heath's hobby being of public notoriety, he was invited to conduct Handel's *Alleluia*.

While I was listening to Dupront sing my praises, I remembered those years 1937–1938 when I had asked him to review Pettazzoni's text for the journal *Zalmoxis*. But I especially remembered that in 1946 or 1947, in his desire to see me be granted a scholarship from the C.N.R.S., he had deemed it appropriate to go see the ambassador of Rumania at the time, the great mathematician Stoïlov, begging him not to put up any obstacles to it, for he, Dupront, could vouch for me and could guarantee that I had never been a "fascist." Stoïlov gave him all the desired assurances, but nevertheless phoned Bucharest to ask for instructions. The response was: *"Nyet."*

15 February

Big party organized by Sibylle at the Beauvilliers restaurant. Around forty friends and colleagues are present. Eugène Ionesco gets up to speak and humorously recalls the "conflict of the generations" that was the war-horse of our Bucharest youth. Henry Corbin and Paul Ricoeur congratulate me, too, the latter saying that my *Patterns* had helped him to free himself from the too-exclusive influence of Karl Barth, and that goes right to my heart. Georges Dumézil recalls the pitfalls that the Rumanian embassy, in 1948, placed with apparent pleasure in my path and, recalling the speech Meslin had given in praise of me, tells me: "In your destiny, who wouldn't see the hand of Providence!"

22 February

Julien Green notes in his journal on 20 February 1945: "Even if my book is nothing, this book must be written and, paradoxically, this nothing must exist, for the writer is created only so that he, himself, creates."

In my case I often think that a writer's books are a little like flowers. We know very well that once cut and put in a vase they only survive a few days, but their beauty is not diminished for all that. Just like flowers, books share the epiphanic modality of existence. They must above all appear, at the risk of subsequently falling into oblivion.

NEW YORK, *24 February*

We arrived yesterday afternoon. Lisette absolutely insists that Christinel tell her, without omitting anything, about the ceremony at the Sorbonne and our party at the Beauvilliers restaurant.

CHICAGO, *26 February*

We returned yesterday afternoon, around four o'clock. The weather is nice, and the air is as mild as in spring. Many books are awaiting me, as well as a pile of letters to which I am going to have to reply.

We have dinner at the Kitagawas', and I learn some bad news: Nathan Scott has accepted the position offered him by the University of South Carolina.

Back home, I immerse myself in the *Journal* of Octav S. I finished the book this very morning in my office at Meadville. What sadness to have all the memories of the years 1933–1938 resurface, not to mention the sadness that emerges in its own right from what Octav S. writes. I did not know him very well. I only saw him when he came to Bucharest from Brashov, where he was a teacher at the lycée. I liked him a lot: What I admired most about him was the sincerity of his writing and his words, no matter what the subject was, whether he was dealing with literature or with a completely different issue of the day. But his novel, *Ambigène,* had, however, disappointed me a little. I had vaguely heard of his passion for Lydia, and the pages in his *Journal* that refer to it are indeed the most moving.

1 March

I reread the few dozen pages of what I've called, not without pretentiousness, my "secret journal." Being certain that it will be destroyed, and thus that no one will ever read it, I don't feel I have to hold back at all. It wins out in spontaneity over all that I've related up until now in my journal, and most especially in the excerpts that have been published from it. I can be more sincere with myself than in the letters I write my friends, or even in my *Autobiography* (although in this respect I have rather been accused of the opposite, that is, that my "sincerity" sometimes bordered on indiscretion). I was both surprised and delighted to read these few pages which finally give me the opportunity to see what, for an author, is the meaning of that return into himself in what is most personal. He discovers himself as he did in front of a mirror into which, as a child, he looked for the first time, *attentively and without fear.*

While rereading what I wrote I go from discovery to discovery. Why did I stress—but differently, and with extreme passion—the subjects that I had, however, dealt with abundantly both in my journal and in other writings? The mystery of the dialectic of the camouflaging of the sacred in the profane, for example. One would think that this is a subject that preoccupies me to the point of obsession. Not content to confront the issue in my works on the history of religions and in my literary writings of the last few years, I must still grapple with it in what I note for myself alone!

3 March

It is quite possible that this "secret journal" is also, among other things, the reflection of my own yearning for a "work" that I have not yet undertaken to write. The fervor with which I rework to better develop reflections inspired by the camouflaging of the sacred in the profane must have a deeper meaning, and I'm just beginning to have an inkling of it. This dialectic of camouflaging is infinitely more vast and goes much farther than all that I've been able to say about it up until now. The "mystery of the mask" is fundamental to an entire metaphysics, for it is the very mystery of the human condition. If it obsesses me so much, it is probably because I don't decide to go into it in more depth, to make a systematic presentation of it, to study it from its own unique perspective, that of philosophical meditation.

It is thus possible that these reflections, because of their intimate character, only amplify better, although indirectly, my remorse in betraying my vocation as a philosopher . . .

9 March

Today I am sixty-nine years old.

My seminar on alchemy has finished. W. T. accompanied me as far as my house, and we walked along Woodlawn Avenue, going back and forth from the Midway to Fifty-seventh Street. Of all those who took the seminar, he is perhaps the most skilled. It's been three years already since he became a member of the Committee on Social Thought. In his doctoral thesis he proposes to broach certain issues relating to the history of sciences through the seventeenth and eighteenth centuries. As often happens during our seminars, we can't keep from discussing *ad infinitum* the reasons why so-called "modern" science saw fit to ignore the Hermetic tradition which had dominated alchemy and iatrochemistry throughout the eighteenth century, and even to deny it all value. As I showed in my seminar, the triumph of Newtonian mechanics had as a result the annihilation of the scientific ideal to which Newton himself had appealed. I will return to this in more detail in my lecture on the "Myth of Alchemy" which I must deliver in Seattle on 29 April. I must in addition examine the issue from a much wider perspective in volume 3 of *A History of Religious Ideas*.

One day justice must truly be done to that extraordinary pleiad of scholars, from Paracelsus and John Dee to Comenius, J. W. Andreae, Ashmole, Fludd, and Newton, who all expected the fulfillment of Western man to occur through an educational reform which involved an integral *renovatio* of Christianity and a new scientific methodology. Just like Pythagoras and Plato, or Chinese thinkers, their ideal was "holistic," in the sense that it embraced the totality of the human person. One must see in their efforts to integrate Christian tradition, alchemical Hermeticism, and scientific thought—above all mathematics, mechanics, and astronomy—as well as in their hope of saving the Christian churches from provinicialism and fratricidal wars, and of establishing the bases for a new form of education, the *last, truly authentic, religious creation* of Western Europe. Their hopes, attempts, syntheses, anticipations, even yearnings, are all the more difficult to judge as they were nipped in the bud.

12 March

Mircea Handoca has just sent me the posthumous book by Comarnesco, *Visages et paysages d'Amérique*. The last part of the book (pp. 419–512) contains the journal he kept during his stay in the United States in January and February 1968. I read it in one sitting, and I am immediately amazed by the prodigious energy of the author, by his extraordinary vitality, well contained, however, by an uncommon will and generosity. As soon as he was able to obtain a typewriter, he undertook to write his journal, which is in fact a long missive intended for his friends in Rumania, in which he wrote everything that seemed worthy of interest: ideas, practical information, impressions, remembrances, statistical facts, etc. . . . . It is quite simply wonderful!

March 1976

Two weeks before concluding my seminar on alchemy I noticed in the window of a bookstore *The Foundations of Newton's Alchemy* (1975) by B. T. Dobbs, and I bought it right away. I was astounded upon reading it. I learned in it that hundreds of Newton's manuscripts on alchemy, in which he had copied by hand essential texts that he annotated as he went along in accordance with experiments he was attempting to reproduce in his laboratory, have been deliberately ignored by scientists for more than two centuries, under the pretext that in their opinion these manuscripts revealed the "mystical and obscurantist activity" of this physicist of genius. In the 1930s the manuscripts were dispersed at auction by Newton's own descendants. Between 1936 and 1939 John Maynard Keynes was able to acquire a small portion of them, but it has been impossible up until now to reconstruct the complete collection. It is thus only on the manuscripts that Keynes possessed, and which he had bequeathed to the library of Oxford University, that Professor Dobbs concentrated her attention, studying them with extreme care. Her examination of these fifty or so manuscripts permitted her to reach conclusions that are as surprising as they are fascinating.

Newton had undertaken to verify experimentally in his laboratory "the whole vast literature of the older alchemy as it has never been probed before or since" (p. 88). Through such experiments Newton wanted to bring to light the structure of the small world, which, according to him, would correspond to that of the cosmological system of which he was the author. Having already recognized in gravitation the force which held the planets in their orbits, he intended to identify the forces at work in the molecular universe. But all his efforts in this area, undertaken without interruption from 1668 to 1696, remained in vain.

More revealing is the role attributed to alchemy in Newton's theology. Like the Hermeticists of the Hellenistic period and those of the Renaissance, Newton believed in a primordial revelation that was hidden, then rediscovered by certain initiates. The latter would have retransmitted it, but in an occult fashion, through fables and myths in order to make it inaccessible to the profane. Newton was convinced, however, that this primordial revelation was henceforth entirely recoverable so long as one attempted to do so by rational, fully scientific methods. This is why he was attracted in particular to esoteric texts, certain that the "true secrets" of matter were hidden in them.

Like many of his contemporaries, Newton believed in the transmutation of metals, as we see in this sentence taken from *Opticks:* "The changing of Bodies into Light, and Light into Bodies, is very conformable to the Course of Nature, which seems delighted with Transmutations." Dobbs writes that Newton never doubted the validity of the principles of alchemy, and that in a certain sense all his activity after 1675 was an attempt to integrate alchemy and "mechanical philosophy" to make them a unitary system. When the famous *Principia* appeared, Newton's opponents claimed that the "forces" he invoked were no more than the "occult qualities" dear to the Hermeticists. In Dobbs's opinion, the opponents were perfectly right: Newton's "forces" did not differ essentially from the "sympathies" and "antipathies" dear to the Hermeticists of the Renaissance. But Newton had given the so-called "forces" an ontological status equivalent to that of matter and motion. In other words, he "quantified" them, thus establishing the scientific bases of all mechanics. As Richard Westfall writes in *Force in Newton's Physics,* modern science is the result of the wedding of the Hermetic tradition with the mechanical philosophy.

30 March

I have just gone over the English translation of the section of *Fragments d'un journal* (pp. 231–571) that will be published by Harper and Row [*No Souvenirs*].[1] I am almost angry at myself for allowing my text to be submitted to such Draconian cuts. It is true that the publisher promised me they would publish the rest of the text "if the book is successful." Still, *Fragments d'un journal* was already the result of a most severe se-

1. Published by Harper and Row, 1977. To be reprinted by the University of Chicago Press, 1989, under the title *Journal II: 1957–1969.*—Ed.

lection, and represented only about a third of the original text. I had eliminated all notations of a strictly personal nature, all allusions to political events, as well as "indiscretions" vis-à-vis my contemporaries. Moreover, I had left aside a good number of more or less technical reading notes and commentaries, considering them devoid of interest for the nonspecialist reader. I was perhaps wrong to do this, for such notes could, on the contrary, be of interest to my readers. After all, the tens of thousands of copies of my works sold in paperback have not been read by specialists alone.

8 April

I complete the preface John Shopp asked me to write for *No Souvenirs*. I worked hard on it, and if I had not been busy with other tasks I would have added a good fifteen pages, so much do I feel the need to furnish certain precisions, to clear up a number of misunderstandings. Many of my English-language readers will probably be very surprised, even baffled, when they discover that I am "also" a novelist, so dominated is the academic milieu by the mythology of scientism. Many still imagine that literary creation and poetic invention are incompatible with the objectivity of research (this is, in fact, a prejudice inherited from the positivist era, but which has not for all that lost any of its prestige). Rare are those who know that men of science worthy of that name think exactly the opposite. Thus twenty years ago Norbert Wiener maintained—and he wasn't alone—that the physicist in no way recorded his own observations objectively, as was believed up until then, but that he actively *interfered* with the experiment in progress. In support of his thesis, he mentioned the role that fell to the observer in the theory of relativity and in the quantum theory.

One must wait another ten or fifteen years for the relationship between scientific and artistic creation to become clear to everyone, including those in academic circles. The present reflections will then have become truisms . . .

9 April

As one may notice upon reading certain pages of my journal, there is another aspect of my activity that deserves greater explanation:

my tendency to integrate, to "combine," different levels of knowledge, whether on theoretical, psychological, literary, or historical planes, etc. . . . I think that contemporary man, and more importantly, men of tomorrow, will soon find themselves obliged and forced to integrate the two forms of knowledge—logical and rational on the one hand, symbolic and poetic on the other. I am also convinced that under the pressure of history we will be forced to familiarize ourselves with the different expressions of extra-European creative genius, such as are found in Asia, Africa, and Oceania. As I've repeated over and over for thirty years, only the history of religions furnishes the discipline that can bring to light the meaning not only of traditional, but also of "primitive" and Oriental, civilizations. In a word, this is a discipline— such at least as I envision and practice it—that will contribute decisively to "globalizing" culture. Up until now, only industrial technology and political ideologies have enjoyed such universalization. With the results we are aware of . . .

16 April

I have just received a copy of the first volume of *A History of Religious Ideas*. I hesitate to reread my book. Its publication comes almost thirty years after that of *Patterns in Comparative Religion* (whose original title was *Prolégomènes à l'histoire des religions: morphologie et structures du sacré*). My latest book only prolongs and completes it. As for the *Source Book (From Primitives to Zen)*, it formed a thematic anthology of religious texts classified by genre: myths, divine figures, rites, ecstatic and contemplative techniques, etc. . . . When I have finished the third volume of my *History of Religious Ideas* the reader will have at his disposal, in only five volumes, the gist of the entire discipline.

21 April

The Marxist dogma according to which it is not man's conscience that determines his existence, but on the contrary, his *social condition* that determines his conscience, is true only insofar as one considers the *human condition to be only as we are given it to live,* thus, "degraded." But all religious traditions insist on the fact that it is precisely up to man to deliver himself from this predetermination and this conditioning. Every tradition has its own method—an ascesis, a yoga—that helps man recover his true identity and pass from ignorance to knowledge, and from the state of conditioning and subjection to freedom.

Thirty years ago, in the conclusion to *Myth of the Eternal Return,* I wrote that Christianity is "the religion of fallen man" (a reflection that has not been very well understood, but that's another story . . .). I would add today that Marxism is "the philosophy of fallen man," the only one that exonerates him from his sins and justifies his resentments.

SEATTLE, *29 April*

I have come to give my lecture at the University of Washington on the "Myth of Alchemy." Professor Weber, whose guest I am, held a seminar last year on the symbolism of alchemy in English literature, and recommended as a reference work the paperback edition of *The Forge and the Crucible.* He tells me that the "problem of temporality" and thus that of the acceleration of time through the *opus alchymicum* literally captivated most of his students.

CHICAGO, *30 April*

This morning at the University of Washington, in Seattle, I held an hour-long seminar with Weber's students. Some of them asked me very pertinent questions, in particular those that referred to the alchemical interpretation of the great scientific discoveries of the seventeenth and eighteenth centuries, such as the circulation of blood, the laws of gravitation, etc.

3 May

I correct and complete the text of my interview dealing with initiation that is to appear in *Parabola,* and as usual I come up against the same difficulty. We live in an age of radical desacralization, where initiatory scenarios survive only in oneiric and artistic realms. But do they only survive there, and there alone? If one agrees with what I've called the "dialectic of the camouflaging of the sacred in the profane," one must also admit another possibility: The initiatory phenomenon could well be perpetuated in our time, before our eyes, but in other forms, so well camouflaged in the "profane" that it would be impossible for us to recognize them as such. All the same, to render this paradoxical situation intelligible, I'd have to develop considerably what I understand by "dialectic of the camouflaging of the sacred," and that would take a good sixty pages . . .

May

In the course of the last ten years I've read a good dozen or so books on Alexander of Macedonia, most of them excellent, particularly those by W. W. Tarn, F. Schachermeyr, F. Altheim, R. D. Milns, and R. L. Fox. I nevertheless believe that the story of the most enigmatic military genius the world has ever known, that of his person and his destiny, still remains to be written. Not that the works that have been devoted to him are without value, but much rather because none of the authors I've read so far present the "phenomenon" of Alexander in its totality.

Historians consider Alexander above all from the angle of the "historic personage," which he indeed was. Other scholars, in the dozens of very well documented studies and articles, have attempted to analyze and discuss the legends that are tied to his name, the dissemination of the *Roman d'Alexandre,* for example, or the different folkloric motifs that, in time, have crystalized around the hero/mythical character. But what Alexander really signified can only be understood when his life is viewed as a whole, the biography of the man needing to be completed by the myth he inspired. Just like that of Buddha or Muhammad, Alexander's destiny only appears in its true dimensions long after his death. To want to establish a distinction between the "history" and the "legend" of Alexander is perfectly chimerical. It is the inheritance of nineteenth-century historiography. The beliefs and legends born after the death of an exceptional character complete and bring new light to his specific role and its importance. Alexander himself wanted to be the image of Heracles or Dionysus. From the life of this illustrious conqueror, popular memory has retained *the exemplary history of a hero* who, not content to conquer the largest empire of antiquity, had indeed decided not to stop until he had reached the "limits of the Earth," so certain was he of finding there the secrets of eternal youth and the means of triumphing over death.

15 May

We go with Charlotte and Nathan Scott to Milwaukee, where we are the guests of Ihab Hasan. It takes us two hours to drive in a torrential downpour, so bad that once having reached our destination we don't even realize that Lake Michigan is only a stone's throw from our host's cottage.

In the course of our conversation we speak above all of the new tendencies in literary criticism. Hasan proves to be as interested as ever in religious symbolism, alchemy, and most especially in Gnosticism. The attraction the Gnosis holds for our contemporaries deserves to be analyzed at length, but differently than Eric Voegelein has done.

20 May

I wanted very much to reread what Julien Green had written in his *Journal* about the period that followed his return to Paris in September 1945. I had myself arrived in Paris at the same time, having preceded him by only a few days. As always happens when I read Julien Green, it was a good two hours before I abandoned the book. But how sad his Christianity seems to me, obsessed as he was by "sin," the "flesh," and other battles between "the flesh and the spirit"! This sometimes reminds me of Gnostic dualism and Manichaeanism. And yet, Julien Green is aware, for he says it on several occasions (but quite timidly out of fear of being contradicted by theologians), that all Christianity is summed up in these words of Jesus: "Be joyful, verily I say unto you, be joyful, for the kingdom of God is at hand!" In other words, and whatever the meaning of the expression "kingdom of God" may be, redemption is henceforth possible, and the Redeemer is among us. The flesh/spirit dualism, the devaluating of life and time, have never belonged, structurally speaking, to Christianity, which in this respect prolongs the Hebraic religious tradition.

25 May
  I wonder whether we shouldn't be more indulgent with respect to the political customs that reigned in Rumania in the nineteenth century, and which so greatly scandalized Hasdeu, Eminesco, or Iorga. All things considered, they were neither better nor worse than those which existed in other Eastern European countries, or even in the West. Here is what Saint-Simon wrote in a letter to his son: "My son, when a man is minister, hold the chamber pot for him. When he no longer is one, turn it over on his head."

28 May
  Dinner at Dr. E.P.'s house, with Mateï Calinescu and his family. Our doctor friend lives in a neighborhood of Chicago that I have not yet visited. Once again I realize how little I know of this city, and I recognize it without shame. Apart from the city's center (the Loop), the neighborhoods that surround the lake, the streets that lead to it, and the campus, this enormous city of more than eight million inhabitants holds no attraction for me. It is the major tragedy of American cities: They don't know how to age and never acquire that nobility shown by the patina of time. As for "ruins," one can see here only abandoned houses with broken windows awaiting the wrecking ball, or vacant lots disappearing under piles of trash, where other houses will be built, which in turn will be demolished ten years later.

2 June
  "Escape into a village to make it the center of the world" (*Journal*, 14 September 1895). Jules Renard's literary imagination sometimes caused him to rediscover traditional ideas or scenarios whose importance undoubtedly always escaped him.

5 June
  In one of his articles, Antoine Faivre cites a passage by Novalis concerning the "return home:" In *Heinrich von Ofterdingen,* the

pilgrim asks Cyané: "Well, where are we going?" And the latter replies, "We're still going home!" And in one of his *Hymns to the Night,* Novalis writes: "Weary of eternal voyages, let us go home to our father's house" (*Die Lust der Freude ging uns aus, zum Vater wollen nach Haus*). And Faivre rightly remarks: . . . the mine worker, "in his alchemical song seems to reply: Carried by (the sea) on its soft green wings, we return to the heart of the fatherland!"

The "return home" corresponds to the path towards the center and to the rediscovery of oneself. Universal literature is rich in completely analogous images and scenarios. The most famous example is that of the *Odyssey:* The long and difficult journey that Ulysses must accomplish before returning home constitutes an "initiatory trial."

WASHINGTON, *15 June*

Visit Kate and Edward Levi; a year ago he resigned his position as president of the University of Chicago to become the attorney general. Their house is superb, majestic. Behind it the yard is as vast as a park.

Evelyn and John Nef come to join us for dinner. Edward tells us that during press conferences at the White House the journalists' questions are sometimes so ferocious that one has the impression that the president is struggling in a veritable lion's den.

PARIS, *25 June*

Renan and modesty: "I've succeeded, I alone in my century, in understanding Jesus and St. Francis of Assisi" (*Recollections of My Youth*).

2 July

I reread, from a distance of twenty-five years, Gide's "Theseus." Superb prose, whose vivacity comes out through the facile irony of the first chapters. But there is nothing else. This "message," to which Gide attaches so much importance, contributes nothing. Writers continue to reinterpret in a more or less personal way the old clichés they've inherited from the Greeks through the voices of the Alexandrian scholars. Gide, as well as all those who have preceded him, derived his idea of the hero from the old mythology manuals, or from Plutarch. From the beginning, the new interpretation he gives of it is already altered by the very nature of the image he has of Theseus, which is that of classical poets and mythologists.

It is regrettable that Gide didn't bother to try to discover the true character of Theseus hidden behind these old clichés. He should have read, for example, *Couroï et Courètes* by Jeanmaire, where he would have learned the true meaning of Theseus' "jump" into the sea, the dance of the swans, the labyrinth, and the initiatory significance of certain notions such as the entrance into the labyrinth and the confrontation with the monster (the Minotaur).

All these episodes—the jump into the sea, the labyrinth, Ariadne, the Minotaur—which Gide reconsiders not without a certain irony, are in fact so many initiatory trials without which one could not attain the condition of hero. These are not notions introduced after the fact by exegetes and scholars, but rather are elements upon which the myth of Theseus itself is based. They belong to a cultural reality which, in *classical* Greece, had fallen into oblivion, or had been camouflaged. If it had been inspired by the primordial image of the hero such as it has been restored to us by certain contemporary scholars, Gide's "reinterpretation" could have been otherwise more profound and more original.

3 July

I do believe that it hasn't been so hot in Paris since 1946. I was living then at the Hôtel de Suède, and the nights were so stifling that I was unable to fall asleep, even after having taken care to wet the floor thoroughly. In complete despair, I had sprinkled my sheets with water and soaked my pajamas in the basin, and this had finally allowed me to fall asleep.

This torrid heat reminded me of that of certain summers in the Bucharest of my youth. In my room on Strada Melodiei, I worked entirely nude with a basin full of water next to me into which I plunged my head every fifteen minutes. Those dog days only ceased at nightfall.

I then went to walk along the boulevards, sometimes all the way to the other side of the city.

Curiously, the stifling heat of these last few days hasn't made me think of India, undoubtedly because it wasn't that humid, exhausting heat that gave one the impression of living in a steam bath. Perhaps also because in Calcutta the houses were constructed to serve in the tropical climate: very thick walls, windows fitted with shutters, next to big trees providing shade . . .

6 July

Visit from Dr. Bratesco, historian of medicine and author of an excellent monograph on Hippocrates and his doctrine. He came accompanied by his wife, whose face reminds me of someone. And with good reason, because she is Anna Pauker's own daughter. Both of them have read *The Old Man and the Bureaucrats*. "But how did you manage," they ask me, "to be so precise in the details?" I told them that the whole story was the fruit of my imagination, and that I had created it as I went along. But apparently they didn't believe me.

PUERTO DE ANDRAITX, *8 July*

We arrived yesterday. We are staying in the villa Sibylle rented.

11 July

The strange pains Sibylle is having worry and sadden us, especially those she feels on her right side. The Paris doctors may well tell us that they are only rheumatic pains; we are not reassured.

20 July

I draft the chapter on the origins of Christianity, or more exactly, I rework, polish, and condense what I wrote before leaving Chicago.

This brings back quite a few memories, those of long ago when I was reading Renan's *Les origines du christianisme. La Vie de Jésus* had not particularly interested me, but *L'Antéchrist,* on the other hand, was fascinating. At that same time, the first book by Paul-Louis Couchoud had been a discovery for me, not to mention many other books, very mediocre for the most part, on the "myth of Christ," or the "enigma of the Essenes." But in the last ten or fifteen years, since the Qumran manuscripts have begun to be deciphered and translated, we have realized that the Essenes, despite their affinities with the first Christian communities, could all the same not be connected to them—far from it.

25 July

I have just received an article from Paris entitled "Une nouvelle Légende des Siècles." It is the one that Georges Dumézil devoted in *Le Monde* to *A History of Religious Ideas,* volume 1. I find it admirable, and whatever the reaction of other specialists may be, Georges Dumézil's support is more than enough for me. I now know that I have not been on the wrong track.

I already owed the success of *Patterns* to Georges Dumézil, thanks to the preface he wrote in 1948. I am also grateful to him for having invited me in 1945 to give courses at the Ecole des Hautes Etudes, and for having put me in contact with Brice Parrain, with whom there was no delay in seeing *Techniques du yoga* published in the collection *Montagne Sainte-Geneviève.*

30 July

Sibylle continues to suffer, although the tests, according to the doctors, show nothing to worry about.

PARIS, 5 August

We returned yesterday from the Balearic Islands. I spent the whole day correcting and transcribing the final pages of my chapter on the origins of Christianity.

Who could have guessed the consequences of the endless postponement of the Parousia. The second coming of Christ, in all his glory that time, as had been announced by the apostles, did not come about. This didn't prevent Christianity from spreading, since for the believers the

Kingdom of Heaven was already of this world because the church was already present in it, and with the church the mystical body of Christ. Because of this, the Kingdom of Heaven appeared clearly only to those believers whose faith was the most authentic and the most fecund. For all others, especially for the Jews and the pagans, the fact that the Christian community and its church in no way resembled the Kingdom of Heaven reinforced them in their conviction that they were not dealing with a *transfigured* human society.

Christianity was hardly born when the sacred was already being camouflaged, for sacrality was only perceived by believers, just as earlier the divine nature of Christ was evident only to Christians. The process of the desacralization of the world, of life, and of history, which triumphs today is due above all to our inability to grasp the mystery of the camouflaging of the sacred in the profane.

10 August

D. Tsepeneag informs me of what Marin Preda told him about those uprooted peasants who leave their village to go look for work in the city. Their entire system of values crumbles. They no longer believe in anything, except for the little schemes and illicit arrangements likely to hasten their success. All feeling of solidarity with the rest of the community, let alone national solidarity, disappears. The peasant transplanted to the city becomes not an egoist, but an egocentric, and this misfortune takes on proportions that would have been unimaginable in our grandparents' time.

Preda concludes from this that the only model, the only source of inspiration and spiritual creativity, was the *village,* which formed a microcosm of norms, customs, and behavior in which everyone found his place, first as a child, then as a young man, then as a father, and finally as an old man.

Such a situation can be compared with what happens, in a much more dramatic way, however, when an archaic society is confronted with our own cultural system. An example of this is found in the Bororo, a tribe of the Mato Grosso, whose huts were grouped in a circle around the space reserved for ritual dances. The circle itself was divided into four sectors by the two axes, one north-south, the other east-west, that cut through it. The entire social and religious life of the tribe was organized around this system of orientation and organic division of the land. But the Salesian missionaries, in their desire to improve the living conditions of the natives, constructed new villages for them along an axis on each side of which were aligned two rows of rectangular boxes.

Torn from the cosmology and the sociology of which the traditional village and its circular structure were the vectors, it didn't take long for the Bororo Indians to lose their identity, to believe everything the missionaries told them, and in the end to no longer believe in anything.

20 August

I have just finished a story today that I wrote in about ten days entitled *Les Trois Grâces*. The day before the eve of our departure from Puerto, I noticed at the bend in a path where I was walking for the first time a group of three villas that were connected in a discrete and unusual way. They were called "the Three Graces." I had stopped to look at them better when a black dog ran up and began to bark furiously.

Back home I already had the plot of a story in my head, or the beginning of one, at least. I thought of the rest of it after having written the first ten or fifteen pages.

CAIRO, *5 September*

We arrived at nine o'clock in the evening. We had left Paris at noon with Simone and Paul Ricoeur, changed planes in Rome, and stopped briefly in Athens. As we get out of the plane, the heat overwhelms us, and in addition, the airport is packed with people. Luckily, Omar, our guide, quickly comes to get us. We give him our passports, and he manages to get us through customs rapidly. He is a slender young man, good-looking, very nice, and speaks English and French perfectly. He takes us to the Hilton in a minibus along with the rest of our group, which includes five couples: a Belgian doctor and his wife; a young French couple on their honeymoon; a businessman and his wife, Belgian as well.

In the hotel lobby Omar reminds us of our itinerary for the next day: Our plane for Aswan leaves at seven in the morning. We must therefore get up at a quarter to four . . .

ASWAN, *6 September*

I didn't shut my eyes all night. From the window of our room on the eighteenth floor of the hotel I spent a long time contemplating the Nile. I had seen it for the first time, awestruck, on a December morning in 1928, from the window of the third-class train car that was bringing me from Alexandria.

Omar drives us by bus to the airport, which is just as crowded as ever even though it is only six in the morning. As we land in Aswan, fatigue hits me like a brick. Luckily, the New Cataract Hotel is quite close. From the balcony of our room on the tenth floor we can see the hotel garden and the inevitable swimming pool. To our right we see the Nile and Elephantine Island, and farther, on the hill, the pink marble mausoleum of the Aga Khan.

After lunch and a little rest, I go down to have a closer look at the trees and flowers in the garden of our hotel. In the afternoon, at five o'clock, a boat ride on the Nile. We dock in a Nubian village of Sehel Island. Of course this is part of our tourist itinerary, as is our being invited to take mint tea in the house considered to be the most picturesque in the village. It is here that we will attend a performance of songs and dances with which we will pretend to be enchanted.

And after all, why be so picky? It would be ridiculous. Tourism is an integral part of today's civilization, just as are television, hi-fis, or paperback books. Moreover, travelers a hundred or two hundred years ago were already attending performances in many ways identical to the one this evening, a bit more authentic, perhaps. It would be interesting to compare the tales of the first European travelers in Egypt, such as Greffin Affagart in the sixteenth century, to those of Chateaubriand, Gérard de Nerval, and Flaubert, and to compare all of those to current accounts. I would wager that there is no break in the continuity of the different stories. It is not so much the content of the itineraries that has changed as their *raison d'être:* The songs and dances were part of a welcoming *rite* in honor of visitors, whereas today they only aim to amuse tourists.

ASWAN, *7 September*

Excursion on camelback first, then on donkeyback, to the monastery of Saint Simeon, which has been abandoned but is surprisingly well preserved. The monks left it when water started to become scarce. Fatehpur-Sikhri, in the Mongolian Indies, suffered the same fate. We then visit the tombs of Egyptian dignitaries.

From the balcony of our room I contemplate Elephantine Island with a sort of fascination. It was on this island that the military settlers from Judaea were garrisoned in the fourth century B.C. Their mission was to defend the Egyptian border against incursions by Nubian nomads. The dryness of the climate preserved certain documents thanks to which the religious beliefs of the Judeo-Aramaeans are known to us today. Once the ties that connected it to the Center, that is, to Jerusalem and its Temple, were slackened, the monotheism proclaimed by Moses degenerated into a syncretic religion: In addition to Yahweh the Jews of Elephantine worshipped a god of harvest and a god of fertility . . .

The religious life of the Jews of Israel and of Judaea would have probably evolved similarly if the Temple and the Prophets hadn't been present, and especially if the terror of History, from Nebuchadnezzar to Titus and Vespasian, had not been inflicted on them.

ASWAN, *8 September*

In the morning, boat ride around Elephantine Island; in the afternoon, visit to the mausoleum of the Aga Khan. The very arid climate agreed with the rheumatism from which he suffered, and eased his pain. On his actual tomb there is a single flower, the rose his widow places on it each morning. Then we go visit the botanical gardens below Kitchener Island, between the rows of superb royal palms several tens of meters high.

The fascination still exercised by Egypt, or more precisely by Egyptian "mysteries" and Egyptian "wisdom," is characteristic of a certain mind set, and must also be attributed to the great creations of Egyptian civilization. It has multiple causes, the principal one being the ancientness of the civilization and its apparently unchanging character. The Greeks, who were completely oblivious to the Sumerians, saw in Egypt the earliest of all civilizations, the one closest to the gods and which conformed best to the divine model. The permanence of forms, maintained throughout so many centuries, proclaimed their perfection. Such reasoning was, moreover, perfectly justified, for from the Egyptians' religious point of view, but also compared to archaic thought, it was *in origins* that perfection was found, and to better appeal to perfection one had at all costs to copy the models that were born of it. The Greeks thought that the Egyptians had succeeded in conserving "primordial wisdom." Later, in the Hellenistic period, saving virtues were attributed to this "wisdom": The Mysteries of Isis and Osiris assured the redemption of the initiated.

But the fascination exercised by Egyptian civilization is attributable to many other things: The Pyramids, so imposing a presence and so mysterious, divinities with heads of animals, and hieroglyphics, too, with their "magical" and enigmatic characteristics, have contributed in no small way.

ABU SIMBEL, *9 September*

Awake at five o'clock. At six there is already quite a bit of animation on the docks of the Nile. A bus takes us to the airport, where we are subjected to a rigorous security check. Could they suspect us of transporting weapons or explosives? After a half-hour flight we land in Abu Simbel. Trees and flower beds surround the airport, but hardly a few hundred meters away we already see the rocky expanse of desert. In less than ten minutes a bus takes us to the outskirts of the temple of Ramses II.

I haven't the words to describe this gigantic edifice with its four colossal statues, each one twenty-seven meters tall, cut out of the sandstone cliff, which guard the entrance to the sanctuary. The impression it creates is all the more extraordinary since we well know that the hill, the temple carved from it, and the four giant statues of

Ramses were still located, only two or three years ago, a hundred meters farther down and some hundred meters farther away, in the place where the immense artificial sheet of water, Lake Nasser, currently extends. It didn't matter that we had been adequately warned; our surprise at seeing it is no less intense. Our guide reminds us that the original cliff was cut into 760 blocks, each of around twenty tons. The blocks, numbered and protected by straw, were hoisted to the height where the whole temple was reconstructed. Quite a feat when one considers that the famous ray of sun that each year penetrated into the sanctuary and lit up the god's face continues to do so even today, at the same hour and the same date.

We then go to have a look, insofar as it is permitted to do so, at the Aswan High Dam. The huge lake extends over the horizon. I can't remember how many millions of cubic meters of water are retained by the dam. It is still true, Omar tells us, that each morning ten tons of fish are taken from the water which, due to the lack of means of refrigeration, cannot be sent to Cairo.

The sixty thousand Nubians who lived in the thirty-three villages that are now submerged had to be relocated. Cubical boxes were constructed for them, built all in a row. They are, it is said, very comfortable, and all include showers and kitchens. But they are also desolately banal and barren of the ornaments, and especially the colors, that were the charm of the traditional dwellings. In addition, the livestock and the camels of the inhabitants are now kept all together outside the village, whereas it was customary for the Nubians to keep their camels *in their homes*.

Ride on Lake Nasser aboard an old motorboat. We go along a rocky coast from the heights of which a vulture occasionally takes flight. What poet will ever recall the villages and the palm groves of this corner of Nubia now drowned under the waters of the lake? Five million palm trees, so it would seem, have been swallowed up.

We land on a dike that protects a little expanse of land where we can see construction in progress. Inattentive to the guide's explanations, I prefer to look at, less than a kilometer away, the columns of the temples on Philae Island, it, too, covered by water. We are assured that some of these temples, most of which date from the Ptolemies and the Roman period, will be saved.

10 September

Our boat left this morning at four-thirty. We come out of our cabins two hours later. The right bank of the Nile is covered with palm trees and sugar plantations. When we stop at Kawm Umbū, our boat is assailed by a cloud of little vendors of "exotic souvenirs." They remind me of their brothers at the ports of Ceylon or India, where I encountered them for the first time. I'm not troubled by these sudden returns into the past. Quite the contrary; there is not a trace of melancholy in me, but much rather a savoring of rediscovered youth.

The first temple we visit on this trip is rather original in its genre. Located on a hill overlooking the Nile, it was reconstructed in the Ptolemaic period on the ruins of a more ancient sanctuary. Since it was dedicated to two divinities, Sebek, with the crocodile head, and Horus, it is really two temples in one. It has two sanctuaries, and two galleries that each lead to a different entrance. Of the frescoes that decorate it, I remember those that represent the ruler offering up a sacrifice to the two divinities, the calendar of festivals, and surgical instruments. In the hypostyle room, the most remarkable frescoes are those in which one sees Ptolemy Euergetes represented as a god, purified by priests, and the coronation ceremony where the pharaoh is offered the double crown symbolizing Upper and Lower Egypt. Also of note is the fresco representing Ptolemy's family which seems to be returning from an ecstatic voyage. Certain figures have been mutilated by Christian Copts.

Back at the boat landing we notice among the multitude of children crying *Bakchich! Bakchich!* a little girl carrying a black lamb in her arms, and a little boy who is standing up on a small donkey.

Our boat slowly goes down the river to Idfū. Immediately upon landing, we are driven to the temple in old wobbling barouches which are surprisingly decorated. The temple of Idfū was already rather familiar to me, for a number of photographic studies and monographs have been devoted to it. Indeed, in itself it exudes the essence of Egyptian religion, and especially of the mythology and the cult of Horus. Its construction, under the Ptolemies, took close to two centuries. Only the temple of Karnak surpasses it in grandeur, and it is most fortunately very well preserved. If I had come to know it as I have today, that is, in a way other than by photographs or books, I would not have changed anything in the paragraphs of *A History,* Volume 1, devoted to Osiris, Horus, and Seth, but I would have perhaps expressed myself more poetically.

Our boat leaves again at five-thirty, and I remain on deck waiting for the sunset. This time, I can't help thinking about my youthful excursions on the Ganges.

I note down some of the thoughts that have been pursuing me in the last five days. "Egyptomania," which flourished in the Hellenistic period, was rediscovered and triumphed in the Italian Renaissance. After Marsilio Ficino, at the request of Cosimo de' Medici, had translated the *Corpus hermeticum* into Latin, the Egyptian "mysteries" doubled in prestige, whence the conviction that Egypt was the source of a "doctrine of salvation," whatever that might have been. It was there, one believed, that Moses, Zarathustra, and Plato had found their inspiration. Francis Yates has admirably brought to light the role played by Hermeticism, whose Egyptian origin was considered a given during the Renaissance and during the period that followed it, when "Egyptomania" was most widespread. The importance of such a belief, that is, that the Hermetic tradition is both universal and very ancient, has not yet been well understood by contemporary historians. In fact, we find ourselves faced with a "deprovincialism" of Western Christianity that is infinitely more radical than that which was attempted, more or less openly, during the Italian Renaissance.

After the great scholar Isaac Casaubon had shown in 1614 that the texts assembled in the *Corpus hermeticum* had in fact been written for the most part at the beginning of the Christian era, it was understandable that Egyptomania lost some of its appeal. But the obsession with Egypt persisted nonetheless, for some claimed that authentic Egyptian "mysteries" were found not in the *Corpus hermeticum,* a collection of Greek texts, but occulted and enciphered in Egyptian plastic art and iconography, and most especially in hieroglyphics. From the sixteenth to the eighteenth century numerous works, admirably illustrated, were devoted to the "secrets" and the "symbols" of Egyptian architecture and iconography. This vogue, so scorned by Egyptologists, has nevertheless strongly contributed to instilling new vigor into the creative, "mythologizing" imagination of the elite of Western Europe.

LUXOR, *11 September*

 Yesterday we attended the performance of a play entitled "The Village Mayor and his Barber," an excellent production of *karagheuz* put on by the ship's company.

 Isnā. We had to get up at six-thirty in order to visit as early as possible the temple dedicated to Khnum, the god in the form of a ram wearing a crown between his horns. I had already seen statues and bas-reliefs representing this god in quite a few museums. What interests me about him is that he is a cosmogonic god. By working with clay on a potter's wheel, he created the egg whence were born both the world and man. My attention is drawn to certain scenes that I intend to examine in more detail in photographs and reproductions I'll be able to find in Chicago: the dance of the priest before the goddess, and the visit of Septimius Severus and his wife Julia Domna.

 The wall that surrounded the temple and its exterior corridor served as a rock quarry at the time of the construction of the city (Isnā today has thirty-five thousand inhabitants). We leave at nine-thirty and arrive at the locks shortly afterwards.

 Admirable Paul Ricoeur! He cannot go without a newspaper, and yet he doesn't seem in the least affected by the news he reads in them! I imagine he can easily go back to work, as if nothing were wrong, just an hour after having finished reading one. To him better than to anyone else applies Hegel's famous maxim: "It is by reading his morning paper that the reader communes with the Universal Spirit." That morning Paul seemed worried, preoccupied, even sad, for it had been impossible for him, either on board or on the quays of the port, to get his hands on any newspaper in any of the languages he knows. He then left with a determined step towards the bazaar, and came back a half hour later calmed down. He had finally found what he was looking for: a local newspaper, written in Arabic, of course, but whose last page included a summary of the latest news in French.

Stop in Luxor. Two kilometers from the river a car lets us out near the ruins of what was once the southern part of the fabulous city of Thebes. They extend over a considerable area.

We go through the passage of the sphinxes, in the form of rams, which led to Karnak, to the north of Thebes. After having visited the great temple of Amon, I close my notebook and put it in my pocket. I find it useless to note down names, dates, legends. Of all our excursions today through the monuments and ruins of Luxor and Karnak, the only memory I really want to keep is that of the sensation I felt upon entering into the hypostyle rooms, with their giant papyrus columns that support the ceiling, and that mysterious light that comes down from openings overhead. What an extraordinary experience for a young poet, a historian, or a philosopher! For it is especially the task of the young to create something entirely new from the beauty offered to us, emanating everywhere in this admirable valley of the Nile.

Purely historical givens are powerless to stimulate the imagination, or even the thoughts, of our contemporaries. Who among us will remember that the temple of Amon was built under the orders of Amenhotep III or of Ramses II? That is only of interest to historians. Luxor and Karnak remain irreplaceable as *works of the spirit,* and no didactic prose can portray this. Perhaps one day we'll be able to really "see" them, otherwise than with the eyes of tourists. May a film maker of genius someday show us the temples and the hypostyle rooms such as we've actually *seen* them today!

LUXOR, *12 September*

The day spent visiting the Valley of the Kings on the left bank of the Nile. It was at one time the necropolis of Thebes. Of course we went to see the tomb of Tutankhamen, but I especially admired the three terraces carved out of rock, in the form of an amphitheatre, of the temple of Dayr al-Bahri, a funerary monument built by Senmout, the most brilliant architect of ancient Egypt, the favorite and the protégé of Queen Hatshepsut.

. . . And I see myself once again in the little room of my childhood. To the left of my work table, mounted on the wall with thumbtacks, was a passable reproduction of the bas-reliefs of the temple of Dayr al-Bahri. Queen Hatshepsut was one of the passions of my adolescence. I would like to be able to reread the article I wrote on her at that time for a popular journal. I had compiled it from the voluminous works of Gaston Maspero and Ed. Meyer on the history of the ancient Orient, and especially after being inspired by one of the chapters in the book by Alexander Moret, *Rois et dieux d'Egypte*. If Queen Hatshepsut fascinated me to such a degree, it was because she had had the courage to instigate a new politics of cultural and commercial expansion, thus breaking with her predecessors' warring politics of conquest, but it was also due to her exceptional destiny. For twenty-two years she had managed to maintain her nephew and son-in-law, Thutmose III, in the shadows, and he was thereby a ruler in name only. The queen governed as a man, and had herself represented on monuments as the incarnation of Osiris, and thus with the false pointed beard characteristic of that god. How tragic was her destiny! Immediately following her death the scrolls where her name had been engraved were erased, and Thutmose's name was inscribed in her place. And two weeks hadn't gone by before the new pharoah, at the head of his army, left to invade Syria and Palestine to quell "rebellion" there. The battle of Megiddo, whose famous fresco I saw yesterday in Luxor, assured his victory, and it is thus that Egypt became "imperialist."

All these characters, their destinies, their conflicts, can be described as Shakespearian, for, in addition to Senmout, that architect of genius, the queen's entourage was comprised of exceptional personalities, beginning with Hapouseneb, who was both prime minister and priest of the god Amon. I wonder why this era, which was at a veritable turning point in history, has not yet inspired any great novelist, Thomas Mann, for example, or any great playwright or poet . . .

At the end of the afternoon we disembark and go to stay at the New Winter Hotel. I remain for a long time in the garden. Omar remembers that as a child he came here to spend the winter with his parents.

LUXOR, *13 September*

Last evening, Sound and Light Show at Karnak. Extraordinary. I can't describe our surprise and our admiration when the first monuments were lit up in the night. One would have said they were emerging from the chaos.

All day long today excursion to Dandarah, whose temple to the goddess Hathor is surprisingly well preserved, and to Abydos, which was the city of Osiris *par excellence*. Wasn't it there, according to the ancient Egyptians, that the head of the god had been buried? It was also in Abydos that were celebrated the famous "mysteries of Osiris," which after more than twenty centuries still obsess European religious thought. I wonder who could have been the last initiate to these archaic, authentically Egyptian mysteries, which preceded the Greco-Egyptian mysteries of Isis and Osiris. This theme has undoubtedly inspired a poet such as Cavafy, but I wonder what a Saint-John Perse could have said about it, if he hadn't been suspicious of "religion," or a Paul Claudel, if he hadn't refused to find his religious inspiration elsewhere than in the Bible.

CAIRO, *14 September*

Arrived this morning; we went to the same hotel as before, the Nile Hilton.

In the afternoon I try to decipher and transcribe the notes I jotted down from day to day in my notebook, then I reread what I wrote on the fascination Egypt has exercised since Herodotus and Plato up to the present, and on the "Egyptomania" that reigned throughout the Renaissance, and even afterwards. Logically, the "demystification" of the *Corpus hermeticum* by Isaac Casaubon having not succeeded in arresting the vogue of Hermeticism, one might think at least that the deciphering of the hieroglyphics would have put an end to speculation on the "mysteries" of Egypt. Nothing of the kind occurred. Certainly, Egyptology became an autonomous discipline, just as did philology, archeology, and historiography, which were connected to it. The cultivated public showed increased interest in the popular works that were written. Egyptian civilization, such as it appeared in the books written by those who were discovering and trying to understand it, couldn't solicit sufficient admiration to inhibit a return to "secrets" and other "mysteries," for the illusion persisted nonetheless. Even after Champollion those who continued to believe in the occult significance of hieroglyphics were numerous. They claimed, among other things, that the hieroglyphics' message, as deciphered by Egyptologists, was only an apparent, superficial one, comparable to the literal and immediate meaning of the text of the Bible. Similarly, the "mystery" of the Pyramids and the Egyptian temples have never ceased to titillate the imagination of Westerners. The mathematical calculations implied in the construction of the Pyramids proved that Egyptian science had surpassed not only Pythagoras, but even Galileo and Newton. Such assertions were not just made by "occultists" and adherents to the sensational alone, for from time to time relatively serious authors took them up, as well. I will limit myself to citing in this regard the success obtained around 1925 by the book written by the Abbé Moreux, *Les Mystères des Pyramides*.

The discovery of the tomb of Tutankhamen, perhaps the only one not to have been violated, and the strange deaths that followed, only helped to reignite the debate, especially among journalists, for whom the sensational side of the event was a true godsend. And an identical scenario was to be reproduced about forty years later, when an eminent French archeologist and Egyptologist, Varille, succeeded in breaking the "secret" of the Egyptian temples and monuments, discovering that for each new construction the Egyptians used as a cornerstone a more ancient element originating from an older edifice. This stone was the "seed" out of which the new monument could grow, an idea that was, moreover, perfectly justifiable. Varille indeed published several prelim- inary studies, but he didn't have time to write his in-depth work based on the detailed analysis of the immense material he had assembled over fifteen years of excavations in the Valley of the Kings, for in 1955 he died in France following an automobile accident. It is said that, since he did not die immediately, he had time to reveal why, at the wheel of his car, he felt compelled to swerve suddenly, which caused him to lose control and slam right into a tree: He apparently had seen, standing in the road and blocking it, a giant scarab . . .

CAIRO, *15 September*

This morning, visit to the National Museum of Antiquities, located right next to our hotel. I write note after note in my book, but I wonder whether I will ever have the time to reread them.

We walked all afternoon around the old city. Only melancholy in this beautiful Ben Ezra synagogue, and how admirable are these Coptic churches! One has only to walk down these narrow streets shaded by a few trees, and between these walls where the light filters through, to fully rediscover a medieval Orient. The memory of my discovery of this same neighborhood fifty years earlier resurfaces, and I experience an intense, indescribable emotion.

CAIRO, *16 September*

A full morning, as the tourists say. Rapid visit to Memphis, where there is hardly anything left but the Sphinx and the immense statue of Ramses II, then to Saqqārah, the necropolis of ancient Thebes, with its Step Pyramid, erected by Imhotep, that other genius of Egyptian art, by order of Pharaoh Djoser at the beginning of the third millennium. Very young, I was already taken with Imhotep who, besides his functions as prime minister, was also an architect as bold as he was original, as is proven by the way in which he erected the Step Pyramid. He was most probably also highly literate and a great scholar, for tradition has it that he was the author of certain philosophical works. The fact remains that his memory was honored for a long time by scribes, even those of the Saitic period who in the seventh century B.C.

proclaimed him a thaumaturgic god and worshipped him in different forms. Certain Greeks even compared him to Aesculapius. It is truly a pity that his statue, which is in the Louvre, is so ugly.

Innumerable *mastabas,* which served as sepulchers for nobles, were built all around the Pyramids, which sheltered and protected the royal tomb. At Chicago in one of my courses I spoke of this solidarity that unified even in the tomb the pharaoh and the nobility.

We finally reach the plateau of Gizeh where stand the three famous pyramids of the three no less famous pharaohs whose names I've known since my first year at the lycée: Khufu, Khafre, and Menkaure. Seeing them again after fifty years, I believe the best description that has ever been given of them, at least in my opinion, is still the one by Flaubert, which I took care to copy down before my departure from Paris: "They have this peculiarity, these mighty Pyramids, that the more one sees them the bigger they seem . . . At fifty feet each stone doesn't seem any more considerable than a paving stone. You approach it, and each paving stone is eight feet high and as many wide. But when one climbs on top, and has reached the middle, it becomes enormous. Up above, one is completely stupefied" (Letter to Louis Bouilhet, 15 January 1850).

CAIRO, *17 September*

I had maintained a rather precise recollection of the citadel of Saladin and of the mosque of the Sultan Hassan, with its superbly beautiful interior court. I saw both of them again this morning.

Then we went to walk around the bazaar of Kan el-Khadili, which was by far what I remembered best of all that I had seen in Cairo years ago. But the automobile traffic and the noise have become infernal.

A few weeks earlier in Paris, while rereading Flaubert's letters written during his voyage in Egypt, I had had the impression that the spectacle offered by the streets of Cairo and the atmosphere that reigned there in December 1928 didn't differ essentially from what Flaubert himself had seen in 1849–1850, at least not in what he himself calls the grotesque element: "All the old comic business of the cudgeled slave, of the coarse trafficker in women, of the thieving merchant—it's all very fresh here, very genuine and charming" (letter to Louis Bouilhet, 1 December 1849).

This visit I haven't had time to take long walks in the streets of Cairo, but I have every reason to believe that the city I knew fifty years ago belongs to a completed past. Who would be surprised by this? Cairo has become a sprawling metropolis with immense slums where several million individuals from all over have come to live packed closely together. Some have chosen to live in the cemeteries, between the tombstones.

CAIRO, *18 September*
        We went this morning to see the National Museum of Antiquities again.

I stay in the hotel and spend the whole afternoon going through the file I brought from Paris. I won't resist the temptation to transcribe here a passage from the *Corpus hermeticum:* ". . . there will come a time when it will be seen that in vain have the Egyptians honoured the deity with heartfelt piety and assiduous service; and all our holy worship will be found fruitless and ineffectual. For the gods will return from earth to heaven; Egypt will be forsaken, and the land which was once the home of religion will be left desolate, bereft of the presence of its deities. This land and region will be filled with foreigners; not only will men neglect the service of the gods, but what is harder still, there will be enacted so-called laws by which religion and piety and worship of the gods will be forbidden, and a penalty prescribed. In that day will our most holy land, this land of shrines and temples, be filled with funerals and corpses. O Egypt, Egypt, of thy religion nothing will remain but an empty tale, which thine own children in time to come will not believe; nothing will be left but graven words and only the stones will tell of thy piety . . . and Egypt will be occupied by

Scythians or Indians, or by some such race from the barbarian countries thereabout."[1]

The least one can say is that this prophecy has come to pass. The fascination exercised by ancient Egypt, its "mysteries," its "initiatory wisdom," has been no less perpetuated into our Western societies. One might even believe that "another" Egypt, one issued from a mythologizing imagination, was recreated and continues to stimulate the oneiric and poetic creations of Westerners.

PARIS, *19 September*

Last evening we attended a sound and light show at the foot of the Pyramids, before going to have dinner under an immense canvas tent. It was in a way an "evening of farewell in the desert."

Arrived in Paris in the early evening. We already know, from our telephone conversation of the day before yesterday, that Sibylle's pain is caused by a metastasis. But we want to keep hoping, nonetheless.

September

22 September: in Amsterdam with Sorin and Liliane. 23 September: excursion to Edam. 24 September: return to Paris. 26–27 September: We do whatever we can to save Ben Corlaciu, who has been on a hunger strike for three weeks so that his wife and children will be authorized to leave Rumania. In addition I must compile my bibliography for the *Cahiers de l'Herne*. 27 September: dinner at Eugène Ionesco's with Stephan Doïnas and his wife. 30 September: I finish the bibliography. In the evening, dinner with Ioan Culianu.

10 October

We decide to stay in Paris to be with Sibylle.

The Belgian Royal Academy of French Language and Literature honored me by electing me one of their members. I will occupy Marthe

---

1. Walter Scott, ed. and trans., *Hermetica: The Ancient Greek and Latin Writings Which Contain Religious or Philosophic Teachings Ascribed to Hermes Trismegistus.* Boston: Shambhala Publications, 1985. Eliade transcribed the French translation of R. P. Festugiere (*Fragments d'un journal II*, p. 300)—TRANS.

Bibesco's seat. For some time I've been trying to read all I can find by this novelist, author of the admirable *Izvor, le pays des saules.*

October

I've read *La vie d'une amitié,* annotated correspondence between Marthe Bibesco and the Abbé Mugnier. The most interesting letters are those from Marthe Bibesco, and yet I had heard so much about that extraordinary Abbé Mugnier! Marthe Bibesco was endowed with a prodigious memory. In addition, all the kings, all the dignitaries, all the monsignors, dukes, princes, famous writers, men of state, and scholars who lived after 1900 were among her friends or her acquaintances. How extraordinary would be the biography entitled *Marthe Bibesco and Her Contemporaries!* The most uninteresting passages are, however, those in which she deals with genealogy, hers of course, but also those of her friends. One senses she was almost frightened at the idea of being a Bibesco, and at knowing that so much blue blood flowed in her veins.

The fact remains that she is a very good writer, and in *Izvor* she gives an excellent representation of the peasant world.

October

Passing in front of a little bookstore, I stop to look at the titles of new paperback books. Why did I suddenly want to buy *Salammbô* in the Garnier-Flammarion edition? The reason for this is perhaps that I hadn't reread it since the lycée, fifty-five years ago. As soon as I was holding the book I felt myself transported back to that summer of 1921 or 1922, and I saw myself climbing into a third-class train car to Constantsa. The heat was devastating. I was going to the summer home in the Baragan, in Sighireni, to be exact, owned by the family of my friend Dinu Sighireanu. He had written me letter upon letter asking me to come spend a week with him, and I had decided to go on the spur of the moment.

While I was lingering on the threshold of that bookstore, a few steps away from the Montmartre funicular railway, I suddenly felt myself plunged back into the atmosphere of that third-class car, with its heat, its dust, even its smells. My nostrils were suddenly filled with the aroma of melons, nougat, chilled drinks, and other diverse and strange smells. I had taken several books with me, but I took *Salammbô* out of my bag. I still see its blue cloth cover. It was, I believe, an edition printed in Germany, right after the war. I had brought this novel on purpose; no one was to ignore the fact that I was already capable of reading a French book in the original . . .

I saw myself seated on the bench in my compartment next to an old man with a gold snuffbox, a student from an institute of sericulture, and a soldier who was looking out the window, his elbows leaning on the door.

The day after my arrival in Sighireni, one of Dinu's two sisters, both of them former students of Notre-Dame-de-Sion, asked me how many times I had reread the first sentence of *Salammbô*. I turned beet red, thinking she doubted my knowledge of French, which was quite modest at the time.

"Only once!" I replied vigorously, believing I was suspected of not having understood everything upon the first reading.

"Only once!" she exclaimed. She then closed her eyes and recited without hesitation: "It was in Mégara, a suburb of Carthage, in the gardens of Hamilcar." "If you don't know that sentence by heart, if you didn't feel like repeating it at least five or six times in a row to yourself alone, then you understand nothing of Flaubert. You'd do better to read something else!"

23 October

While rereading *Itinéraire de Paris à Jérusalem*, I come across a historical point that I had long since forgotten. It concerns the Parthenon. Until 1687, the monument was still more or less intact. Father Balin, a Jesuit, who wrote down his impressions during his travels in 1672, had noticed this a few years earlier. I vaguely remembered that the propylaea and the temple of Athena had been destroyed by Venetian artillery, but I had forgotten under what circumstances. Chateaubriand wrote: "A bomb falls on this latter edifice, breaks open the vault, sets fire to barrels of powder, and blows up in part an edifice that honored less the false gods of the Greeks than the genius of man.''

Let us regret in passing Chateaubriand's narrow-mindedness concerning religion manifesting itself in such an inopportune way! To which Greeks were the gods ''false''? But the rest of the passage deserves to be contemplated and retained. Morosini, who ''with the aim of embellishing Venice with the debris of Athens wants to pull down the statues from the Parthenon's facade and smash them . . . ''; Lord Elgin, who, while taking down the bas-reliefs of the frieze, mutilates the entire facade . . .

26 October

Through Cioran I learn that Raymond Queneau has just died. We had met again last autumn at Editions de l'Herne, where he had come to submit material for the *Cahier* that was being prepared on him. He was as I had always known him, a little sadder, perhaps, and more melancholy. He admitted to me that day that he had twice reread *Fragments d'un journal* from cover to cover.

Certain memories resurface, among others that of my emotion the day he proposed I write the introduction to the three volumes of *Histoire des littératures* in the Pleiade collection. My French ''career'' was only just beginning then, and yet it was I who was the lucky one, whereas he could have chosen from among dozens of writers who were just as competent. Or yet that unforgettable scene that was played out in his office. With an unfortunate gesture of my arm I had knocked over the inkwell he had in front of him. The ink immediately spread over all the pages of a file he had just opened. Feeling terrible, I didn't know where to stand, but my crestfallen look was able to amuse Queneau. He smiled dreamily, all the while agilely wiping up the ink that had spread from one end of his desk to the other. I watched him do it, my handkerchief in my hand, not even daring to extend my arm to help him sponge up that black pool from which I could not move my eyes.

He did not seem angry for all that, although not one of his papers had been spared. Later, I told myself that he wasn't displeased at being shocked, and that the absurd and the unusual must remind him of his past as a poet and a surrealist.

October

8 March 1936, Marthe Bibesco wrote to the Abbé Mugnier: "Petworth is so large that the legend was born in the region of the chambermaid employed to close the curtains at nightfall, and to open them the next day, and whose work never ceased! She is the Danaides of shadow and light."

This legend, if it is authentic, is a telling example of mythological creation in England between the sixteenth and the eighteenth century. Since no description could more concretely portray the immensity of such a construction, the popular imagination borrowed the language and scenario of tales.

7 November

Impossible to close my eyes all night. A plot for a story pursues me to the point of obsession. I had had a preliminary idea for it in the bus that took us to Dandarah. I draft four pages.

8 November

Someone calls me from Brussels to say my reception at the academy has been postponed until 19 February. So much the better, since this will allow me to finish my story.

We have dinner with Sibylle, as we do almost every day.

20 November

Small contribution to Jean-Jacques P.'s "sources." How many times did I hear him say: "I know it is very easy to malign the unfortunate!" All the while agreeing with him, I especially liked his way of making that statement, which I found word for word last evening in *Itinéraire de Paris à Jérusalem*. What a memory he had! Speaking of Robert Hutchins he liked to say: "He has the sad eyes of those who have for a long time watched the horizon.'' That is what Marthe Bibesco wrote about King George V.

I glance over some of the correspondence I received in Portugal between 1941 and 1945. In a letter from Bucur T. I rediscover what Emil Cioran declared at the time, that is, that the only letters he liked to write were petitions . . .

December

The influence of exiles of German origin on American public opinion has been and continues to be considerable. The "case" of Ernst Jünger is in this respect particularly telling. In France, although Jünger had arrived with troops of the occupation, a good twenty of his books have been translated and published. In the United States, none. The journal *La Table Ronde* devoted a special issue to him. In the United States he is not even mentioned as being among the representatives of contemporary German literature. I remember von Blankenhagen's indignation when he learned that the journal *Antaïos* was to be published in Stuttgart under Jünger's and my direction. It was in vain that I replied that *On the Marble Cliffs* constituted the only book of interior resistance that appeared in Nazi Germany. The French people who lived for four years under the German boot are more qualified than anyone else to have an opinion on the Jünger case. It was while reading the preface that Marshal Juin wrote for *Oranges d'acier,* recently published in paperback, that all this came back to mind.

25 December

We have a family Christmas with Sibylle and a few friends, for the first time since 1955.

28 December

In the last few days, on 22 December to be exact, I finished the little novel I began on 6 November. I haven't yet given it a title. At first I had called it in Rumanian *Youth without Age;* the equivalent French title would be *Le centenaire.* Christinel has finished typing its 115 pages. I note down a few random observations: (1) For the first time since I've begun writing novels I wrote the sixth and final chapter before finishing the fourth and beginning the fifth. The conclusion of my novel had come to me one evening, and since the fourth chapter didn't especially interest me, I immediately jumped to the sixth and had finished it in a few hours. (2) It was the first time, too, that I decided to keep all my notes, rough drafts, and preliminary manuscripts, the original text and the first transcription. (3) I decided to write this novel after a night of insomnia in the course of which the story's beginning, and the meaning I had to give it, suddenly came to me. (4) I had initially thought of it last summer, in Egypt, while we were going from Luxor to Dandarah. We had had to get up at four o'clock in the morning, while it was still dark out, and during the trip I dozed, only waking from time to time to add a new "vision" to the plot that was already being developed.

I don't really know what to think of this last-born of my literary prose. While reading it over yesterday, it seemed to me to be "up to snuff." I find, however, that certain episodes are written in too summary a fashion.

30 December

Received a visit from I.C. The news he brings from Rumania is just as depressing and troubling as ever: From the age of four, children are raised entirely by the Party, etc. . . . He tells me about the scene he witnessed on New Year's Eve 1944–1945, which I was unaware of. I.C. was at the time one of the editors of *Scânteia Tineretului* (The Spark of Youth), the Party weekly intended for young people. In a large room were assembled, before a well-plenished buffet, around a hundred communist journalists and Party members. A quarter of an hour before midnight Georghiu-Dej, one of the principal communist leaders of the time, made his entrance amidst roars of applause. A few moments later the lights were turned off, and when they were turned back on at the twelfth stroke of midnight, one could see Gheorghiu-Dej standing up on a chair, urinating blissfully on the banquet table. Everyone there applauded him.

The next morning, I.C. submitted his resignation, and it was written in extremely violent terms. It was this, and above all the way in which it had been written, that was the real reason for the proceedings that were instituted against him. At a second set of proceedings he was even sentenced to death, then pardoned, but still had to purge his crimes with a total of eleven years in prison.

PARIS, *8 January 1977*

I always put off until later, without really knowing why, writing what I hardly dare call my "literary testament." I must, however, hurry up. In their current condition, that is, in cartons and files scattered here and there, both in Chicago and in Paris, my articles, my unpublished manuscripts, my journal, my correspondence—all this is in a state of indescribable chaos that would be the despair of any commentator of my works. I must at all costs write down in detail where all these documents are located, the way in which their publication can be envisioned, and especially who should be in charge of seeing to this. I'm quite frightened that numerous chapters of volumes 2 and 3 of *A History* will never be identified given their present condition, scattered throughout several hundred files, some in my Meadville office, others at home on Woodlawn Avenue.

10 January

I reread, almost from beginning to end, volumes of Scandinavian mythology. I am still just as amazed to notice that the end of the world (*ragnarök*) was already evident in the cosmogony—barely even outlined—of the *Edda*.

And once again I ask myself the same question: How was it possible, psychologically possible, for an entire generation of *Hitlerjugend* to be raised in the cult of such a *pessimistic* mythology, which prophesied apocalyptic battles among gods, heroes, and demons, at the end of which all would perish and the world would be destroyed.

CHICAGO, *18 January*

We returned via Montreal four days ago.

Joe Kitagawa tells us about the funeral of Norman Perrin, who died last summer following a heart attack, whereas he had been operated on for cancer of the kidney some five years ago . . . After the religious service, G. invited those in attendance to the Quadrangle Club, telling them that Norman had wanted it that way, and that the requiem in his honor should culminate with champagne, or with any other beverage one might want . . .

I much admired Norman and his competence in New Testament theology, as well as the courage he had shown in the course of his illness. One day he had told us how he had come to be a professor at an American university. During the war he had been a member of a British patrol in the desert. Beaten with fatigue, dying of thirst, he and his fellow soldiers were dragging themselves along with difficulty when they ran into another patrol, which happened to be American. The commanding sergeant, who was brimming over with goodwill, immediately asked them if they'd like to have some ice cream . . . Since they had come to expect as much from Americans, the English believed him to be making a joke of dubious taste, but they pretended to play along. The sergeant insisted, and asked everyone what his favorite flavor was—vanilla, strawberry, chocolate? The English replied as seriously as they could. The American sergeant then asked for the desired quantity: "A pound per person, is that enough?" "I say!" exclaimed the English, who could hardly keep from laughing.

Upon which the American sergeant took his walkie-talkie, pulled out its antenna, and placed the orders he had just taken into the mouthpiece, then gave the coordinates of the place where they were located. A half hour hadn't gone by when an airplane appeared in the sky, a parachute opened, a container landed, and a few minutes later everyone was leisurely eating the portion of ice cream he had ordered. "If I ever get out of this war alive," Perrin told himself, "I will move to the United States! With such an abundance of means and such organization, the smallest American university must be superior to the best European university . . ."

20 January

I was very touched to read the poem that Bruce Lincoln, one of my former students who two years ago became my assistant, left on my desk before leaving. I'd like to cite an excerpt from it here:

In a wood-paneled study atop the grey
Seminary, a man nearing seventy sits
At his desk. Laden shelves sag under polyglot
Volumes; the excess spills to tables,
Chairs and floor while folder-waves flow
Across the room. For a while he reads,
Puffs pipe, twirls letterknife,
Chews an imported biscuit. Many
Secrets of the Whare-wananga are his . . .
Likewise Midewewin, Djunggawon,
Ngakola and more; Vedas, Eddas and
Soft shaman's songs. Possessing all Zalmoxis taught,
He muses, writes, chats with the occasional
Visitor.

Wisdom passed down from his fathers
Wisdom passed on to his sons.

Bruce Lincoln
August 19, 1976

When one speaks of the birth and expansion of Christianity, we must insist on the fact that in the course of the first two or three centuries of its existence, it competed with analogous ideas, beliefs, and religious techniques, some of which were on a very high spiritual level. And yet it was Christianity, that creation of an ''obscure Jew,'' that ended up triumphing.

30 January

I've just received a copy of the new printing of the French edition of *The Old Man and the Bureaucrats*. The first printing was thus sold out in just two or three weeks. It's the first time one of my novels has been successful in France, and I owe this to Marcel Brion, who gave enthusiastic praise of it on television.

The German translation (*Auf der Mantuleasa Strasse*) was at least just as successful. I congratulate myself: This will perhaps convince publishers to undertake as soon as possible translations of my other "fantastic" stories. Perhaps one day I will succeed in being known as an author of a *complete works,* and not just as a historian of religions, an exegete of myth, or a mere novelist.

How absurd and pernicious is the "Christian vision" of certain believers, who are, moreover, very sincere. So it is with Julien Green, who doesn't hesitate to write on 7 August 1972—and thus at over seventy years of age!—"We'd like to know who is saved. Are the majority of men doomed to the flames?"

I have trouble imagining how a Catholic writer can still, in our time, take these archaic images and metaphors at their literal meaning.

2 February

I think again of that professor who several years ago had invited me to give a course at the London School of Architecture, and whose name obstinately eludes me. I would have a lot of trouble finding his letter, which must be in one of the numerous cartons where I pile up my correspondence. I had to refuse his invitation, of course, not without expressing all the interest I would have had in giving the course. Once again the "exemplariness" of all competent exegesis of religious symbolism burst forth in front of my eyes.

A long time ago an architect had written me from Athens to say that the "true function of a bridge" had not been apparent to him until he had understood its symbolism while reading one of my books by chance: The bridge is that by which one passes from one modality of the real to another, from a certain condition to a different condition, from life to death, among other things (consider the image of the bridge in mythologies of death). He also told me about his own discoveries concerning the structure of cities and houses, because he saw in them the striking confirmation of what I had written on the meaning and function of habitations, seen as an *imago mundi,* and a "Center of the World."

7 February

I'd like to find the letter from that architect whom I was thinking about a few days ago. I had answered him, kindly, of course, but too briefly. He would have deserved a longer letter, and especially a more detailed one. In particular I should have insisted on the fact that for a historian of religions, that is, for a man who has spent a good part of his life looking for the meaning and the finality of a number of divinities, myths, images, and symbols, in a word, for a hermeneut of religious universes, the praise he receives from his teachers, his colleagues, and his students counts much less in his opinion than that of "nonspecialists." What a hermeneut appreciates the most is to be read and understood by those who work and create in domains close to his: the plastic arts, music, literature, literary criticism and history, architecture, psychology, etc. . . . One must not see in this a manifestation of the well-known and basically innocent ambition of all scholars to be understood by others than those in their specialties. But given the nature of the documents with which he works, the historian of religions is aware that his exegesis can eventually stimulate, through a curious process of anamnesis, the creative faculties of all those who passionately wish to know what the human spirit is capable of.

10 February

I'm having enormous difficulty working, but luckily I work all the same. There were days when I had to write more than ten or so letters.

PARIS, 16 February

We arrived yesterday morning. I've caught cold, a good flu, probably. And to think that in two days I will have to deliver my acceptance speech in Brussels . . .

20 February

We've been in Brussels since the day before yesterday. I felt so under the weather—it's certainly the flu—that I was quite afraid of not being able to deliver my speech.

Marcel Lobet was waiting for us at the train station. We are the guests of the Fondation Royale. I go to bed right away, first stuffing myself with medication. The next morning, my condition has not improved. Nevertheless I go to the luncheon given by the academy, to which have been invited G. Sion; the president, Maurice Piron; Professor Prigojine, whom I had met in Chicago; Pierre de Boisdeffre; etc.

In the afternoon at three o'clock, Maurice Piron gives me a medal. Photographs. Then we move off towards the lecture hall. Lobet, in a long introductory speech, covers me with praise. It is my turn now to speak. I feel at the end of my strength, and I have to catch my breath after almost each sentence. Quite fortunately, by the way, for the sound system had been badly regulated.

The quotes from Marthe Bibesco that I cited were very long, but I had wanted to stress one of the least-known aspects of her work. In any event that allowed me to evoke Rumanian popular spirituality.

Next, long conversations with diverse individuals. J. Duchesne-Guillemin had come, from Liege, to see me, as had Sorin and Liliane, who had arrived from Amsterdam. I was able to have an hour's visit with them both at the Fondation Royale.

Evening reception at Dehollain's. He had invited us to Chez Jean, that admirable restaurant very near the Grand-Place. Completely intoxicated by the medication with which I had stuffed myself, I was unable to do justice to the meal and had to limit myself to some vegetable soup and a few potatoes. Our evening went on until close to midnight. As for Sorin and Liliane, they were full of energy.

That night I plunge into a deep sleep. Fever, dizziness, and probably a liver attack. The shock treatment I imposed on myself for three days, without results, by the way, has something to do with it. Return to Paris today on Sunday 20 February. In the evening, dinner with Sibylle.

25 February

A few years ago, a New York avant-garde painter had announced the unveiling of his latest creations, and had sent out a good number of invitations. On the appointed day, the walls of the gallery were completely blank, with the exception of a few inscriptions in which the painter had summed up his ideas on aesthetics. In addition, loudspeakers had been set up in the gallery. The "exhibition" consisted of this: The artist masturbated on the podium, and the loudspeakers amplified his groans of pleasure throughout the gallery.

The event was commented on abundantly in all avant-garde publications.

1 March

Sibylle went for a three-week hospital stay under the care of Dr. Israel, the great cancer specialist. It's strange to see the extent to which the prestige that surrounds him has given us all hope again, beginning with Sibylle.

4 March

"Ah! What I would give," says Gide, "to write a good fantastic tale!" (*Les Cahiers de la petite dame,* vol. 2, p. 380, 10 May 1934).

From a detective novel by Marjory Allingham: "How wise I was to let you marry me!" It's the husband who's speaking.

7 March

Terrible earthquake 4 March in Rumania. As Cioran said, it took only two minutes to destroy what was most modern in Rumania, its industry. No one can evaluate the damage yet, but it is enormous. The number of victims is unknown. Some foreign correspondents speak of two or three thousand dead, others of ten thousand. I tried in vain to reach my sister Corina by phone, but there were several hundred calls waiting to go through. Sorin was, however, able to speak to her on the morning of 5 March. Her house didn't suffer too badly. No victims either among our friends.

8 March

For three days I haven't been able to do anything, so devastated am I by the misfortune that has befallen my country. Just a few years ago Rumania was stricken by catastrophic floods; in addition the country had to undergo the earthquake of 4 March.

Among the victims, numerous writers, musicians, and artists. Bakonski and his wife, as well as a few others, perished under the rubble of their apartment building. I never knew Bakonski personally, but I appreciated his style, his talent, and his scholarship.

Alexandre Ivasiuc was in the street and was going under a balcony when the ground began to tremble. The balcony crumbled and Ivasiuc, crushed, died immediately. I remember the few days we had spent together in Chicago. I especially remember the description he had given us of the Rumanian prisons where he had shared a cell with Paul Goma. He was also in the camps of the Baragan, where he had spent five years. He nevertheless always claimed to be a Marxist, and, he added, "as a writer I am what I am, but my true vocation remains philosophy, and if the history of Rumanian culture retains my name, it is as a philosopher that I wish to be remembered."

10 March

With a few friends I celebrated my seventieth birthday yesterday. I will not try to take stock. Now that I have forever crossed the threshold of old age, now that I am well and good an "ancient," I realize that I have not yet completed my *History of Religious Ideas,* nor my *Autobiography.* I have not even yet begun that short treatise on *Homo religiosus,* in which I want to show in a systematic way all that I believe I have understood in the course of fifty years of research and reflection.

11 March

Saw at the Théâtre de la Ville, in the company of Eugène and Rodica, *Jacques ou la soumission,* in the production by Pintilie. "An impressive performance from all points of view," I heard a spectator say at the exit. Eugène tells us that he liked the play, although he did not always recognize his primary intentions in it, nor even the dramaturgy that he had imagined and which had seemed so evident to him while he was writing the text. It happens that a director, through his own genius, manages to recreate a play, and it is this that allows classics of dramatic literature to be given new life. It is nonetheless true that for a contemporary author such a "recreation" can appear suspect, for he sees in it a beginning of the alteration of his work.

20 March

Through a letter from William McGuire I learn that Vaun Gilmore died last September. I hadn't seen her for four or five years. Upon the death of her husband, who was a doctor, she had left New York and had settled in Virginia.

I had met her for the first time in 1950 in Ascona, where she had come, as she did every year, in the company of John Barett and Herbert Read to attend the Eranos lectures and to meet Jung. Along with Barett she represented the Bollingen Foundation; just like he, she spoke excellent French. One evening when we were on the shore of the lake in front of the Tamaro Hotel, where the conference participants were staying, we had a long conversation into which also joined Louis Massignon, Henry and Stella Corbin, Herbert Read, the Reverend Beirnard, and a few others. I don't remember how I came to tell them about my short-lived position at UNESCO in 1948, where Theodore Besterman had managed to get me in as a five-month replacement for an office worker who had gone on mission to Lebanon. I especially dwelled on what I had learned from my colleagues who, originating in diverse countries, worked as I did in the Department of Information and Bibliography. At the time, in 1948, the greatest fantasy was to be recruited as an office worker. It is thus that a young man from Switzerland, who had just passed his exam to be a train stationmaster, learned by chance that UNESCO was looking for applicants. He applied and was hired. When he became tired of doing nothing apart from reading newspapers in the office he had been assigned, he announced that he was going "to the library," and he was never seen again. Another worker was assigned to a "six-month project" consisting of drafting a directory of all the chairs in sociology that existed in the world. One day when I was working in his office and was consulting the references assembled on his shelves, I noticed several international directories in which were listed all the chairs in sociology that existed at the time. A less than conscientious typist could have completed the "project" in three days at the most.

But why do I wish to bring all that up today? Perhaps because I'm not sure I noted it down in my journal at the time, and also because Vaun Gilmore had been very amused by the story. She had never forgotten how I had enraptured her by telling her, on that same evening on the lake, the story of the young New York journalist who had come to Paris to do a story on UNESCO and who never left, for he had managed to secure a position in the Department of Cultural Information, or something close to that.

Vaun was very tall, very blond, and had a marvelous laugh. She could have been very beautiful if she hadn't had the onset of a goiter that made her neck swell up. Her doctor convinced her to have it operated on. He undertook the procedure himself, and sometime later he married her. I want to believe that they knew perfect happiness, at least in the beginning of their marriage, that is, before her husband himself was operated on for cancer, which shook him up both physically and emotionally. Once having become a widow Vaun finally consented to tell her friends what the years that had preceded her husband's death were really like for her.

27 March

Dinner with Sibylle. We don't yet know what the results of the chemotherapy will be, but the forced solitude of the nights spent in the hospital is visibly weighing on her.

CHICAGO, 4 April

Christinel stayed in Paris with Sibylle. I feel very tired.

19 April

Yesterday we opened the colloquium on Judaism sponsored by the Divinity School. In the evening after our dinner at the synagogue, Zwi Werblowski gave a lecture on Lurianic Kabala. Joe Kitagawa had asked me to say a few words on the Christian Kabalists of the

Renaissance. I agreed, although those Kabalists were only familiar with the "classical" Kabalas alone, such as the *Zohar* and all those of the twelfth and thirteenth centuries. My talk, which I had to improvise, lasted only a quarter of an hour. Back home, I felt full of remorse at never having devoted the least article to a subject that has, however, fascinated me ever since my university years. It is true that I don't know Hebrew, but the Kabalists of the Renaissance wrote in Latin. In addition, knowing Hebrew is not enough in itself to grasp the meaning of the Kabala.

20 April

I've received a lot of correspondence from professors of English literature or of philosophy after the publication of *No Souvenirs,* the translation of a portion of *Fragments d'un journal.* Their enthusiastic letters only anchor me in my conviction that I was right to publish in my lifetime excerpts from my journal. Here is a passage from a letter sent on 14 April 1977 from M.C., who had taken my courses in 1968–1969: "No one has made me realize as you have the extent to which myth profoundly covers and encompasses my entire existence. Reading your personal 'odyssey' has a rejuvenating, initiatory, cathartic effect on your reader." Could a writer of today want anything more?

25 April

The preface by Elémire Zolla for *Il superuomo e i suoi simboli nelle letterature moderne* (vol. 5, Florence, 1977) holds a surprise for me. I learn that Disraeli, in his novel *Lothair* (1870), predicted that following the decline of Christianity one would see the growth of a cult of the superman, having as corollaries a neopagan exaltation of the race, as well as the decline of a culture based on books. Disraeli had already portended that an "Aryan" doctrine would triumph in Germany, and that a "return to Sparta" would be witnessed there, just as Italy would know a new Caesarism. "Of such principles a great renewal is at hand," he concluded.

In that same year, 1870, Melville published his novel *Clarel.* In it he wrote that in the future two political forces, and only two, would confront each other in Europe, the Roman Catholic church and communism, and that the church would be defended by "demo-Christian" (the term is his) parties. He also foresaw the decline of the "Frontier Spirit" in the United States and, in a more or less distant future, the bloody growth of race riots in American cities. Zionism didn't exist yet, but he was already predicting the conflict that would involve Arabs and Jewish colonists in Palestine.

5 May

I am reading *Hope against Hope* by Nadezhda Mandel'shtam. I've rarely read a more authentic and more convincing account. And yet, as she herself writes: "How can we not think of all those who, outside, refuse to believe us . . ."

7 May

Christinel has come back from Paris. Sibylle's condition hasn't changed. In any case, no improvement since last winter—on the contrary.

May 1977

How easy it is to go from the realm of bibliography to that of the philosophy of culture! In the last few days N.F. came to see me to compile the list of my books that have been translated, which the publishing house where he works needed. He was very surprised to note that Japanese translations will soon be the most numerous, and he asked me how I explained this. I answered that I had never thought about it, and that it was possible that publishers had had their attention drawn to me by Professor Hori, who was the first to translate my books into Japanese and has contributed much to their success. But N.F. did not seem convinced.

I saw him again this evening, and he appeared transfigured. His radiant air was all the more surprising as he is practically never seen smiling. For an entire half hour he spoke with volubility. Even though it is difficult I will sum up here some of his thoughts: (1) The Japanese are more sensitive than Westerners to the systematic interpretation of religious figures and symbols. (2) This is all the more valid in my own case as I have dedicated myself to the exegesis of symbols of cosmic structure. (3) In other respects, the Japanese show an extraordinary instinct, almost "divinatory," in foreseeing what will become of the diverse currents of contemporary thought. For N.F. there seems to be no doubt that historico-religious hermeneutics will "very shortly" be successful. (4) Very often the Japanese surpass, after having copied them, their European models; the best "Swiss" watches, the best "Bavarian" beer, are often found in Japan . . . (5) In other words, all that I've tried to do up until now, the Japanese will soon do, "and much better."

I must point out that N.F. is a remarkable bibliographer. I would only have to give the titles of his latest two contributions in this area for all specialists to know who he is, for the initials N.F. are obviously my own invention.

I had spent almost the entire day at the library. In the evening I came home tired and listless. My sadness disappeared all of a sudden when, having arrived at a crosswalk on Woodlawn Avenue, I had to stop to wait for a green light. A group of young blacks and hippies in rags, their hair blowing in the wind, were crossing the street with measured steps, despite the red light, to the great exasperation of the drivers compelled to stop to let them pass, and who reacted by honking their horns loudly and with strong epithets. The "walkers' " triumphant air and their pride were something to be seen. Hadn't they just given new proof of their disdain for rules, and of the little respect they had for authority and the norms set by the odious Establishment?

They were only too visibly members of that contentious faction that occupies all the screens in the movie theatres as well as on television, and of the "revolutionary youth" upon which, thanks to the power of the mass media, all eyes are fixed and which is able to monopolize public attention. Looking at their eyes, one guessed their feeling of high self-esteem and their legitimate pride. Hadn't they just shown courage and risked their liberty, perhaps even their lives? And one also guessed their faith in the coming of that revolution that would finally win out over that awesome American Establishment destined to crumble like a castle made of cards.

And I suddenly wanted to laugh, for their wishes could indeed very well become reality. And if the Establishment were ever to perish due to this type of behavior alone, we will discover—with stupefaction perhaps, but not without laughing—that the contemporary history of the so-called free world surprisingly resembles a Charlie Chaplin film.

Five or six years ago Auden had been invited to read in public his own translation of Scandinavian epic poems. I hadn't seen him for a long time, and I was struck by the wrinkles that cut into his forehead and face and gave him a strange expression. There were about a dozen of us seated around a table at the Quadrangle Club. I had arrived a few minutes before we sat down. Auden was drinking little mouthfuls of gin. According to Richard Stern, he was already on his fifth or sixth glass. I approached Auden and reminded him of our first meeting in Paris in 1950 or 1951, at a reception organized by the Congrès Européen pour la Liberté de la Culture. He told me that he, too, remembered, and that I had spoken to him about a translation of his poems into Rumanian by an author whose name I had forgotten, and which still escapes me today. We sat down, and Dora served the wine. Auden hadn't finished his soup, and he had already emptied two glasses. He had served himself the second and, to be safe, had taken care to keep the bottle within arm's reach. By dessert, he had finished it off himself. Auden fascinated me by his elocution and the high standards of his speech. When I asked him whether the fervor he had apparently felt in translating excerpts from the *Eddas,* with the help of a linguist, of course, had echoed the mythological content of the poems, he answered that what interested him most was the eschatology, that *ragnarök* announced by the *Völuspá,* and that he regretted that in many places one had to be satisfied with simple allusions, when they existed, and that the essential elements had to be looked for elsewhere, in another poem, in the *Vafthrúdnismál,* which belongs to another poetic universe.

He had time to empty several glasses of cognac before accompanying us to Mandel Hall. He read his poems for almost two hours, and was dazzling. The timbre of his voice brought out all nuances, without the slightest false note, without the slightest error in tonality. It was absolutely extraordinary. I learned later that that very afternoon he had drunk, all alone in his room at the Quadrangle Club, a good half bottle of whisky.

31 May

Spent the evening in the company of B.B., first at the Quadrangle Club, then at our house where our conversation went on until around midnight. I hadn't seen him since 1966 in Rome, and then quite briefly, despite a separation of thirty years. This time we can talk at more leisure. Of all my contemporaries he is one of the few not to have experienced prison and torture, or in any case, he refuses to talk about it. A former judge, he collaborated on certain literary journals. Since then, having become an art critic, he is one of the great specialists on Brancusi. He has published numerous studies and monographs in specialized journals.

What is striking about him, as about many others, is his *will* "to be involved with culture" despite everything. One would say that he maintains the following reasoning: Insofar as I am still allowed to study and interpret Brancusi's works, I remain a creator, and thus I am *free.* He could add that for the present, and for a long time to come, this freedom is the only one we still have. The day is perhaps not far off when all of Europe, and perhaps even the entire world, will know the fate which is ours today, we intellectuals of Eastern Europe. I don't know how the Western elite will react *then,* but in any event our *past* will plead in our favor, for we will have behind us those thirty, fifty, or even hundred years of suffering during which it has been necessary for us to adapt in order to continue to "create," or quite simply in order to survive. But we haven't wasted our time. No one will be able to claim that our past has been but a long succession of lost opportunities.

NEW YORK, *16 June*

I spent almost the entire day at the Metropolitan Museum. I think about the first months of my stay in Paris in 1945 and 1946. At that time I went almost every day to spend an hour at the Louvre. I wonder what became of the notebooks in which I jotted down my "impressions" then. As it rarely happened that I transcribed them into my journal, I also wonder what I would experience in rereading them now, thirty years later . . .

PARIS, *18 June*

We arrived tonight. Today we went to see Sibylle. She has lost a considerable amount of weight since last March.

21 June

I spent yesterday and today assembling "biographical notes" for the *Cahiers de l'Herne.* I experience a curious sensation, that of drafting the curriculum vitae of someone else, whom I know well, but in whom I don't always recognize myself.

27 June

I am in the process of transcribing from diverse notebooks and scraps of paper my journal from the years 1971–1972. I don't always manage to reread what I wrote, since there are so many abbreviations and mutilated words. Luckily I have enough "notes and observations" written at more leisure, although they are not always precisely dated. To tell the truth, while writing them I expected to gather them one day into a volume, *Carnets,* but not in any chronological order.

29 June

Having gone to Editions Belfond, I meet Claude Bonnefoy there and make the acquaintance of Claude-Henri Rocquet, with whom I am to prepare our next volume of *Entretiens*. He is a professor at the school of architecture in Montpellier. I have before me a young man, nice, very open. The way he is dressed—his sandals and his beard of a Himalayan hermit—make him look like a painter from Montmartre, or like the head of a neo-Hindu sect in Chicago.

I tell him right away the extent to which I feel panicked when I know my words are being recorded. He tells me again what Bonnefoy has already told me, and which made me less hesitant, that is, that I will be able to correct the text of *Entretiens* once it is typed up, to rework certain passages if I judge their content to be insufficient or approximate, etc. To reassure him I put on a tight smile, which didn't prevent me from once again being plagued by doubts as soon as I had stepped outside.

1 July

The first truly summer-like day. In the evening at the Ieruncas', I meet Father D. Staniloaie, professor of theology. All three of us listen to him—Monica, Virgil and I—tell us about the situation of the church in Rumania. But what's the use of repeating here what everyone already knows.

2 July

It is still just as hot, and the sky is still just as blue. In the afternoon, from three to five o'clock, first recording session with Rocquet. I have no reason to congratulate myself. When he had come to see me the day before yesterday, our conversation had gone on for a while, and I had answered all his questions quite naturally, for the good reason that he had come without his tape recorder. I had even hoped that he had given up on any sort of recording and would be content to take notes from which he would draft the text of our conversations. But if he came without his machine it is quite simply because it wasn't working . . .

3 July

I told Rocquet yesterday about the great pieces of luck that have marked my life: Of the three children my parents had I was the middle one, which kept me from being too spoiled by them, unlike my older brother and my younger sister. My parents tolerated my pranks. I wasn't yet seventeen when they let me go with seven of my lycée friends on a sailboat trip that would take us, the only ones on board, from Tulcea to Constantsa. It took me years to admit to them that we had been caught in a storm from which we had escaped only by miracle. At twenty-one, as soon as I had my diploma, they got together the money I needed for my trip to India, which wasn't easy for them, for they weren't rolling in money—quite the contrary. I was also lucky enough to escape the dangers that awaited me in London in 1940 at the time of the bombings, after having been lucky enough to be appointed cultural attaché there. From that time I had to live far from my country, which kept me from sharing the fate of my compatriots. But there are many other events and circumstances in which I believe I recognize the intervention of Providence and about which I have never yet spoken. I promise myself to do so one day, without omitting anything.

5 July

I have just read *Entretiens avec Marcel Duchamp,* and I am dismayed. This man was never interested in anything except games of chess. The self-importance with which this revolutionary speaks on art is amazing.

8 July

Three recording sessions in the course of the week. Our conversations are all the more fascinating as I find that Rocquet is a fervent fan of some of my books, in particular *Fragments d'un journal* and *The Old Man and the Bureaucrats.* If that cursed microphone weren't between us these conversations would certainly be much more spontaneous, precise, and even more interesting.

Rocquet is taken with place Charles-Dullin. He likes to hear the chirping of the sparrows in the old linden trees, and he doesn't tire of seeing the pigeons scatter around the theatre. "We have worked well!" he exclaims after each session, and I pretend to share his enthusiasm.

July

I must read that book by a Hegelian, H. F. Augustus Damerow, *Die Elemente der nächsten Zukunft der Medizin, entwickelt aus der Vergangenheit u. Gegenwart* (I don't know when it was published). He maintains that the history of medicine is organically inseparable from universal history, and to all the crucial moments of the latter has always corresponded a surge in medical innovations. This assertion is corroborated by multiple examples which I find in *Romantische Medizin* by Werner Leibbrand: The advent of Christianity meant that sick people no longer had to fear being considered inferior beings, and one began to see in illness a purifying trial and a sign of election. The medical profession was from then on thought to have a religious function, whence the importance accorded to medicine in monastic orders, notably at Sankt Gallen, Fulda, and Reichenau.

In the Renaissance the renewal of art corresponded to the beginnings of anatomy. Whereas sculptors were rediscovering the "classical body," da Vinci was fascinated by anatomy.

Paracelsus, too, was a reformer, to the same extent as his contemporary Martin Luther. The great geographical discoveries had as a counterpart the discovery of that new continent, the human body: the anatomy of Andreas Vesalius in the sixteenth century. Moreover, Harvey's theory on the circulation of blood is inseparable from the physics of Galileo.

Damerow's reflections can be compared to the recent work of Debus on iatrochemistry, Paracelsus, etc. . . . and to my own remarks on Newton's alchemy and seventeenth-century Hermeticism. All of this should be taken up and commented on in more depth. Since then the history of Western thought has never known another "holistic" period.

My work is not suffering from the heat, which is, however, oppressive. I've succeeded in writing a good dozen pages. In addition, I've come across this quote which will delight Cioran: "Life is short, but one is bored all the same" (Jules Renard, *Journal*, 24 May 1902).

Chtchedrine claimed, in one of his pithy reflections, "that there doesn't exist one parcel of their land that the Russians haven't covered with spit." (I don't dare to wonder whether one couldn't say as much about us others, Rumanians . . .).

21 July

Ugh! Seventh—and last—recording session with Rocquet. According to him, the definitive text will be "one of the most interesting and most useful."

I still think that if there hadn't been a microphone between us, our conversations would have been much more spontaneous, and I would have been able to show more originality and especially more daring.

On the other hand, we quickly agreed on what the title of the work will be: *L'Epreuve du labyrinthe* [*Ordeal by Labyrinth*]. For me, in any case, Rocquet's questions about my childhood and my adolescence in Rumania, my Indian years, my stays in London and Portugal and the men I had the opportunity to meet there, my arrival in Paris, then in Chicago, not to mention those he asks about my work in Indianism and the history of religions, then my literary activity, both in Rumania and in France, were just so many "initiatory trials": I suddenly found myself propelled back into a fabulous past, that of the Rumania I had to leave in 1940 and which since then has become for me like a piece of paradise. It is there that for thirty-three years I lived an existence that remains engraved in my memory even in the most minute detail, but of which I now discover only secret dimensions, so much so that I see in it a "personal mythology," and not my life as I truly lived it. "Initiatory trials," I say, because I sometimes had the impression, once alone, that I had "strayed," that I was groping along in a labyrinth. It took me hours to find myself again, and, along with myself, to find present reality. I had a similar experience ten or fifteen years ago while I was writing my recollections of childhood and youth.

LA VALETTE, *August*

Oani had rented this immense cottage hidden in the forest, barely six kilometers from Toulon, a long time ago. He had rented it so we could all spend our vacation together, for we thought that Sibylle would be able to join us. But Sibylle is confined to her bed on the rue Lamarck, and her body is nothing but a wound. She insisted, however, that we go spend at least two weeks in Toulon. As soon as we return to Paris Christinel will stay with her along with the nurse, and Jacqueline will come in turn to stay here until the first of September.

Arthritis, unless it's gout, tortures my right hand, and I have difficulty writing the preface to *Forbidden Forest,* the English translation of *Forêt interdite,* which will be published by Notre Dame University Press. I'm all the more upset since I would have liked the preface to be rather long, which would have allowed me to comment in more depth on what I call the "necessity of narration." In my journal, but also in lectures, I've already made numerous allusions to this *existential need* to listen to or to read a "tale," whether it is a myth, a fairy tale, a history, a short story, or a novel. I have, however, never had the opportunity to deal with the subject in its entirety.

During the ceremonies in memory of Pushkin, and speaking about the destiny of the Russian people, Dostoevsky glorified "our ability and our tendency to rebuild the universal and panhuman unity between all the families of the great Aryan race. Yes, the significance of the Russian man is incontestably European and universal. To be a true Russian primarily means (remember this well) to be the brother of all men, a *panhuman,* if you wish. All our Slavophilism and our Westernism, you see, is but a great misunderstanding between us, although it is historically necessary . . ." (*Journal d'un écrivain,* N.R.F., 1958, p. 633. [Translated here from the French. Available in English as *The Diary of a Writer,* New York, George Braziller, 1954]).

What is saddest is that Dostoevsky could very well have been right if . . .

Among Dostoevsky's admirers, very rare are those who remember this admission in the *Diary of a Writer:* "There is only one supreme idea: the immortality of the soul. All others, however profound they may be, are only the continuation of it.''

We went to spend two days in Eygaliere, at the home of Ioan and Ileana Cusa. Christinel calls Paris almost every day. We're not told very much, but we guess the rest . . .

Ioan drives us to Gordes, to the abbey of Senanque, in Aix. I realize with melancholy that I didn't yet know the real Provence.

18 August

Return to Paris.

19 August

Christinel went to spend the night at Sibylle's. Luckily, we are dealing with an exceptional nurse. It's impossible for me to find another adjective or another term of comparison; only one suits her: Her presence and her behavior are truly ''angelic.''

24 August

Sibylle expired today at two-thirty in the morning. When I saw her yesterday for the last time she was sleeping, but I felt that the end was near. She had suffered all too much. Especially in the last months she was a martyr. But she so much wanted to live and to conquer her illness. . . It would be useless to add anything more.

September

Probably too few of my readers will understand the true significance of what I once considered to be my magnum opus. As I have written it up until now, *A History,* volumes 1 and 2, only satisfied me in part. I should have written it ten or fifteen years earlier, at the time when I was in ''good shape.'' I nevertheless hope that volume 3 will turn out better. In any event, this *History* has an autobiographical significance for me (obviously secret). In the twilight of my life I review *one last time* the entire history of religious beliefs and ideas, from their

origins to the present. I have the impression of seeing in this my entire
life gathered into one sole instant, into that very instant that precedes my
passage *into the hereafter.*

I have just learned a number of fascinating details about the origins of
traditional thought (*philosophia perennis*) which René Guénon brought
to light, quite simply from books on philosophy and occultism from the
beginning of the nineteenth century. Actually René Guénon ended up
discovering late in life the *real* sources, both Oriental and Western, of
esoteric traditions, and above all understood their meaning . . .

But this "issue of origins" also has another facet. One could say that
these apparently banal books which dealt with philosophy, freemasonry,
and occultism, and which Guénon read in his youth, were all that
remained at the beginning of the nineteenth century, degraded, mutilated, and even camouflaged, of the content of the Western esoteric
tradition that was partially rediscovered in the Renaissance.

I've read almost the entire *Cahier de l'Herne* devoted to Gombrow-
icz. Of his writings I was only familiar with his *Journal,* of which I had
read excerpts, and a novel whose title I've forgotten.

He wanted to prove that he had dissociated himself from his
aristocratic birth: In restaurants he made a point of picking his teeth with
a fork . . . What else could he do to prove to everyone that, although
of noble birth, he felt free to act "otherwise"?

When he arrived in Argentina he lived in misery. He would follow
funeral processions all the way to the cemetery in order to be able to eat
the cakes offered in memory of the dead, as was customary practice
among the poor. But he was immensely proud, and he always refused
to join any of the literary circles that existed in Argentina, so much did
he consider himself to be an exceptional and unique individual in his
genre.

CHICAGO, *14 October*

We have been back since the day before yesterday and are dead
tired. Christinel hardly slept more than two hours, and she's fighting

against a tenacious flu. As for me, I feel completely exhausted, undoubtedly because of the multiple medications I must swallow. There are pills for gout, for a chest cold, etc. . . . It's true that for some time everything's been attacking me at once: arthritis, gout (luckily, the series of ten injections I was given won out over the pseudo–writer's cramp that was preventing me from writing), ears that are plugged up due to a nasal allergy, my eyes (the onset of cataracts is fighting against the treatment I've been following for three months).

17 October

I'm feeling a bit better. Yesterday I decided to give up the gout pills I had been taking for six weeks. I don't know whether they were to blame, but I had the impression of being a wet rag.

19 October

From seven to ten o'clock in the evening, joint seminar with Frank Reynolds, one of my former students who became my colleague a few years ago. Its theme is "Classics in the History of Religions from Max Müller to G. Van der Leeuw." Among those in attendance are about forty students. The Curtis Room, the largest lecture hall in Meadville, is almost full. J.T. gives a very well-structured analysis of Robertson Smith's theory on rites, and it is followed by discussion. I speak up to say that to analyze the theories of Max Müller and Robertson Smith on myths and rites amounts to taking up Faust's monologue: "In the beginning was the verb." This was also Max Müller's opinion, for whom *numina = nomina*: Divinities were first *names*. Faust proclaimed the contrary: In the beginning there was the act (Robertson Smith maintains that rite preceded myth, which is not only subsequent to rite, but is secondary to it and was only invented to justify it).

I remember the seminars with Paul Tillich, which were played out in this same room a long time ago. My comparison with the prologue of *Faust* would have certainly got a rise out of him! He would have renewed our debates with great spirit, and it would be at our house, late into the night, that our discussion would have ended.

But the students were still intimidated. And I had the impression that I was seeing most of them for the first time.

October

In a letter I received dated 8 September from a young professor of ethnology, I come across this passage: "I come to wonder how 'anthropologists' expect to be real students of man without familiarity with your work." These few lines obviously please me very much. Nevertheless I am perfectly aware that I don't have much to expect from them, at least not for the moment.

20 October

Superb day, hot and luminous like in August. I am all the more aware how much my vision has deteriorated recently. The blue of the sky, the trees, the buildings, all seem fuzzy and indistinct, as if seen through a cloudy window. I constantly feel like taking off my glasses to wipe them . . . My ophthalmologist has assured me, however, that the onset of my cataracts has been arrested.

I remember Papini trying to inscribe one of his books for me, his head glued right up next to the paper, the day I saw him for the last time.

Met by chance in Staver's Bookstore one of my former students, G.O., now a professor at a university in one of the southern states. I notice very quickly that something has changed, both in his behavior and in his way of speaking.

"I feel more and more attracted to politics," he tells me. "I must admit that I've learned a lot recently from reading Marx."

Amused, I interrupt him a moment to tell him about the attacks of the "new philosphers" against Marxism. He seems visibly moved, and even upset. "In Paris," I tell him, "some people consider Marxism to be dead and buried."

"Really," he says, pensively.

The prestige and even the magic of Paris and of French culture! G.O. must be saying to himself that if Marx has gone out of style in Paris, why should he waste his time reading him . . .

3 November

It was with much interest, but not without melancholy, that I read *An Illustrated Life* of Mark Twain. The book is abundantly documented, and the text is based on admirable drawings and photographs of the period: scenes of cities, houses, boats, facsimiles of pages from newspapers, portraits of Twain himself and his contemporaries, etc. . . . It is the authentic image of an America that I would have liked to know. Certain landscapes aside, that America of less than a century ago has almost completely disappeared.

10 November

Knowing that I have always refused to give courses or lectures at other universities, J.S. was very surprised to learn that I will spend three weeks next March at the University of North Carolina, where Chuck Long is a professor. He asks me what made me decide to accept. I jokingly answer that it is because of Duke Bernhard. Hadn't he found a copy of *Faust* in the possession of an Indian of North Carolina . . . (See the letter from Goethe to Zelter dated 28 March 1829.)

I have the impression that J.S. believed me . . .

19 November

In the framework of the colloquium *Religious Studies and the Humanities: Theories of Interpretation,* sponsored by our department, I gave a lecture on literary imagination and religious studies. It is the first time that I speak in public about my literary writings and their relationship to the history of religions, such, at least, as I conceive it to be. I didn't have enough time to develop more than a few ideas. I said first of all that a literary work is an instrument of knowledge. The imaginary universes created in novels, stories, and tales reveal certain values and meanings unique to the human condition which, without them, would remain unknown, or, at the very least, imperfectly understood. I also emphasized the existential necessity of *narration*, whatever the form chosen by the writer to express himself may be. The "death of the novel" proclaimed by some following *Finnegan's Wake*,

Glasperlenspiel, or *Doctor Faustus* doesn't seem obvious to me. One can at most speak of the death of the realistic, psychological, or social novel, or of models that have become outdated (Balzac, Tolstoy, Proust, etc.). But true epic literature—that is, the novel, the story, the tale—cannot disappear as such, for the literary imagination is the continuation of mythological creativity and oneiric experience. Narration has infinite possibilities, for infinite are the number of characters or "events," both in life or in history and in the parallel universes forged by the creative imagination.

All the same, I did not emphasize sufficiently the similarities between religious phenomena and literary creation. Just as all religious phenomena are hierophantic (in the sense that they reveal the sacred in a profane object or act), literary creation unveils the universal and exemplary meanings hidden in men and in the most commonplace events.

23 November

I discover only now an article by Thomas Mann, "The Making of the Magic Mountain," which appeared a long time ago in the *Atlantic Monthly,* but which was taken up as the preface to the novel in the recent Modern Library edition. In the article Thomas Mann affirms from the start that *The Magic Mountain* is "a novel of initiation." A study by Howard Nemerov, "The Questor Hero," had caused him to discover that *The Magic Mountain* is essentially a "quest for the Grail," and it is the *lapis philosophorum,* the *aurum potabile,* the elixir of long life, that are being sought in it. In *The Magic Mountain,* writes Thomas Mann, "there is a great deal said of alchemistic, hermetic pedagogy, of *transmutation.* And I, myself a guileless fool, was guided by a mysterious tradition. . . . Not for nothing do Freemasonry and its rites play a role in *The Magic Mountain,* for Freemasonry is the direct descendent of initiatory rites. In a word, the magic mountain is a variant of the shrine of the initiatory rites, a place of adventurous investigations in the mystery of life. And my Hans Castorp . . . has a very distinguished knightly and mystical ancestry: he is the typical curious neophyte—curious in a high sense of the word—who voluntarily . . . embraces disease and death, because his very first contact with them gives promise of extraordinary enlightenment and adventurous advancement, bound up, of course, with correspondingly great risks."

And in concluding Thomas Mann affirms that his hero, too, is in search of the Holy Grail: "Hans Castorp is a searcher after the Holy Grail." But the novelist realized this only after reading Nemerov's study. I would be curious, however, to know whether this revelation caused him to discover more profound aspects concealed perhaps in his other works, *Doctor Faustus,* for example.

25 November

It's snowing as if it were the middle of winter, and it's very cold. In Meadville my desk disappears under a pile of books, files, letters, papers, and notecards. Exasperated, I try to sort it all out a bit, and I come across a bunch of notes filed under the heading "Journal." I take one of them and read: "Chicago, 17 January 1977. In the taxi coming back from the Loop there was this sign: Cancer cures smoking."

27 November

For almost three days it hasn't stopped snowing. I don't really feel like working. I manage not without difficulty to write a few letters.

28 November

I've just learned that Monica L. was the victim of an assault on the very doorstep of her house, and that she was badly beaten up. Christinel was able to talk to her on the phone, barely a few hours after she returned from the hospital. No cranial injuries, very luckily for her.

This attack is part of the campaign of intimidation that has followed the "scandal" in which Paul Goma, the Rumanian dissident, was implicated. It took place on the eve of Goma's arrival in Paris.

November

A year ago I had received a little book, *The Futility God* (Mansfield, Ohio, 1975) which its author, Jack W. Hannah, had sent to me. When it arrived I hadn't had time to read it. I found it again recently and I looked it over. I learn from it that Morgan Robertson, a minor American novelist, quite mediocre, moreover, and long since forgotten, published in 1898—I stress the date—one of the most ordinary of novels, completely sentimental and devoid of any literary value, but stupefying nonetheless. It's the story of the shipwreck of a trans-Atlantic steamer, *The Titan*. Its resemblance to its near homonym, the *Titanic*, which went down in 1912, is extraordinary. The *Titan*, as Robertson had imagined it, was a 45,000-ton ship. As for the *Titanic*, it weighed in at 46,328 tons. When it struck an iceberg, the *Titan* was traveling at a speed of 25 knots; the *Titanic* at 22.5. The two shipwrecks, the imaginary and the real, took place in the month of April, and the two steamers where making the crossing from England to New York. The *Titan* struck an iceberg at 21:45, and the *Titanic* at 23:45. In both cases, the shipwreck occurred for the same reasons, that is, the ship's excessive speed given the season and the fog. The *Titan* is supposed to have sunk nine hundred miles from New York, and the *Titanic* went down thirteen hundred miles away. The former was 800 feet long and 80 feet wide; the *Titanic* measured 883 feet by 93 feet. Both were constructed entirely out of steel. The *Titan* had forty thousand horsepower, the *Titanic* forty-six thousand. They could accommodate respectively 3,000 and 3,320 passengers, including the crew. The *Titan* belonged to a company from Liverpool; the *Titanic* flew the flag of White Star, whose headquarters were also in Liverpool. The two steamers had a British crew and were driven by three turbines. Almost all the 2,000 passengers of the *Titan* perished (Robertson doesn't indicate how many of the crew were lost). Of the 2,208 passengers and crew members on the *Titanic*, 1,517 drowned. The *Titan* had twenty-four lifeboats, compared to twenty on the *Titanic*. The *Titan* was equipped with nineteen watertight bulkheads, and the *Titanic* sixteen, which closed automatically as soon as they came into contact with water . . .

When Robertson wrote his novel, the biggest steamer existing at the time was 680 feet long and displaced only 18,915 tons, and the most power attained by a trans-Atlantic ship was thirty-two thousand horsepower. No ship was driven by three turbines. Robertson described the *Titan,* then entirely a product of his imagination, in terms identical to those used later in praise of the *Titanic:* "the biggest construction ever built by man," and in addition, "entirely unsinkable." Just as troubling is the number of people Robertson imagined had drowned— about 2,000—and all the more since from 1892–1901, the years in which Robertson wrote his novel, 3,250,000 passengers had made the crossing between England and the United States, with only 73 victims. From 1902 to 1911, 6 million people made that same crossing and there were only 9 victims. The number of 2,000 victims imagined by Robertson was thus, in 1898, so fantastic as to be inconceivable.

Jack Hannah rightly estimates that we are dealing with an authentic "premonition" that must be analyzed from a theological perspective. This is what he attempted to do in writing *The Futility God* (what an admirable title!). However, his manuscript didn't interest any of the big publishing houses, and this was in the United States, the only country, it is claimed, where theology is not a "dead science."

1 December

Last evening I began my last seminar of the year, which will continue through the three winter months. A student, C.B., gave a report on the work of R. Pettazzoni. After the coffee break, general discussion. I tell the students that Pettazzoni remains, in a certain sense, my model. I thus repeated what I had already said a few years ago in Santa Barbara in the closing session of the colloquium on my work. I had specified then that by "model" I mean what a historian of religions actually *does,* and not *his way of doing it.* Pettazzoni is a historicist, whereas I am not. In numerous circumstances our respective opinions differ, when they are not completely opposed. Nevertheless, his example encouraged me to follow in his footsteps. Pettazzoni is perhaps the last scholar who undertook to study and to understand the history of religions *in its totality;* he never allowed himself to limit his activity to a single area, although he was considered to be one of the great "specialists" in Greek religion. He didn't hesitate to tackle problems of a general nature: origins of the idea of God, Hellenistic mysteries, structures of mythological thought, confession of sins, etc. . . .

"It's really too difficult!" exclaimed a student, one of the best of the group.

I could only shrug my shoulders and breathe a sigh, and everyone burst out laughing.

5 December

"To die brutally in trenches or little by little in a factory, it's almost the same thing," wrote A. K. Coomaraswamy in 1937 in *What Is the Use of Art, Anyway?*

6 December

We call Corina in Bucharest. We hear her even more clearly than if she were in New York. She had the flu for two weeks, but is doing better, and we share her hope that we will be able to see each other next summer.

7 December

It's been cold for two weeks. It's snowing like it snowed back home, in that Rumania of fifty years ago.

I'd like to find the passage where Marx wrote: "The worker, just like the machine, is an invention of modern times." It is one of the rare reflections by Marx that is unanimously accepted, by "moderns" as well as by traditionalists.

8 December

It's still snowing, but the wind has let up. At one in the afternoon Giovanna Breu comes to interview me at Meadville for *People* magazine. Her photographer joins us shortly afterwards. He's a nice, bearded young man who has arrived from Paris.

The interview lasts a good two hours. Then we all three trudge across the snow to Swift Hall, where I must attend Juan Campo's thesis defense. The photographer asks me several times to stand still, and aims his camera at me, using as a backdrop the buildings that seem most photogenic to him.

At the end of the day I immerse myself in the biography of Ananda Coomaraswamy. I was already somewhat familiar with it from reading the chapters that Roger Lipsey had sent me, in manuscript form, seven or eight years ago. I also remember the first letters I received from Coomaraswamy in the 1930s. I had sent him a copy of *Yoga, essai sur les origines de la mystique indienne*. He rightly brought to my attention that the word *mystique* was a bad choice, for yoga was also *something else*. I had asked him to collaborate on the journal *Zalmoxis,* and he immediately accepted. Indeed, he liked to contribute articles to more or less obscure little journals published in South India, Ceylon, or Portugal . . . He submitted the manuscript of an admirable article, "The Philosophy of Medieval and Oriental Art," which Lipsey is currently reprinting in the first volume of the *Selected Papers*. Then, three or four days later he began sending me letter after letter, all very brief, to indicate a modification in the text, to add a quote, correct a bibliographical note, etc. . . . He continued to do this even after his article had been typeset, and he significantly reworked the proofs. The publication of another of his articles, it, too, magnificent, "Svaya matrina: Janua Coeli" was even more epic. I would need dozens of pages to tell about what was a true adventure: Additions were counted in the tens, and several sets of proofs were necessary. Then I left for London. The composition of the second volume of *Zalmoxis* having been completed, the plates were melted down. When, a year later, it had to be reset, the manuscript couldn't be found, and we had to use the proofs. But numerous corrections had become illegible, and the article appeared with mutilations that in places made it incomprehensible. I nevertheless sent the offprints to the author, first from Lisbon in 1941–1942, then from Paris in 1945, but I was a bit embarrassed. Luckily, almost every copy of *Zalmoxis I* and *II* were destroyed in the American bombings of 1944.

10 December

In the speech he delivered at the banquet given in his honor on the occasion of his seventieth birthday, Coomaraswamy spoke of a certain Dr. John Lodge, a great expert in Indian art, who had a position at the Museum of Fine Arts in Boston. Dr. Lodge, said Coomaraswamy, wrote very little, but he will be remembered for this aphorism: ''From the stone age until now, *what a comedown!*''

16 December

Superb day. This morning attended Gallagher's thesis defense: ''Conversion in the Beginnings of the Christian Era.'' I must note in detail—but when?—everything I think about ''Conversion through Books'' in present-day Europe: Franz Rosenzweig, Papini, Father Jean de Menasce, etc. . . .

I return to my office at Meadville, but I don't feel like working. From my window I watch the workers who are taking down the wooden staircase that used to go down from Channing House to the garden. A few days ago Mike had noticed termites in it. A balustrade on the first floor was already half-eaten from the inside. If it hadn't been noticed, and if someone, in a year or even earlier, had leaned against it . . .

I remember the autumn of 1956 and the beginning of the winter of 1957, and the little apartment we lived in then in that same building. I can see the squirrel who had entered by the dining room window while Christinel was in the bath, and who was nibbling at a box of candy. A few weeks later another squirrel—but perhaps it was the same one—had also come in through the barely open window and, not knowing how to get out, had begun to gnaw at the wood of the window frame. And I can especially see that bird whose bluish reflection had for an instant passed in the mirror while I was shaving. At first I thought I was the victim of a hallucination, and I was frightened. I was at that time unfamiliar with the ''jaybird.'' It is when it opens its wings to take flight that it appears in all its ideal bluebird splendor.

20 December

It is not without emotion that I put down Céleste Albaret's *Monsieur Proust* tonight. The book had been brought to my attention by Cioran one October day, at the Café La Martiniquaise. We had met an hour earlier, Cioran, Ionesco, and I, at Editions Belfond, where a photographer was waiting for us. Then, all together, we had gone to the place Fürstenberg since, as I had told Claude Bonnefoy, it was there in September 1945 that we had seen each other again, all three of us, for the first time in a long time, shortly after I had arrived from Lisbon. The photographer took multiple shots, and photographed us in different poses: talking, looking at each other, Eugène laughing, speechifying, raising his arms to the sky, and Cioran letting him go on, seeming resigned, polite, and melancholy. Then Eugène left us, for he had to go quickly to a work session at the Academy.

Our group having dispersed, I went with Cioran to La Martiniquaise so we could warm ourselves up. He ordered, as he usually did, a pot of herbal tea, and I a cup of coffee.

While I'm writing these lines in my office at Meadville, and am glancing outside from time to time where large snowflakes are falling, I wonder why on that day, in that room way in the back of the café where Cioran and I had taken refuge to be better isolated, we didn't think of recalling that fabulous Paris of right after the war when we were all three poor, all three unknown, and yet quite determined—although without too many illusions and each for different reasons—to remain what we had already been in Rumania: writers. How funny it would have been to talk about the time when Eugène pinned all his hopes on being employed as a representative of Ripolin, whereas he had just left us a few minutes earlier, cutting his goodbyes short, anxious to avoid having his colleagues on the quai Conti wait for him . . .

But a respite from nostalgia. I then listened to Cioran tell me how enthused he had been in reading *Monsieur Proust.* He would never have imagined such devotion, an altruism as complete as that of this kindhearted woman. Preceding all whom France counted among its intellectuals and writers, she was the first to be aware of the originality and the importance of Proust's work. I then asked Cioran if he reread *A la recherche du temps perdu* with the same fervor as before. He admitted that he preferred *Le Temps retrouvé,* and that he had reread it at least three or four times.

"But that's the most depressing part of *A la recherche!*" I exclaimed.

"Exactly!" he replied. "It's also the truest . . ."

PALM BEACH, *24 December*

We arrived on 21 December. The Ocean View Hotel held for us the two communicating rooms we had last year. Lisette's is not far away.

As we were leaving Chicago it had started to snow again, and we thought that flights were going to be cancelled. Our plane took off with an hour's delay and we were disagreeably surprised by the cold and the overcast sky that awaited us in Palm Beach. The next day the sky had finally cleared, but it was still just as cold. In this same place, four years earlier, and again on Christmas Eve, we walked around in shirt sleeves, and the beach was covered with people. I remembered the garden, where at that time there were butterflies and hymenoptera in abundance, and lizards that ambled across the hotel pathways. Luckily, the flowers are still just as beautiful, and this morning I noticed on the walls and in the bushes enough lizards, some of which were no bigger than a strand of yarn, to cause a resurgence of childhood memories.

Since our arrival I haven't worked very much. I haven't even answered the few letters—urgent, however—that I had brought from Chicago. Instead I take long walks on the ocean front, walking into the wind. In addition I sleep like a log, as if I had been deprived of sleep for several nights in a row. I have to force myself to reread the material I have been assembling for some time relating to archaic Chinese religion. Last evening I started the book by Ping-Ti Ho, *The Cradle of the East*.

26 December

We have dinner almost every evening at Lydia M.'s, and I take my daily walks alone or with Christinel. As for Lisette, she prefers the beach. She has discovered she has a fascination for seagulls, and she never tires of watching them catch pieces of bread in the air.

Shortly after midnight I finished reading the book by Ho. If what he says is true, all current hypotheses on the origins of Chinese culture, that is, that agriculture, ceramics, metallurgy, would have come to China from Mesopotamia and the Balkans, fall apart. One must see here one more argument in opposition to the "diffusionist" theory. Henceforth, any attempt at a universal history will have to take into account at least three autonomous centers of civilization: the Middle East, China, and Central America. But perhaps there have been more, the Balkans, for example, and Africa, as well. Some authors have long maintained that African agriculture is of local prehistoric origin.

I envy and pity at the same time whoever will one day undertake to write *A Universal History*. In truth, for some time the species has been singularly scarce! The last, and also the best, history of this sort is the one by McNeill, *The Rise of the West,* and it dates from 1963.

I envy any such potential author, for the horizon he will have before him was still unimagined only ten or fifteen years ago. But I pity him, too, for I suspect he will have trouble maintaining three or four parallel narratives, two or three of which (Middle East, Africa? China, Balkans) unfold almost simultaneously.

28 December

I preferred that Christinel and Lisette accompany Lydia to Miami, and, alone in my room, I spent almost the entire day transcribing the contents of diverse scraps of paper, the usual sources of the notes from which I write my journal. I don't always manage to reread what I wrote, and, exasperated, I crumble up my paper and throw it into the wastebasket. I regret this. Those few lines which had become illegible perhaps contained thoughts or remarks that I would have liked to have kept.

29 December

It's very mild today, for the first time since we arrived. Usual walk along Gulf Street, then Middle Street, which I particularly like, for at this hour of the day it is almost deserted. I stop to look once again at that wonderful cottage surrounded by tropical greenery, its palms, its baobabs, which each time I see it reminds me of Ceylon. What an admirable house! One would think it had been conceived especially for a writer! For a novelist, that is, not for a historian of religions . . .

It's not yet noon, and the beach is already packed. The waves have calmed down, and with them have disappeared the groups of young people who practice surfing.

30 December

The air is becoming increasingly mild, and I can walk in shirt sleeves on the ocean front, despite the wind.

Artificial and almost supernatural cleanliness of this city. There are streets where one would be ashamed to throw down a cigarette butt. And yet sometimes a vacant lot throws a false note into the wise harmony of the proud, elegant apartment buildings which rise up from among the palm trees. Undoubtedly, a house must have been torn down. Several years have gone by and, new construction having to wait, brambles and thistles have taken possession of the abandoned lot. This means that in the height of the tourist season one sees in places piles of old boxes, empty bottles, dirty papers. Along these vacant lots the sidewalk is broken, weeds grow out of the cracks, and this at hardly a few steps from majestic homes, villas built in Hispano-colonial style. If the car that young, elegant woman in an evening dress is getting out of had stopped a few meters farther away, the beautiful passenger would have stumbled into a crack in the sidewalk, would have got her feet caught in Coca-Cola cans . . .

Ultramodern city. One has no neighbors here.

31 December

It's hot, too hot, even. I spend the day writing, first my journal, from my disparate notes, then the preface to the French edition of *Mademoiselle Christina.*

Dinner at Lydia's, then we go home. Christinel reads *Monsieur Proust,* and I the poems of Vasile Voïculescu. Memories quickly surge up. I think about those years 1934–1935. In those days I would meet Voïculescu, either at the Radio or at the Society of Rumanian Writers. One evening General Condeescu, president of the society, had invited us to dinner at a fancy restaurant in Bucharest, Voïculescu, Professor Herescu, and me. The dinner went on until dawn.

It was Voïculescu, again, who had the idea for that luncheon which the Society of Rumanian Writers offered in my honor in May 1937 at the Capsha restaurant. It was in response to the press campaign that had been unleashed against me in which I found myself accused by C. Kiritzescu, then by Cocosh, in the newspaper *Neamul Românesc,* of writing "pornography." Memorable luncheon! Among the guests were the general Condeescu, Professor C. Radulescu-Motru, Al. Rosetti, C. C. Giurescu, Nae Ionescu, Ionel Teodoreanu, and many others whose names I've forgotten.[1] Except for Rosetti, all have been dead for a long time. C. C. Giurescu was the last to disappear; it will be a year this autumn.

In the days that preceded my departure from Rumania, Voïculescu and I met frequently. After my arrival in Paris, I received from him in 1946–1947 several letters in which he told me about his new passion for India, the Upanishads, and Buddhism. He managed to send me the manuscript of a "fantastic" story, and his poem "Farewell Freedom!" which I immediately published as the frontispiece to the journal *Luceafarul* (*Morning Star*). I later learned that he was living in isolation, poor, forgotten by all: He refused to "collaborate."

Then shortly after his death in 1963, surprising publication of some of his works: *Derniers sonnets imaginaires de Shakespeare* (imaginary last sonnets of Shakespeare) (which I already knew of in part through Father Scrima, who had brought some of them to Paris). Finally, a collection of his "fantastic" stories in two volumes.

PALM BEACH, *4 January 1978*
Arrival at the airport an hour early. In the cafeteria we are served the ubiquitous ham sandwiches to be washed down with coffee. Around us are other travelers, the same ones, it seems, as ten days ago, or ten years . . .

There are Americans who can work anywhere, in a cafeteria or on board a plane. I saw a professor who, during the flight from New York

1. This luncheon gathered together the most visible representatives of Rumanian culture at the time: writers, university professors, novelists, journalists, publishers, etc. . . . Cf. *Autobiography, Volume 1: 1907–1937, Journey East, Journey West,* p. 323.— C.G.

to Los Angeles, recorded all his correspondence (a good hundred or so letters) into a miniscule dictaphone . . .

CHICAGO, *5 January*

Bad surprise when we get home: The snow on the roof melted, and in the living room drops of water are falling from the ceiling.

From seven to ten in the evening, seminar on methodology in the history of religions.

6 January

Wrote eleven letters. But since I write them by hand, I hurry, and my writing suffers from this. One of my former American colleagues has published nothing since his doctoral thesis. He is held in esteem, however, and is even admired for his great erudition in bibliography, for the lectures he gives, and especially for his massive correspondence. Each day he dictates between ten and twenty letters to his secretary. And when she's gone, he records almost as many on his dictaphone . . .

9 January

Anniversary of our marriage. Twenty-nine years already.

Outside the wind is glacial. It's $-20°C$. But the sky is crystal clear.

I reread the documents assembled by Coomaraswamy on "death during life." Eckhart: "The Kingdom of God belongs only to those who are definitively dead." And Plato, of course, with this famous passage: "True philosophers practice death," etc. . . . Which made Rumi and Angelus Silesius say: "We must die before we die." Indeed, only those who are truly dead will be able to be resuscitated. Rumi notes "a man who is dead and who, however, walks on land like the living; yet he is dead, and his soul is already in heaven . . ."

10 January

In the *Naladiyar*, Tamil collection of didactic verses probably dating from the sixth century, I come across this praise of the wife:

"The chastity of a woman is like a sharpened sword in the hand of a valorous warrior."

12 January

I noticed today in a bookstore a new edition—paperback—of *Patterns in Comparative Religion.* This is the eighth edition. Through my own fault, this English edition of my *Traité d'histoire des religions* has earned me in all and forever only $300. When in 1951–1952 Payot let me know that an American publisher wanted to translate *Traité,* and that they were offering us either the usual 7 percent royalties or a flat fee of $600, I begged him to accept the latter, for I was in terrible need of money. The $300 to which I was entitled assured me, twenty-five years ago, a good month of tranquility (we were living at the time on rue de la Tour, and we weren't paying any rent).

14 January

Among the fifty or so books which I donated today to the Meadville library there were the two big volumes by Professor B. Weinberg, *Literary Criticism in the Italian Renaissance.* I remember my last meetings with the author. We spoke above all of French poetry, of Paris where he had lived in 1950, of Florence. He was a scholar, both ironical and shy. At the university when he met with students in his office, he always left the door partially open. So as not to cause any gossip . . .

16 January

Long letter, very moving, from a refugee teaching today in Canada. In it she tells me about her misadventures when, three years earlier in Rumania, she had dared to "slip something in" concerning me during a seminar at the Faculty of Arts. "Watch your step!" she was told. "And don't let us catch you again!" But she did it again, and even proposed to Professor Al. Dima, chaired professor in her department, that she use me as the subject of her doctoral thesis. Dima, shocked by so much audacity, hurried to the door, double-locked it, threw his coat over the telephone—*"micro oblige!"*—and exclaimed, choking: "You want to kill me! What's wrong with you? You will be happy when they have thrown us both out of the department. This is pure folly . . ."

17 January

The campus is disappearing under the snow, which is still falling. Julia, my California student, told me the strange impression she had on seeing snow for the first time.

I hear someone knocking at the door, and I get up to go open it. I'm irritated because I don't like students to bother me outside office hours. Vicky enters. This student, who is in her fifth or sixth year at the university, was first fascinated by Tibetan, then by the history of religions, then by symbolism, and abandoned them all one after the other. She's holding a book and gives it to me. It's a book she bought at a secondhand bookstore in Rumania, where she accompanied her father two months earlier. She decided to make me a gift of it. It is a hard-bound book, with a red leather cover. I open it: The paper is thick, and the text is entirely written by hand in an old-fashioned script in black ink. I read the title: *Le règne de Saturne changé en siècle d'or* . . . All of it translated from the Latin of Huginus Barma by Mr. Pi. Th. An. in Paris, at the expense of Pierre Derieu, MDCCLXXX.

Once alone, I leaf through the work with curiosity, and not without melancholy. How could such a manuscript have managed to land in Rumania? To whom did it first belong? And above all, why did someone bother to recopy this text by hand when the book had already been published in Paris in 1780?

25 January

Large snowflakes are falling. My desk is disappearing under files, and I try to impose a little order on it. I would have really liked to have found the envelope containing my most recent notes for chapter 31 of *History,* but I have to give it up.

Last evening, third seminar, this time on Van der Leeuw. The first two, on Freud and Jung, or more precisely on their respective contributions to the understanding of the religious phenomenon, were excellent. A student had alluded to my "Jungianism," and I thought at first that he wanted to talk about archetypes. Given how interesting the subject was, I invited him to develop his thoughts. "You were always with Jung during the Eranos lectures in Ascona," he merely replied.

I had to hold myself back not to be sharp. In the end I thought it preferable to escape with a quip:

"In that case," I told him, "you must also consider me to be a Unitarian." Indeed, the office where I work is located in a building that belongs to the Unitarian church . . .

26 January

More snow. The campus is again covered with its white blanket. Dreamily, I look out the window. I had found the notes I was looking for in vain, as I didn't feel like working. This silence that surrounds me has something supernatural about it. Outside there are no cars, no sounds of voices. One would think one were in a little mountain village, in the winter, in the last century.

27 January

Yesterday afternoon a young man with blue eyes and a flamboyant beard asked me, excitedly, to please see him today "for an hour, or even forty-five minutes," because, he claimed, "it's an extremely important day for me."

He came today at one o'clock in the afternoon carrying a bag. Out of it he took a bottle of white wine, a cardboard box containing two glasses, and a few sandwiches. He was disappointed to learn that I had just eaten, and he asked my permission to eat in front of me. He then uncorked the bottle of wine, which was chilled, and we clinked glasses. "This is the most important day of my life," he told me. "Not only is it my birthday, but it's been exactly three years today since I learned that my cancer was cured . . . "

At twenty-one years old, when he learned he was suffering from lung cancer that was spreading, he had believed he was condemned. The doctor had warned his parents that he had at most eighteen months to live. He underwent intensive treatment, cobalt therapy, perhaps, but I'm not sure I understood this very well. Still, he benefited from very recent therapeutics, in use for less than five years. Each treatment session left him drained. He spent nights reflecting on his fate: Why him? Why so young? etc. . . . Finally, one fine day—quite exactly 27 January 1975, after one last control test, his doctor announced that he had been definitively cured. A strange impression had invaded him then: He felt as if he had *really* been "reborn," for the good news had been given to him right on his birthday.

He finally finished his story, not without having interrupted it with expansive gestures and bursts of laughter. "Isn't it a miracle?" he kept repeating. "I can't believe that it is to technology, that dreadful technology that is poisoning our atmosphere and polluting the entire world, that I owe my recovery!"

This summer he will receive his diploma as Master in Religion. What will he do next? He doesn't really know, himself. He intends to go see cancer patients going through treatment in hospitals and talk to them about "miracles" of science. After having swallowed two sandwiches and emptied several glasses of wine, he asks my permission to be photographed next to me and asks a secretary to take the picture. He insists that we both hold a glass, while with his free hand he holds up three symbolic fingers . . . Last year he had asked Langdon Gilkey, his professor, to participate in the same ceremony.

Why, indeed, did he come to see me? I didn't know him at all and had seen him yesterday for the first time. Suddenly I realize that I don't even know his name.

29 January

Last evening we invited the Ricoeurs and the Lacocques to a restaurant, Army and Lou's. The establishment is owned by a black whose wife is Belgian. They make a very nice couple. I've known them for about two months, and their restaurant is somewhere on the south side of Chicago, around twenty blocks from where we live. To get there we first have to go through the black neighborhood, which is disappearing under the snow. From time to time we notice on either side of the street abandoned houses with broken windows. Some of them, a few stories high, must have once even been pleasant. The effect is sinister, depressing.

5 February

Temporal cycles are shorter and shorter: geological, biological (life of the species); historical (duration of cultures); individual (the human person) cycles. But man alone knows their true "significance," and he alone is capable of freeing himself of Time.

7 February

Randy hasn't succeeded in completely clearing our roof of the snow that covers it. Enough of it remained so that while melting the water falls drop by drop into the living room.

The typewriter Christinel is using to type my latest manuscripts isn't working: The letter *a* is off, and I must go over all the texts by hand.

My watch, too, has given up. I had to ask Christinel to call me at the office around eight-thirty if she wanted me to arrive in time for dinner.

14 February

Thomas W. told me today that he had been shocked, and even indignant, indeed furious, to learn that "Thomas" is not a true *name,* but an Aramaic word meaning "twin."

When I expressed surprise at his irritation, he remained nonplussed, being content to smile uncomfortably.

"To tell the truth, I don't know why, myself," he finally replied. "The *why* escapes me. It's instinctive, stronger than I, as if it came from the unconscious."

9 March

I'm seventy-one today. And I have completed neither the second volume of *A History of Religious Ideas* (I'm still writing the final chapter), nor my *Autobiography.*

This evening, in the taxi coming home from the Italian Village Restaurant where we spent the evening with Joe Kitagawa, his wife Evelyn, and David Tracy, I kept saying to myself, "I must act quickly! I must devote myself exclusively to my works in progress . . ."

But I well realize that that is useless, and that one doesn't change. Come what may.

CHAPEL HILL, NORTH CAROLINA, *13 March*

Chuck Long came to pick us up at the airport. We spend this first night at the Carolina Inn, but as of tomorrow we will move to the house that has been reserved for us. Chuck assures us that it is admirable and located right in the forest. So much the better, for it would have been difficult for me to bear living for three weeks in these two rooms without kitchen or refrigerator, and especially without any kind of table to work on.

CHAPEL HILL, *15 March*

I never tire of contemplating, through the bay window, and sometimes for more than an hour straight, the birds that rush over to eat the seeds we threw out for them. There are cardinals, which I recognize by their beautiful red feathers, and other sparrows with blue crests, whose name I always forget.

It's truly the most beautiful house I've ever lived in. And it is indeed lost among the trees.

20 March

I worked all day on the last chapter of *History*. In the evening, discussions with students. Since I've been in Chapel Hill, there's something planned for me on the "itinerary" almost every day. On 15 March, from two to four o'clock, discussion with professors from Duke University and from Chapel Hill. On 19 March, cocktails and dinner at the department. And I had to give a lecture.

21 March

Every night around midnight, the forest is filled with mysterious sounds. Perhaps they are only dry branches falling through the boughs already filled with sap, or oak twigs that the wind has pulled off the tree, or a wild animal going through the woods.

I don't tire of listening to these unfamiliar noises that make me think of those in the Carpathans of my youth, whose echo still follows me, and of those that reached me from the nearby jungle in my *kutiar* in Rishikesh, on the banks of the Ganges.

22 March

Yesterday I was able to work at complete leisure and didn't stop until close to evening, as I was to give a lecture on "The Myth of Alchemy."

This afternoon, second seminar at the department. In the evening, discussions with Dr. Peak's students at his home. The questions raised are not only in the realm of the psychology of religions. The students ask me, more or less directly, to talk about *me,* to tell them about my Indian experiences (why did I go there so young, at twenty-one years old? Why did I choose yoga as the subject of my doctoral thesis? Why did I leave the Himalayas?). They also ask me to talk about Jung and the Eranos lectures in Ascona. And even about the "Paris existentialists" . . .

24 March

Yesterday and today, worked from morning to evening. Luckily the house is so beautiful and so comfortable (Mary Stevenson and Jay Kim have come to join us, but we could easily house two or three more guests), and the neighboring forest is so enchanting, that I would be ungracious to resent the obligation I have to meet with so many people.

It's been an eternity since I've seen spring *surge up* so closely, and all around me. This little city, framed by hills, lost in greenery, suspended on the edge of steep slopes, is metamorphosed from day to day: The trees are covered with flowers, new plants jump out of the ground, new birds make their appearance . . .

27 March

On the 25th, reception at Professor Tysen's. The next day, reception at Chuck Long's, where I was able to see many colleagues and former students again.

28 March

In the evening, lecture: "Literary Imagination and Religious Structures." Then I have a few friends over to the house. Mac Ricketts is among us. Long conversation with Chuck.

30 March

Yesterday, anthropology colloquium. In the evening, from eight to ten o'clock, discussions. Victor Turner, Mary Douglas, Beidelman were present. Today, at the department, third seminar. In the evening, dinner and reception at Professor Peacock's, an anthropologist. Our discussions go on until very late.

CHARLOTTESVILLE, 2 April

Chuck drove us to the airport, and at two-thirty we flew off towards Richmond. I would have liked very much to visit the city, and to have the opportunity to travel around Virginia. Another time, perhaps. Charlotte and Nathan Scott were waiting for us at the airport. Two hours later we arrive here in Charlottesville, where we're their guests in the house they recently bought. It's a superb house, very bright, surrounded by large trees. Bookshelves everywhere.

Long conversation, about our friends in Chicago, about the book Nathan is writing.

3 April

In the morning we visit the campus of the University of Virginia. I remind Nathan of certain passages from Julien Green's *Journal*. I am amazed in noticing that the students' rooms have been preserved such as they were in the time of Edgar Allan Poe. And we stop for a moment to look at the one he had occupied.

In the afternoon we go up to Monticello, the home of Thomas Jefferson. They have made a museum out of this noble and stately home. It was Jefferson himself, that prodigious scholar, who conceived the design of the University of Virginia and its campus.

In the evening, dinner in the company of three colleagues of Nathan's and their wives. I wonder what Marcel Proust would have thought if he had been told that some fifty years after his death one of the most eminent exegetes of his work would comment on it and would devote works to it at a university founded by Jefferson . . .

CHICAGO, *4 April*

Charlotte drives us to the airport, where we take the plane to Washington. Two-hour wait there before making the connection to Chicago.

I always experience a sort of fascination at the spectacle of the concessions and corridors of a big airport. Especially here in Washington, D.C., the city where more than ten thousand (at least, I would imagine) diplomats, secret agents, and commercial, military, and cultural attachés gravitate in the service of close to two hundred embassies, legations, and consulates . . .

In Chicago I discover the pile of letters that has accumulated in our absence, and a great number of new books. Among them, Ioan Culianu's on my work as a historian of religions. It's the first of its kind written by a Rumanian, the only one of my fellow-countrymen who is an authentic historian of religions.

6 April

Usual morning walk to the Midway. I go down Fifty-eighth Street (to admire the flowers at 1320), then come back on Fifty-seventh Street. I suddenly remember that encounter I had several years ago at about the same time of year, since I can still see the lilacs that were in bloom. Two men, one older, the other still young, had approached me smiling. I had put on a smile, too, while wondering with whom I was dealing.

"We've already met," said the older of the two, "only once in New York, at the congress . . ."

That brought back no memory, and I nodded my head without saying anything.

"We had just brought up certain essential issues," he continued, "indeed those that our congress is committed to discussing. And you were in complete agreement with us."

"Oh yes! I remember," I exclaimed. "Everyone had indicated what he considered to be most important: structure of myths, religious symbolism, etc. . . ."

The man was visibly surprised, but he continued to smile.

"My recollection is not as precise," he continued. "Nevertheless, our group approved Tom's proposal, that is, that the following year an entire day would be devoted to discussing the three problems brought up."

It was I this time who was nonplussed.

"The three problems," he specified, "that Roman civilization proved incapable of resolving: that of the Teutons, that of the Persians, and that of the nomadic Arab tribes . . ."

Since then I continue to wonder with whom my mysterious colleague could possibly have confused me.

10 April

A young man insists on seeing me. He tells me his name, which I have since forgotten, and our conversation lasts barely five minutes. He is passing through Chicago for a few days, he tells me, and is staying at his sister's. Knowing how busy I am, he has simply come to shake my hand and to tell me how he had heard about me: in a dream. It was in a dream, he assures me, that he learned my name, and that a voice told him to obtain my books and read them.

At that time, two or three years earlier, he was an atheist. He had just completed a long sea voyage (as a steward on a big steamer). No sooner had he landed than he went into a New York bookstore and asked for "any book by Mircea Eliade." He was given a paperback edition of *The Sacred and the Profane,* and he began reading it while walking away. All the same, he admits, "that day I didn't understand very much of it . . ."

12 April

Beginning of a colloquium that will last three days, organized by Norman Girardod at Notre Dame University: "Mircea Eliade or the *coincidentia oppositorum.''* I had promised to attend it, but, having too much to do—among other things, choose all the documentation and illustrations for Rocquet—I had decided not to go.

14 April

A young Jesuit came to get me yesterday at two in the afternoon. We arrive at Notre Dame around four o'clock, in time to hear the end of Mateï Calinescu's paper. (An excellent paper. He had given me the text of it some time ago.) I took the opportunity to see Chuck and Jerry Long, Jay Kim, Mary Stevenson, Mac Ricketts, etc. . . . Also present are Virgil Nemoianu, Saliba, Dudley III (these last two have just published their theses on my work). After dinner in Washington Hall, Florence Hetzler of Fordham University gives a paper entitled "Introductory Remarks on Eliade and Brancusi," which is followed by excerpts from *Endless Column,* admirably directed by Miles Coiner, who himself plays the role of Brancusi: The stage is empty, except for six desks on the left and two others on the right. It is there that the young girl and Brancusi interact.[1]

I listen attentively to Florence Hetzler's paper. I already know that reading *Endless Column* in Mary Stevenson's translation, had made Florence Hetzler want to go to India to verify whether what I had Brancusi say (in the play) on Indore, the labyrinth, etc. . . . was true, and that she had managed to do this. Listening to her paper, I didn't understand very well whether her intention was to summarize and comment on *the play,* or to present and analyze what she had seen herself or discovered in India. Up until then, I thought that certain motifs in the play, such as Daedalas, the labyrinth, light, silence as a primordial element in music and poetry (and whose equivalent Brancusi sought in architecture), came entirely out of my own imagination. In any case, I don't remember reading anything that had influenced me. But listening to Florence Hetzler, one sometimes came to believe that it is to Brancusi himself that one owes those motifs, and that he had been concerned with them during his lifetime.

1. *Endless Column*—play written by Mircea Eliade and inspired by the work of the sculptor Brancusi.—C.G.

How strange is the destiny of this *History!* I've been working on it for
ten or eleven years, and I find myself forced to draft the last chapters of
volume 2 in all haste. I have to mention that the book went into
production in May 1977!

30 April

Urs von Balthazar's bibliography of the last ten years is truly
amazing. And yet, he says he devotes himself essentially to the
publication of the work of a Swiss woman doctor, exceptional works,
according to the great theologian. Forty volumes have already been
published, thanks to him.

2 May

Visit from Mike M. He expects to give a course this fall on
religious psychology at the University of San Diego. The titular
professor died recently, right in the lecture hall while he was teaching a
class on death, religion, and psychology. Half the people in the room
fainted.

5 May

Last night attended the lecture given by Siegfried Unseld on
Hermann Hesse. "Here we are finally together!" he exclaims. He's a
man full of energy who evokes kindness, seems untiring, and always
has something funny to say. He likes to talk, and especially to engage
in dialogue (he listens attentively to all the questions he is asked, and
then answers them). After his lecture, where he spoke very well, and
even *con brio,* without the slightest nervousness, we go to honor him
with champagne at Morris Philipson's home.

Siegfried Unseld tells me of his enthusiasm for *The Old Man and the Bureaucrats*. He asks only to publish my ''complete works'' in German translation, and would like me to prepare an outline for him in this regard. He will come to Paris in June or July to discuss the matter with me.

6 May

This morning on Woodlawn Avenue, visit from Dr. Unseld, who insisted on seeing us again before he leaves for San Francisco. He immediately asks me to prepare the outline for my complete works. He envisions the publication of around ten volumes, and I hesitate to tell him that there should be, in my opinion, a good half dozen more.

7 May

All day yesterday until almost midnight, then today until six in the evening, Dennis Doeing came to work in my office in Meadville. He thought he'd be able to complete the bibliography of my articles and the reviews of my books, but that will take him still quite a bit more time. It is moreover with a certain melancholy that in order to help him I've immersed myself in my files from the years 1942–1943, or 1948–1950. I hadn't opened them in at least fifteen years. To extract them from drawers and bookshelves where they were lying dormant, we had to proceed with true excavations and rearrange hundreds of books.

10 May

After a long period of cold, rain, and grey skies, finally a glorious day! Stroll on campus, where the tulips are finally in bloom (our garden is full of them). I believe I am going to begin to live again. Since my return from Notre Dame University, I felt rather under the weather: stomach aches, esophageal pains, vagotonia, drowsiness, fatigue, etc. Without this last chapter of *History,* volume 2, which I must finish as soon as possible, all that wouldn't bother me unduly.

27 May

With Mateï Calinescu and his family, in the afternoon, at the Rumanian church for the baptism of their son.

May

One has only to open a newspaper to realize that we are condemned and that we will not escape from condemnation without a miracle. And yet, this doesn't prevent people from continuing to live as if nothing were the matter, and some even continue to *create*. I feel reassured. In saying that, I'm not really thinking of those who are content to "exist" in relative unawareness of what awaits us. I only admire those who persist in working, in *creating*, just as if our world had a good millennium of peace and "progress" before it. They are like that poet who composed his verses seated on a barrel of gunpowder, all the while knowing he could be blown up from one moment to the next, but refusing to let himself be dominated by fear, and who had only one idea in mind: to write in the most authentic and the most perfect way possible.

6 June

I've begun to work again as in the best of days: twelve or thirteen hours a day, not counting innumerable letters. In addition, I'm preparing quite a few packages of books to send off.

8 June

Superb weather. After the lecture given by Jacob Neusner, informal reception at the home of our colleague Morris Janowitz. I set to work at seven-thirty, and we have dinner at eleven-thirty. Strange sensation of *freedom*, as if time and schedules didn't exist. To do what one *wants*, even if in the end it is only that which one is indeed obliged to do.

9 June

It's still just as nice out. One would think it were the middle of summer. I am invited to lunch at the Disciples House by J.A., the young man with the flamboyant beard who had come to see me last January. He has received his diploma. Still just as joyous and as confident, even though he is getting ready to go back into the hospital; some of the doctors are afraid his disease has still not been completely cured.

11 *June*

At last, at ten in the evening, I've finally finished the last chapter of *History,* volume 2. I immediately gathered up the files containing (for how many years?) materials for chapters 29 and 30, and I threw a good armful of them into the trash . . .

13 *June*

I send my manuscript to Payot and write quite a few letters.

I see one of my students who tells me he intends to write a "study" to prove that the *morphology* (the "structures") and the *history* of religions are the counterpart of the famous distinction established by Saussure between *language* and *speech,* between the synchronic and the diachronic. While listening to him, I remained thoughtful. All he was doing there was repeating what I had said myself on multiple occasions, notably during my courses in the history of methodology. How could my student have *forgotten* what he had only so recently learned? But it happened thus: He had completely forgotten that which had interested him most, only to subsequently discover it again, *by himself.*

NEW YORK, *16 June*

Arrived last evening. I immediately set to work on the index to *History,* volume 2.

Today, spent almost all afternoon at the Metropolitan Museum: Claude Monet exhibition.

NEW YORK, *20 June*

The index is completed. Saul Steinberg exhibition. Since we arrived, the trash has not been collected. New York has the very look of a city in a state of siege . . .

PARIS, *22 June*

Arrived yesterday morning. Still dazed and drowsy.

24 *June*

Dr. Unseld invited us to the Méditerrannée Restaurant, along with his son and Edith Silbermann. I sign the contract for *Le centenaire,* and we discuss future translations: *Şarpele* [*Andronic et le serpent*], *Noaptea de Sânziene* [*The Forbidden Forest*], *Nuntă în Cer* [*Noces au paradis*].

30 June

Lots of people to see. Almost every evening we have dinner at friends' houses.

It's getting more and more difficult for me to keep this journal. I limit myself to noting down in a notebook the names of those I met during the day. I'm quite afraid of one day regretting my current negligence: I should at least have noted the essence of our conversations, or certain news that I received from Rumania.

2 July

Received a visit from Serban Cioculescu and his wife, who have both just arrived from Rumania. Although we haven't seen each other for more than thirty-eight years, I find he's almost unchanged. We spend the whole afternoon chatting, and in the evening we go have dinner at the Carlos restaurant.

Cioculescu is negotiating with Payot to acquire the translation rights for a Rumanian edition of two of my books: *Zalmoxis* and *History*. It seems that the powers that be want to publish them as soon as possible. I indeed wonder why . . .

Through Cioculescu, I learn quite a lot about certain Rumanian writers, Camil Petrescu, among others, who died tragically, as well as about G. Calinescu, Al. Rosetti, Zaharia Stancu, etc. . . . One day when Cioculescu had some business at a publishing house (Editura Univers, unless I'm mistaken), he saw Constantin Noïca arrive, accompanied by M., who was in Bucharest at the time to negotiate the sale of translation rights to her novel, *It Never Dies*. Noïca was carried away by this: "To be able to have two versions of the same passion written forty years apart, would be magnificent," he said. They then discussed terms, or royalty, for the Rumanian translation. The head of the publishing house proposed a figure.

"How many dollars is that?" asked M.

The sum seemed paltry to her. In any event it wasn't transferable out of the country.

Noïca, unless it was the interpreter, then suggested that M. donate the original manuscript (in Bengali) to the library of the Rumanian Academy.

"How many dollars are you offering me for it?" M. asked again. No one dared mention a figure. In any case, the academy has no foreign currency at its disposal . . .

5 July

Yesterday evening spent in the company of Jerry and Muriel Brauer, Cioran, Paul and Simone Ricoeur. Jerry shows us a clipping from an American newspaper: During National Airlines flight 51 from Miami to Los Angeles a pretty, young blonde causes a stir in the first-class cabin, a bottle of champagne in her hand, and completely nude. She's laughing and dancing with joy. Perched on a seat, she announces to whoever wants to hear that she has just inherited five million dollars. She learned of it hardly a few hours earlier. Jerry maintains that such an incident only confirms what I've said: Ritual nudity proclaims the return to paradisiacal beatitude. With this small exception: Under these circumstances the described happiness was caused by the sudden arrival of five million dollars . . .

15 July

We took refuge for two days, the thirteenth and fourteenth of July, at Eugène's "mill" to escape the din of the loudspeakers on place Charles-Dullin. Especially so as to be able to chat peacefully among ourselves.

26 July

It's always the same story. I *must* prepare the paper I have to give 29 July at Cerisy. I also *must* write, between now and 1 August, the little text on myth that I promised Yves Bonnefoy. But I can't think of anything but the story whose plot came to me a few weeks ago, and whose beginning I have just thought of.

CERISY-LA-SALLE, *29 July*

"Literary Creation and Initiatory Scenarios." This was the subject of my series paper for the "Places and Figures of the Imaginary" organized by Vanda Bannour and Maurice de Gandillac (the latter having invited me, I couldn't refuse). The debate that ensued was quite animated, intelligent above all.

This finally gave me the opportunity to know those famous "Décades de Cerisy." There would be too much to say about it; I will do it some other time.

EYGALIÈRE, *2 August*

At five o'clock we take off for Marseille. Ioan Cusa is waiting for us at the airport. The weather is magnificent. At the end of the evening we arrive at the Mas du Tilleul.

3 August

How I would like to be able to begin my novella! But I can't allow myself to do it, at least not before having completed the little text on mythology Yves Bonnefoy is waiting for.

"The only poetic fact in the life of thousands and thousands is their death" (Emerson, *Journal,* August 1842).

4 August

The weather is consistently beautiful. The surroundings are made to order to relax, write, take walks. And to think that we know so little of Provence . . . Ioan and Ileana are hosts such as one rarely encounters.

Afternoon at the Abbey de Sénanque, where we listened to the concert given by the Boston Camerata (created in 1954 by Narcessa Williamson, and which has been under the direction of Joel Cohen since

1958). Jewish music of the Middle Ages and the Renaissance in Spain, Italy, and Germany. The singers are accompanied by period instruments.

The concert is quite simply extraordinary. I note down certain pieces, in the hope of being able to find recordings of them: works for minstrels by Matthew the Jew (thirteenth century) and by Suskint von Trinberg; Hebrew liturgies of the Italian Renaissance; *Canticum hebraïcum* by Louis Saladin (1670).

5 August

Christinel has finished typing the text for Yves Bonnefoy. I can begin my story.

Oani and Lili arrive from Marseille.

"The sky is the daily bread of the eyes" (Emerson, *Journal*, 25 May 1843). An entire theology summed up in a witticism.

6 August

Five pages written. As usual, I imagine the action of my story as I progress in writing it. But this time, the beginning of it is so strange—"mysterious"—that the subject itself is starting to obsess me.

7 August

Overcast sky, for the first time since we arrived in Eygalière. I work all day long. Five more pages written. I still don't know "what will happen next" . . .

8 August

I wake up tired, out of sorts. I set to work, but my heart isn't in it. I limit myself to transcribing and correcting what I've already written. At the end of the afternoon I do manage to write a few pages.

9 August

Incomparably beautiful day. I write from morning to night: close to twenty pages. But I am almost certain that I'll cut out most of them.

PARIS, *10 August*

In Eygalière it was just as beautiful as yesterday, but surprisingly cooler. We arrive at the Marseille airport at three-thirty, and at the end of the afternoon we are once again at place Charles-Dullin.

"If you are not his slave, you are his enemy" (Racine, *Alexandre*). That is true for all dictatorships.

CERISY, *11 August*

Departure from Saint-Lazare around three o'clock. It's cold. In Cerisy we find Rodica, Marie-France, and Eugène, as well as G. Ionesco, Tsepeneag, etc. . . .

CERISY, *12 August*

At three o'clock I improvise a little report on light and transcendence in the work of Eugène Ionesco (I am only developing the article already published in English in *The Two Faces of Ionesco,* edited by Josette Lamont and Melvin Friedmann).

In the evening we attend a particularly excellent "show": *La Lacune,* with Maurice de Gandillac in the role of the academician, and especially *La Leçon,* with Marie-France in the role of the little girl.

PARIS, *13 August*

Departure from Cerisy at one o'clock. The beauty of twilight in Paris. During the trip, animated discussion with G. Ionesco and Tsepeneag.

Yesterday, I forgot to mention X.'s surprise when I told him that historical upsets and crises can prove propitious to spiritual creation. I had to remind him (but perhaps I didn't convince him) that if the discovery of agriculture constitutes a decisive stage in the history of humanity, it is *above all* because it made possible new religious creations.

21 August

During the afternoon and evening, long walk in the Marais with Jay and our friend Margot Rik. I am finally able to see this Parisian neighborhood such as it was around fifty years ago, that is, without cars (Cioran is quite right in saying that Paris rediscovers its nobility of yesteryear annually, two weeks in the month of August).

22 August

Most scholars and poets aren't aware that Humayun, son of Babur and the father of the famous Akbar, died in January 1556 after having slipped and fallen down the stairs of his *library* in Delhi.

30 August

During the entire week I worked seven or eight hours a day. I have already recopied more than one hundred pages, which I've just given to Christinel. Although in my opinion I have so far written only half my novel, I was anxious to know what it would produce upon a first reading. There always comes a time when I am absolutely no longer aware of the value of what I write.

1 September

Yesterday I received the first copy of volume 2 of *A History of Religious Ideas*. Last night I dreamt again of that magnificent city, built on hills, filled with greenery, and dotted with gardens and parks. I was looking for the "rue de Bellechasse" without success. Yet I knew where it was located. From time to time, very rarely, I ran into passersby. Yet I didn't dare ask them for directions, thinking they were as I was, strangers in the city.

Christinel has finished typing the first 110 pages of my novel. Her enthusiasm comforts me.

2 September

I wrote all day long. In addition, I've found a title for my novel: It will be *Nineteen Roses*. In the evening, dinner in a pizzeria with Giza and Dinu.

5 September

Lisette arrived yesterday from New York. I went out today for the first time in twelve days in order to go to Payot to sign review copies.

In the evening Ioan Culianu and Jacqueline come over for dinner.

8 September

I temporarily stop writing my *Nineteen Roses.* During the evening, from nine to eleven o'clock, I meet with Yannick Bourdoiseau, whom Virgil Tanase brought to interview me. Supposedly an interview, it is rather a conversation we have, while the photographer tries his luck from all angles in my office. As usual under such circumstances, I feel half-paralyzed and can hardly speak.

9 September

Cultural significance of the three "religions of the Book": They announce and prepare our alphabetical culture, civilizations based on what is *written,* and no longer on *oral* tradition.

10 September

I had a visit from Al. Rosetti, accompanied by his son. He tells me an anecdote about G. Calinescu. The latter had at home a great number of birds in cages which he kept in a room in the basement of his house. As soon as they heard their owner's footsteps, they all began to sing. And in the very hour of the religious service of the fortieth day following the writer's death, *all* the birds, without exception, died.

11 September

Reception at the home of François Parlier, where I am given the Cross of the Legion of Honor by the ambassador, Philippe Olivier. His speech is beautiful, but much too laudatory. Then he pins the cross to my chest and gives me the certificate of knighthood. For the occasion we had invited some forty friends and acquaintances. Unfortunately, Mariane Parlier was not among us. She had to stay in Tourrette to see to her guests.

I'm not used to "official honors," and I have never really wanted them. One gets used to them with much more difficulty than to obscurity or to a lack of success.

AMSTERDAM, *12 September*

Christinel and Lisette left today for Rome. A few hours later I took off for Amsterdam. Sorin and Liliane were waiting for me at the airport. In the evening we phone my sister Corina in Bucharest, then we stay up chatting until late into the night.

STOCKHOLM, *13 September*

Arrival at four o'clock in the afternoon. René Coeckelberghs and Gabrielle Marinescu came to get me at the airport. We're going first to Uppsala. Only today I realized just how beautiful the cathedral is under the rays of the setting sun enveloping it in a golden cloak. We amble aimlessly around the city and go into an immense bookstore.

We have dinner at Cattelin's Restaurant. On the way back we go through the old sections of Stockholm, both noble and austere. We run into a group of students who are a bit tight, and I ask my hosts how these young people find the money to drink, when alcohol is so expensive in Sweden. It seems that to hasten their euphoria, they pour a little glass of vodka into their bottle of beer . . .

I stay in Coeckelberghs's guest room; he lives in a large and bright apartment building a few kilometers from Stockholm.

STOCKHOLM, *14 September*

Paul Goma arrived this morning from Paris. In the afternoon we visit the Strindberg museum together, at 85 Drottninggatan, where the writer lived the last four years of his life, from 1908 to 1912. The house only became a museum in 1973. It is not without melancholy that I go through the rooms of this dwelling that was once very bright and elegant. I am consoled when I approach the window on the fourth floor whence, on the evening of 22 January 1912, Strindberg watched the procession organized in his honor by the workers of the city, who had come to give him the fifty thousand kronor of the "anti-Nobel" prize. The sum had been collected through public subscription after the Swedes had become convinced that Strindberg would never be given the real Nobel prize. More than ten thousand people participated in the

JOURNAL III, 1970-1978   (320)

torchlit procession that took place that evening. Strindberg appeared on the balcony, took off his hat, and greeted the crowd. The ovations were unleashed and were interminable. As for the fifty thousand kronor, the anti-Nobel prize laureate made a gift of them to Stockholm's poor.

Strindberg died a few months later, on 14 May 1912. I learn that the daily paper that reflected the opinions of the Swedish Academy devoted only six lines in all to the death. But the *Dagens Nyheter* devoted five entire pages to it. Strindberg's funeral procession was followed by more than sixty thousand people. The religious service was celebrated by the archbishop of Uppsala, Nathan Soderblom himself, the great Orientalist, historian of religions, and one of the founding fathers of our discipline.

In the evening, the four authors whose books will be presented to the public tomorrow by Coeckelberghs Bokförlag (Paul Goma, two American poetesses, and myself) are René's guests at the magnificent and picturesque Stallmästaregarden restaurant. This "historical" restaurant (it dates from the eighteenth century), will, however, be demolished to make way for a highway.

Back at the house, long conversation until around two in the morning with Gabrielle, René, Goma, and me. We talk about what we take most strongly to heart: the existence of God, difficulties of monotheism, the significance of desacralization in modern societies, but also the "mysteries" of the Nobel prize. According to those in the know, the prize in literature this year will be awarded to Graham Greene. The proof of this is that Bonniers have begun a massive reprinting of the eighteen or twenty titles by Greene that have been translated into Swedish . . .

STOCKHOLM, *15 September*
        Busy day. At two o'clock reception organized by René at Coeckelberghs Bokförlag for journalists, critics, and friends. Among those invited, the minister of culture, the president of the National Bank, etc. . . . The editor of this (admirable) collection of Swedish translations of great international poets makes a brief presentation in

English. One of our American colleagues follows him, then I am invited to speak on the relationships between mythology and literary creation. Copious buffet, French wines, whisky, cognac.

In the evening we go to have dinner as a group—there are about twenty of us—in a French restaurant nearby. Next to me is Ulla Wikander. We speak a lot about Rumania, which she knows very well, and of Stig, whom I've not been able to see, as he is immobilized in his apartment in Uppsala with his arm in a cast.

SIGTUNA, *16 September*

Magnificent walk. The ruins, the cemetery. Little city built on the edge of its gulf, whose houses date back several centuries. Some are still inhabited and keep their furniture of the period, the beds in particular, and the lamps. What a pity it truly is that Christinel is in Rome! (I suddenly realize that this is the first time we've gone on separate trips).

PARIS, *18 September*

I have just read the last page of the manuscript of the journal[1] Paul Goma kept at the time of his battle for the rights of man in Rumania. I had begun reading it in the plane coming back from Stockholm. What an admirable book! This time he is not dealing with the terror of the years 1950–1960, but of the vicissitudes of a police "investigation." Paul Goma notes with a certain detachment, and sometimes even with humor, the picturesque elements of his conversations with friends or unknowns, and especially of his dealings with the officers of the *Securitate*. If I had the means, I would give myself the luxury of buying several thousand copies of it and sending them to intellectuals and journalists all over the world, if only to make them aware of the efficacy of their public declarations, or of their signature at the bottom of a telegram of collective protest. Who could say how many Eastern European writers and intellectuals would have been saved if their Western colleagues had taken the trouble to speak up at the right time.

1. Published in French under the title *Le Tremblement des hommes* (Ed. du Seuil, 1979).—C.G.

PARIS, *21 September*

Press cocktail party organized by Jean-Luc Pidoux-Payot, right in Payot's bookstore, in honor of the publication of volume 2 of *A History of Religious Ideas*. There is a crowd: scholars (Georges Dumézil, Marcel Détienne, etc. . . .); philosophers (Paul Ricoeur, etc. . . .); writers, journalists. After only an hour, I can no longer take any more. I seem to lack air, I'm suffocating. I take refuge away from everything in a little room where I can finally sit down. A little group of guests and sympathizers come to find me and subject me to a battery of questions. I respond as I am able (I'm quite afraid of having disappointed them, and they must have thought that I had been suddenly overcome by age, or that I was under the weather . . .).

22 September

During the afternoon, visit from Catherine Clément, who came to interview me (at the reception yesterday I had agreed to do it, upon the insistence of Odile Pidoux-Payot). Since Catherine Clément is a psychoanalyst, and in addition a student of Lacan, I feared she would ask me questions on religious experience, language, the structures of the imaginary, etc. . . . whence my reticence. Indeed, I have a lot of trouble expressing *out loud* what for me must be reflected on and thought out *in writing*. Luckily, our conversation was quite agreeable: recollections of youth, of my stay in India, relationships between scholarly research and literary creation, etc. . . .

29 September

Yesterday from three to five o'clock, discussion/interview at *L'Express* with Jean-Louis Ferrier and Sophie Lannes. Rocquet's presence reassures me. I feel somewhat at home, which makes me forget there is a tape recorder. To certain questions I could, however, only reiterate what I had already told Rocquet last year (*Ordeal by Labyrinth* is soon to be published). Their promise that I would be able to review the text of the interview before its publication in *L'Express,* in order to edit out repetitions and inadvertencies, calms me.

At three o'clock in the afternoon, the first of the recording sessions with Olender for the radio station France-Culture, to which I agreed, again upon the insistence of Odile. There will be five in all. I'm afraid I was particularly awful. Knowing that I will have to repeat, in bad French, what I've already put forth in writing on multiple occasions in my books, was enough to deprive me of all my faculties. The presence of a microphone paralyzes me and rids me of all spontaneity.

5 October

I feel under the weather, and I have to postpone to a later date my interview with Olender for France-Culture. For the final program he suggested I discuss "the terror of History," a subject I've already dealt with in chapter 4 of *Myth of the Eternal Return*. I reread the chapter in question and I realize how wrong I was *not to have reread my books* while writing the second volume of *History of Religious Ideas*. Under the circumstances, my obsession with keeping on top of the most recent publications on a specific subject has been of particular disservice to me. My text would have been otherwise more lively and original if I had been content to take up and develop the ideas already contained in my own books.

7 October

At three o'clock, another interview, this time with Dominique Grisoni for *Le Magazine littéraire*. As soon as it's over I get a phone call from Cioran, who tells me that Henry Corbin has died. I feel a great sadness overwhelm me, as if a whole section of our lives, Christinel's and mine, had just crumbled. Henry wasn't only a friend, he was above all a *witness*.

At five o'clock, fourth recording session with Olender. It's a real catastrophe. After a quarter of an hour, I have to give it up.

In the evening I go to visit Stella. Henry didn't know he had cancer and that he was condemned. Stella herself only knew for a few months, the doctor having judged it wise to inform her. Henry didn't suffer. He died in peace, so sure was he that his guardian angel was waiting for him.

8 October

I can't stop thinking of Henry. He had just turned seventy-five. He died having accomplished almost everything he had promised himself to do. As for what remained, it is probable that he wouldn't have failed at the task, if only he had had a few more years in front of him.

Evening spent at Barbaneagra's. More than forty people are there. Despondency, lassitude, sadness.

CHICAGO, 23–24 October

I've felt sick for several days now. Is it my stomach? My liver? I continue to feel exhausted, sleepy, stunned. Everyone keeps telling me that I did too much in Paris, what with the interviews, recording for the radio, the receptions, etc. It's possible. But how is it that this period of despondency follows a week when I felt perfectly well, and when I was able to work without any difficulty? (I had even prepared chapter 31 of *History,* volume 3.)

25 October

This morning I am in worse shape than ever. Christinel calls Dr. Cohen, and he asks that I be brought to Billings Hospital, where, from one in the afternoon, I go through a general checkup. Two doctors then come to do additional examinations: electrocardiogram, blood tests, etc. . . .

26 October

Slept little and badly. In any event, I don't have an internal hemorrhage, since no trace of blood was discovered. While waiting for the results of the other tests, the three doctors speculate that my fatigue and my pain are due to an excess of acidity provoked by the aspirin which I swallowed in massive doses for a whole week to ease my arthritis. I took as many as eight tablets a day.

27 October

This morning I had to take two big glasses of barium meal on an empty stomach, and they took an X ray of my stomach and intestines.

It was the specialist O.R.L.'s turn to examine me. He finds nothing abnormal. And yet my throat is still just as dry, my voice is hoarse, and I am in the same state of exhaustion. The weather has been superb for a good week already. Never was an autumn more beautiful . . .

30 October

I slowly recover. This autumn is of unequaled beauty, and I don't believe I'm the only one to feel this way. The passersby whom I run into on the street seem drugged.

I continue revising the text of my *Autobiography* (second part: "India"), which Grigoresco is to translate into French.

At the end of the afternoon, I stop in front of the Green Door Bookstore. One of my students, having seen me, comes to congratulate me for having left the hospital, then he takes a piece of paper out of his pocket and gives it to me.

"It's a newspaper clipping I've copied for you," he says. "I think it will amuse you." It's a news item taken from the *Vecerny Pravda* of Prague: Having learned that her husband was cheating on her, Vera Czermak threw herself out of the window of their third-floor apartment. She is currently in the hospital, and out of all danger. Her fall was broken by the passerby upon whom she fell. It was her husband. He died on the spot . . .

5 November

The weather is still just as beautiful. The trees are slowly shedding their leaves in a golden light. I take my usual walk along the Midway before settling down to work. Last evening I again reread and corrected chapters 11 and 12 of my *Autobiography*. Christinel is also of the opinion that I must leave such as they are the passages relating to the Maitreyi, Sorana, and Nina episodes (I had thought about omitting the first, and shortening the other two). The text that has already been typed goes to the autumn of 1938. My first plan was to stop the first volume in the spring of 1940, that is, at the time of my departure for London. However, I think I should add two more chapters in which I will recount what I lived through from April 1940 to September 1945, when I arrived in Paris. It was only then, in the autumn of 1945, that the *true* rupture took place, and that I entered into a *new life,* that of exile and poverty. I had to learn to write in a language different from my own, and to address an audience completely different from the one I had won over up to then, and which I had "shaped" in the Rumania of the years 1928–1940.

9 November

I receive *Les Nouvelles littéraires* of 26 October, which contains my homage to Georges Dumézil, who was elected to the French Academy just today. I'm angry at myself for having been so banal, so uninspired during my conversation with him (if only there hadn't been a microphone between us!). But in volume 2 of my *Autobiography,* I do intend to recall my relationship with G. Dumézil and the friendship that has linked us for more than fifteen years. I will speak of the opposition he had to face, from J. Vendries (our conversation of 1947) to Zaehner (our discussions since 1965). Fortunately, Georges Dumézil has been able to *live* (he's entering the French Academy at the age of eighty!) and thus to *pursue* his work, that is, correct and refine his earliest formulations on the Indo-European tripartite system (*Jupiter, Mars, Quirinus,* 1941; *Mitra Varuna,* 1940; etc.). Twenty years ago he had already, through his work, commanded the attention of all his foreign colleagues. But if he had had to stop all activity around the 1960s, I wonder how many French scholars would know of him.

15 November

In a letter I receive from Rumania, this popular legend is told: One day a saint persuaded himself that the most beautiful homage he could pay to God would be to sing for Him, on earth, the same songs of glory that the angels and the cherubim raised up around the celestial throne. But to whom could he apply to learn them? The saint then remembered that the Devil, before his fall, was one of the angels. And the saint, who his entire life had prudently stayed away from the demon, began to invoke him night and day. Finally the Devil appeared. Very circumspect, he inquired into the reasons that had suddenly made him so important to the saint. Of course, he agreed to teach him the celestial songs, but under the condition that the saint promise him his soul in exchange. A sort of duel developed between them: Who would possess the other? One day, however, when the exhausted Devil had fallen asleep, the saint took a rope, tied him up, and started to beat him, crying, "Sing! Sing!" Seeing that the beating had no effect, the saint threatened to sprinkle the Devil with holy water. Terrorized, the Devil then began to sing the hymns of glory that he had learned when he was an angel.

The hymns reached up to Heaven, and God, having leaned out over His throne of clouds, was very moved to see that the singer was none other than the Devil. He immediately had him reinstated into the place he had lost in the choir of the angels. But seeing also that the saint was in ecstasy, so beautiful were the songs, God took him by the hair and threw him into Hell, for, through his fervor, he had succeeded in lifting the punishment, nonetheless eternal, that God had inflicted on the demon.

NEW ORLEANS, *17 November*

Because of the storm, our plane leaves three hours late. We arrive in New Orleans at eleven o'clock at night, and at our hotel after midnight. We are let out at the Lafitte Guest House, 1003 Bourbon Street, where we have a room with a bath and a huge balcony on the second floor. We don't tire of contemplating the lights of the city and of listening to the sounds that rise up in which the strains of diverse music are all mixed up together. All of a sudden I remember that student who had asked to see me, and with whom, two weeks ago, I had made an appointment for this very day. I saw her this morning. She wanted to have certain points in the *Bhagavad-Gita* cleared up for her, and had prepared several pages of notes to show me. I think about her disappointment when she noticed, after ten minutes, that I was listening to her distractedly. In fact, I was listening for the arrival of the taxi that was to drive us to the airport.

18 November

After breakfast, which we take on the balcony, we go into the city to see the different hotels where the other members of the congress are staying. Right next to the Lafitte Guest House old houses with patios and cast-iron grillwork testify to New Orleans's Spanish past.

With Evelyn, Ane-Rose, and Joe Kitagawa we hire a carriage which takes us to the French Quarter. Useless to enumerate the streets and houses of yesteryear that seemed most picturesque to us. On the way back we stop at "Jean Lafitte's Old Absinth House since 1806," where we are served "the best coffee in the city," or so they claimed.

In the afternoon, long walk in the Vieux Carré and notably in Saint-Peter Street, that street which is so picturesque and so lively despite the invasion of tourists. Numerous stores are decorated with paintings. There are some in windows, on walls, and even on doors. It doesn't matter that for the most part they only reflect the disappointing mediocrity of dilettantes. What enchants me is the very life of this street, these houses with cast-iron balconies, the passersby one runs into, most often very young, quite open and good-natured. One would think they were all on vacation, even though that is not the case.

We pass in front of the famous Preservation Hall, where we will try, today or tomorrow, to get tickets to listen to the old jazz tunes.

This evening, not one available seat at Preservation Hall. We have dinner with André Lacocque, Jay Kim, Norman Girardot, and Alf Hiltebeitel. Then we go to the Maison Bourbon, where there is another famous jazz ensemble. We listen first standing up in the street, then after a half-hour's wait we are told that a table is finally free, right next to the piano, the trumpets, and the tenor Vicenzo XXX. I have the impression of leaping back into the past and of reliving my youth and adolescence.

19 November

This morning, walk in the French Market, then we leave to look for a restaurant. We have lunch on the patio. At a neighboring table I see Gadamer. I greet him, and he signals me to come join him. But no sooner do we sit down at his table than I see a whole group from our congress arrive. I get up, assuring Gadamer that I'll come to listen to him at three o'clock in the big auditorium.

Christinel and I have a lot of trouble finding seats. David Tracy also speaks, as a replacement for Paul Ricoeur, who is ill and had to stay in Chicago. We hurry to leave the room after having listened to their two papers. I had hoped to be able to leisurely leaf through the publications exhibited in the lobby by more than thirty publishers, but I am constantly approached by colleagues or former students, surprised but delighted at my presence at this annual meeting of the American Academy of Religions (I hesitate to admit to them that I'm here not for the meeting, but for the city). I am also approached by unknowns, such as that tall bald man who, after introducing himself, shakes my hand warmly, and congratulates me. Because, he tells me, he was once a "fundamentalist," and only became "religious" after reading my books . . .

20 November

That colleague I pass looks at me with shock, surprised, it seems, not to see me on the verge of decrepitude, or at the very least, in retirement.

I have the same impression every time I meet, I won't say "adversaries," but so-called historians of religions with whom I am in disagreement and who, more precisely, refuse to admit the importance, and above all the scope, of our discipline (at least, such as I conceive it). They would be satisfied with the smallest parcel. Indeed, what's the use of having a whole woman? An arm is enough, or a breast, or a knee . . . In short, their dream is the little "specialty."

And I understand that my presence in the United States is upsetting to them. Without me, each one of them could have become the great master of a little "specialty": neo-Babylonian religion, for example, or Vedic, or Hellenistic . . . that would have freed them from having to worry about "general issues": the structure of myths, high gods, the problem of evil and redemption, etc. . . . . How tiring to be forced to read books by colleagues and other specialists on China, India, Egypt,

Islam, or the "primitives," when in the good old days when the history of religions wasn't yet considered to be a *complete and autonomous discipline,* it was quite happily enough to repeat what your professors had taught you . . .

But they are not the only ones whom my presence bothers. There are also certain theologians and certain so-called philosophers of religions. For the former, no problem: The world is divided between those who believe in the *Revelation,* and those who don't, the "pagans" *(Belial).* For the latter, those who call themselves philosophers of religions, there are only complications which they would gladly do without! It was once enough to acquire a few vague notions on "paganism" pantheism, or monotheism, and one was free to build oneself a little personal "philosophy of religions . . ." And to think that one is now obliged to delve into the study of archaic religions, or to try, for example, to decipher the meaning of the myths of the Australian aborigines . . .

CHICAGO, *22 November*

I reread the notes I took in New Orleans. They seem so mediocre that I wonder whether they deserve to be recopied. I tell myself, however, that in ten or twenty years, all these little nothings could well be fascinating for whoever reads them (it won't be me . . .). It is from this accumulation of minute facts that it becomes possible, if not to reconstruct, at least to get an idea of what an era, a city, a whole part of the life of a human being could have been.

26 November

I spent all day yesterday and today revising *Zalmoxis: The Vanishing God* with a view to its translation into Rumanian. I add new bibliographical references and draft a short preface. Since the time of the book's publication and its multiple translations into various languages, it will have been necessary to wait eight years for the Rumanian authorities to finally decide . . .

2 December

We saw Marcia and Ted Johnson again yesterday at the Croissans', for the first time in four or five years. Last autumn we had learned that their son had died in a car accident. Marcia gives us, in a strong voice that has recovered its serenity, the details of the tragedy. She was at the university where she gives courses in instrumental music, when the hospital alerted her by telephone that her son had had an accident, not specifying that the accident had been fatal. Marcia went to the hospital, her guitar under her arm, and it was in seeing her son's body that she understood and could no longer move. Incapable of uttering a word, or even of crying, she sat on a chair and started singing softly, accompanying herself on the guitar, her child's favorite tunes, as well as those of her husband, and her own.

I don't know of any writer capable of evoking such a scene without falling into low-level melodrama. Chekhov, perhaps . . .

3 December

At noon, another interview, this time with Leslie Mailland of the *New York Times*. (Indeed, this is the year for interviews. In four months I've given more than during the last ten years.) The young journalist has studied the history of religions, first at Chicago, then at Harvard. Most of her questions refer to religious manifestations, beliefs, and institutions in contemporary societies. She asks my opinion of the recent ritual massacre in Guyana ordered by Jim Jones, the head of the "People's Temple," a politico-messianic cult. She insists, and gives me the exact number of families, young and old people, and children Jones ordered to be massacred or forced to commit suicide . . . I have to admit to her that the only information I have on this subject is from the few sensational reports I've read in the press. The subject is much too serious, much too complex, too, for an explanation of it to be advanced lightly in the course of a conversation. In order to respond I would first have to study the background of this messianic community, and know the exact *facts,* and especially what truly happened during the days that preceded the massacre.

16 December

For several days I've done nothing but grade exams and write letters. I've written a good twenty, in addition to those dictated to

Catharine Bell. In any case I couldn't have done anything else, so much am I thinking of our approaching departure for the Yucatán and Guatemala with Paul and Simone Ricoeur. Since our departure is set for the day after tomorrow, I can't undertake any serious work, whether it be the revision of the third part of the *Autobiography,* or my journal, or even my novel *Nineteen Roses.*

This afternoon, long conversation with J.P., who arrived from Montreal two days ago. He is preparing a thesis on me, and he has read all that he could find, including my stories, translated by Mary Stevenson, which have not yet been published. His questions are very pertinent, but I wonder whether my answers will be of any use to him. On the one hand, "inspiration" abandons me when I have the impression I'm repeating myself, especially if I'm speaking to only one person (before an entire class it's different, for I couldn't expect the students to know my ideas on the subject in question). On the other hand, the more J.P. talked to me about what was of particular interest to him (psychoanalysis, semiotics, etc. . . .), I felt less and less concerned with our dialogue. I've wasted too much time, when I was young, and even long afterwards, in such "dialogues of the deaf" . . .

MÉRIDA (YUCATÁN), *18 December*

To be sure not to miss our flight for Memphis, which was to leave this morning at seven-forty, we preferred to spend the night at the Hilton, right next to the airport. Bad surprise: A room with bath there costs seventy dollars, with the bonus of the noise of all the takeoffs and all the landings that occur during the night.

Breakfast in Memphis, where we wait an hour for our connection to New Orleans. A third plane finally lands us in Mérida at two o'clock in the afternoon. As we get out of the plane, we are completely shocked by the heat: Over 32°C., whereas this morning in Chicago the temperature hovered around 0°C. Our rooms are reserved at the Maria del Carmen Hotel. Tropical garden, with its ritual pool surrounded by round tables on which multicolored parasols throw a bit of shadow. In the lobby, a Christmas tree with its electric lights, just like in the United

States, and dozens of suitcases, as a group of American tourists are preparing to leave.

We go walk around the center of the city. Magnificent public garden, the Plaza Mayor, where stand the cathedral and the governor's palace. Under Hispanic-Moorish arcades, stores, cafés, and restaurants are all crowded together. Paul Ricoeur, guide in hand, gives us some elementary information: Mérida, the capital of the Yucatán, was founded in 1542, replacing T'ho, the former Mayan metropolis. T'ho was destroyed, but the blocks of stone from the city, some of which were decorated with very fine Mayan sculptures, were preserved to build the cathedral (sixteenth-century), the Casa Montejo, and other aristocratic Spanish dwellings. The army that took possession of the Yucatán was commanded by Don Francisco de Montejo y León. The Casa Montejo, Paul Ricoeur tells us, citing his guide, is today the most ancient private dwelling in all America that is still occupied by direct descendants of the man who built it.

We return to our hotel in a little carriage pulled by one horse, and we eat dinner there. The restaurant, decrepit, melancholy, makes me think of the one Eça de Queirós described at the end of the last century. But where? And in which novel?

UXMAL, *19 December*

While waiting to get sleepy, I read a good part of the information I've brought on Mesoamerican civilizations.

At the beginning of the afternoon a rental car takes us to Uxmal in less than an hour. The driver parks his car in the shade, and we head off towards the ruins. The first monument we visit is the pyramid built in honor of Kukulkan, the divinized hero, the Plumed Serpent of *quetzal,* analogous to Quetzalcoatl of the Aztecs. The pyramid was restored under the direction of Cesar Sáenz. It is also called the Haunted House. In fact, we are in the presence of a group of five temples, each one built at a different period in time. We climb the great stone steps with difficulty, and stop after about fifty to contemplate the other neighboring structures, after having found them on our map. Some have still not been explored in depth. Alone among us, Paul insisted on climbing the stairs to the top, in order to be assured one more time—and in this he wasn't wrong—that the dizziness and the chest pain which had caused him to spend ten days last month in the university hospital were not due to heart problems.

Next we go see, right near by, the quadrilateral of Chac, the god of rain and storms, where this evening we are to attend a Sound and Light Show. I limit myself to noting in the margins of the guidebook—but these margins are so narrow—a few observations that I will develop later when I have time. It takes us a half hour to climb the Sun Temple, which is also called the Governor's Temple, then we go back down as far as the esplanade of the Ball Court. This involves a rite that has fascinated me for a long time and which I do hope to deal with more in detail in the chapter of the third volume of *History* devoted to Mesoamerican religions. The Casa de las Palomas also deserves to be seen. It is in the process of being uncovered, and only the facade has been exposed. Although we stayed a good half hour looking at it, I didn't manage to fully understand everything on it.

Basically, it is the stucco decorations of the exterior walls that create all the beauty and value of the site of Uxmal, and give it all its meaning. One can only be fascinated at the sight of that bas-relief, for example, which decorates one of the walls of the pyramid of Kukulkan, and which represents a man's head emerging from the mouth of the Plumed Serpent of *quetzal* (according to Cesar Sáenz, the head symbolizes the sun). And everywhere there are images of reptiles of all sizes. There is much to say about this obsessive symbolism of the serpent. The cosmological meaning of it seems obvious to me: the night before Creation, fertility, birth and rebirth . . .

I'm writing these lines in all haste on the patio of the Villa Arqueológica Restaurant, near its pool, which is enclosed by yellow walls. Children play under the parasols, between immense vases of flowers. We're waiting for the dinner hour. I feel grumpy, melancholy, so much do I regret that we can't stay here two or three days more. Then each one of us, whenever we choose—in the morning or evening— could go back to see our "favorite ruins."

CHICHÉN ITZÁ, *20 December*

Yesterday evening, under the luminous, diversely colored beams of the Sound and Light Show, I finally saw the iconographical "plot" of the god of rain unfold. Luckily, the commentary that accompanied the show was clear and unpretentious. It included excerpts from the mythology of the god Chac, with background music of strange and unknown tunes, punctuated by strikes of a gong and flute melodies. After the show we returned through the forest smelling the strong odors of the jungle.

We left this morning with the same driver who had brought us to Uxmal yesterday. We go through a few more or less prominent towns. Some of them seem to huddle around a well-maintained plaza, with ancient trees, in front of the church. Others gather together tiny little houses, almost huts, lost in vegetation, climbing plants, and bougainvillea. After nine hours on the road, we arrive at Chichén Itzá, and we get out at the Mayaland Hotel, located right in the middle of a tropical garden. Paul succeeds in getting us a bungalow in the back of a park: two rooms with terrace, in the shade of flowering trees. No immediate neighbors, the nearest bungalow being about twenty meters away. From time to time the birds scream out their metallic cries. Hidden in branches, they remain invisible. I experience intense joy in walking along the paths that wind through the vegetation, and in trying to identify the tropical flowers that sprout up from between the rocks.

In the afternoon, our first visit to the ruins. Most of them begin a few hundred meters from the hotel, on either side of the road. We proceed slowly, so dense is the traffic. Near the entrance, vendors of souvenirs, lemonade, and Coca-Cola display their wares for tourists of all ages.

From reading books I already had an idea of Chichén Itzá, all the more since I had obtained a collection of reproductions. But only a photographer of genius could succeed in capturing the secret of archeological vestiges, and especially those of Central America. I need only cite as an example that immense, extraordinary pyramid that dominates the landscape and stands in the middle of a plain completely empty but for one lone tree right next to the monument. The pyramid is built of nine superimposed platforms. On each one of its sides, facing the four cardinal points, stone staircases lead to the summit where the sanctuary of the god Kukulkan is placed (populations originating in Uxmal, where the ceremonial center in honor of this god was located, introduced their cult into Chichén Itzá). All the while listening to the explanations of the guide, I leaf through my book for more detail, and I take notes in my notebook. I think it's useless to transcribe them here.

I won't forget that platform where the skulls of victims offered up in sacrifice have been preserved like quarry stones in a wall, nor that skeleton with a snake around its legs, nor even that great rectangular ball court measuring ninety meters long by thirty meters wide, surrounded by twelve-meter-high walls upon which spectators probably sat. It is the largest ceremonial ball court known today. They are, however, numerous: I've seen the one in Uxmal and, in 1969, those in Monte Alban and Xochicalco. They are found in all ceremonial centers, with the exception of that in Teotihuacán, and they are mentioned in all the manuscripts we have been able to preserve. In all probability, the contest between the two teams engaged in the match would symbolize the confrontation of antagonistic forces, in other words, the creative dialectic that alone could assure the continuity of cyclical life. But there would be too much to say about it, so inexhaustible does the symbolism of the game seem to me.

I must also note the exceptional acoustics: A mere murmur at one end of the enclosure is heard at seventy meters . . .

The name given to the principal palace bears witness to the naiveté and the "provincialism" of its discoverers. When they saw this building, seventy meters long and thirty-five meters wide, its innumerable rooms, its sculpted staircases, and its doors decorated with hieroglyphics, Francisco de Montejo's soldiers thought that it was a monastery for women, whence the name they gave it, Las Monjas, and which has been maintained.

We cross a few hundred meters between scattered trees to go see the tiny little lake of strange beauty that spreads out about twenty meters below at the foot of the rocks.

On our way back we cross the road and go into the second archeological site. Before reaching the first uncovered monuments, you must go through the forest for rather a long time. I continue to take notes, but I'm quite afraid of never being able to reread what I've written, so much have I abbreviated the hastily pencilled words.

From on top of the platform of a temple we see our hotel. It seems quite close, less than a kilometer away, and we decide to return to it by cutting through the forest. We do hope to find a path that will take us to the road. But after walking for a half hour, we realize we've gone astray. After resting under a giant cedar, we retrace our path.

I won't forget the end of this evening on the patio of the hotel. The silence in the garden is disturbed only by the murmuring of the fountain. We stay a long time chatting on the terrace in front of our bungalow.

ISLA DE LAS MUJERAS, *21 December*

Three hours on the road. We go through Valladolid, the first capital of the Yucatán. Magnificent park and, quite obviously, church, the latter of very beautiful colonial style.

We arrive in view of the ocean and reach the boat landing just in time to take the boat to that famous "Island of Women." Offshore we still see the palm trees on the banks we have just left. I will have to do some research on this island to find out how it got its name. As soon as we get off the boat we are approached and proposed diverse excursions in motorboats, but our only wish is to find a place for lunch. We are directed to a little restaurant nearby which overlooks the port. A quarter hour after our arrival, the room is already full. We have our best meal since we've been in the Yucatán: Lobster is the specialty of the island. We have rarely eaten any better, and they cost a lot less than a mediocre meal in Mérida.

We then walk around the streets adjoining the port. Many picturesque restaurants, a number of brightly painted houses, and flowers or flowering trees everywhere. "Artists" abound: Improvised studios and shops display their paintings everywhere. The light seems to be more beautiful here than on the mainland, especially more golden, as in a legendary Provence.

Excursion on a glass-bottom motorboat which allows us to see the depths of the sea. We see fish of all varieties and all sizes. When we throw pieces of bread or cookies overboard, they flock together in a mob under the hull, the largest chasing the smallest, in a frantic scuffle.

On the water's edge we notice colonial-style villas. The road has been skillfully laid out between the beach and the forest.

We then go through a sort of strait between large rocks and the garden of a sumptuous villa with a private beach and boat landing. We wonder who might live there.

Suddenly our pilot shuts off the craft's motor. We are above a school of fish. They press up against each other by the thousands and remain almost immobile. We don't understand what could have provoked such a gathering of adult fish. But we are told that fishing is prohibited in this area.

Once again, we arrive just in time to get the return boat. It is packed, and we have to make the crossing standing up. Numerous groups of South Americans, young, noisy, overflowing with gaiety. The palm trees on the shore are far away, bathed in the light of the setting sun.

We are delighted to return to our Mayaland Hotel. At night I reread my notes and transcribe them.

MÉRIDA, *22 December*

Day of rest. Walk through the city. We go see certain sections again. Correspondence.

Happy men imagine they have succeeded in uncovering all the secrets of Mesoamerican civilization. Men such as José Díaz-Bolio, a "well-known poet in Yucatán," as he is introduced in the *Guide to the Ruins of Chichén Itzá* (Mérida, 1971), and the author of a successful book (three editions), *La serpiente emplumada, eje de culturas*. The guide opens with this sentence: "In 1942, I discovered that the rattlesnake was the principal religious symbol of the Mayan populations." Explanations follow: The Mayans believed that each year the rattler's tail grew by a segment. They thus imagined that the rattlesnake was able to calculate the passing of time, and this is why they considered it a solar god.

MEXICO CITY, *23 December*

At the Mérida airport, a bad surprise: Our plane tickets for Guatemala are no longer valid since we didn't call to confirm within seventy-two hours preceding our departure. All our plans are going to be upset. We had already reserved our rooms in Guatemala City, plane tickets for Tikal, etc. . . . Luckily, Paul manages to get us seats in a plane this evening for Mexico. We arrive at eight-thirty and go to the Carlo Hotel, Plaza de la República. I go out, quite determined to walk around the streets adjoining the plaza, but I had forgotten that we are at an altitude of more than two thousand meters. Fatigued, I have to go back to the hotel.

MEXICO CITY, *24 December*

No way to find the address, nor even the phone number, of Eric T. We call N. Petra, but in vain.

At the end of the morning, visit to the National Museum of Anthropology. We stay until closing time. Without any doubt, it is one of the most beautiful and best-conceived museums of its genre. One need only look with even the least attention at the collections exhibited in chronological order throughout a dozen or so rooms, and read the very brief explicative notes, to quickly form an idea about the complicated history of these still rather little known Mesoamerican civilizations. I take note upon note in my book and in the margins of the excellent museum catalog, written by the museum's director, Ignacio Bernal.

What is both fascinating and mysterious is to note the decadence, then the ruin, of all these centers of civilization. At a certain period, between 200 B.C. and A.D. 150, the populations of the valley of Mexico began to gather in Teotihuacán, the renowned ceremonial center, where, among other monuments, the Pyramids of the Sun and the Moon were built. The age of glory of this new cultural synthesis extended from 350 to 650. It was followed by decadence. Teotihuacán fell into the hands of "primitive" tribes who descended from the north, and the city was destroyed. Nevertheless, in time the conquerors let themselves be civilized by the conquered, or the Toltecs, "the artists and the scholars," in the language of the conquerers. The new syncretist civilization lasted from 900 to 1200, then new hordes descended from the north, the Aztecs, or *Mexica* (in the beginning they were called "Chichimecs," or "nomads"). I won't talk about the mythical establishment of their metropolis of Tenochtitlán in 1325: The God Huitzilopoctli had ordered the ceremonial center to be built in the place where an eagle would be seen devouring a snake.

No sooner do I arrive at the hotel than I realize that I didn't take any notes on the different phases of Mayan civilization, which, however, left its mark on all the Yucatán and Guatemala. It was without any doubt the most innovative of all the Mesoamerican cultures due to the passionate interest it nourished in chronology, astronomy, mathematics, and music. Even more important, certain Mayan populations have been able to survive up to the present, and to maintain in part their original culture. Certain "enigmas" could undoubtedly be clarified with the help of the oral traditions of their latest representatives.

We have dinner in one of the rare restaurants that have stayed open on Christmas Eve, then go to midnight mass. The huge cathedral is full of people: flowers, lights, the odor of incense . . .

MEXICO CITY, *25 December*

From eleven to two o'clock, the elevator is broken. We are forced to stay in the lobby since our rooms are on the tenth floor. It's very warm. Outside, in the Plaza de la República, I notice big butterflies with red or orange wings.

Yesterday and today we went to walk around the neighborhoods we had particularly liked at the time of our last visit in 1965. We saw again today the cathedral of Santiago Tlatelolco, which dates from the sixteenth century and was built on the ruins of the palace of the last Aztec rulers. Here is a translation of the text of the commemorative plaque placed facing the cathedral: "On 13 August 1521 the city of Tlatelolco, despite the heroic battle of its defenders, led by Cuahtémoc, fell into the hands of Hernán Cortés. It was neither a victory nor a defeat, but the painful birth of the half-breed people who make up the current population of Mexico."

Long stroll in Chapultepec Park, more animated than ever on this Christmas Day. Numerous *negocios* have installed themselves all around it. The most picturesque are the little open-air scenery stands where you can be photographed in old-time cars, or next to shepherds and wise men, in front of the stable where Jesus was born . . .

I find it strange that I've never heard nor read anything about the life of Count Jean-Frédéric Waldeck. He was one of the originators of Mesoamerican archaeology, and dedicated forty-three years of his life to it. It was at the age of sixty-six that he was suddenly taken with a passion for Mayan civilization. It is claimed that he died in Paris following an accident: Having noticed a pretty woman, he had turned around a bit too quickly in his tracks. He was 109 at the time . . .

GUATEMALA CITY, *26 December*

Following the advice of our driver, we got up at dawn this morning to arrive at the airport before there were too many people. Despite this precaution, the airport is already packed, and there is an enormous line in front of the counter where we are to have our tickets validated and our bags checked. Luckily, Paul was with us . . . Without him we could only have returned to our hotel and spent the rest of our vacation in Mexico City.

Last year's earthquake completely destroyed Guatemala City. The sidewalks are broken, and certain neighborhoods make one think of a bombed city. Before landing we had been able to see the cabins and the encampments where some tens of thousands of homeless have found refuge. I wonder, however, if the filthiness that abounds in our neighborhood is also a consequence of the earthquake. After walking around for a half hour, we go back to the hotel. Luckily it's the Colonial Hotel, an old patrician dwelling, remarkably cool and calm, with a patio, a fountain, and a parrot in a huge cage. I spend the better part of the afternoon reviewing my file of notes on Mesoamerican religions.

As soon as the sun sets, the city is metamorphosed. Having gone at random into one of the streets to the left of the hotel, we soon come out into a park, weakly lit, but still very animated. At each step vendors propose delicacies, trinkets, and souvenirs. Most often they are children, old women, or ageless men.

Excellent dinner in a Spanish restaurant. The patio, where all the tables are taken, is surrounded by rooms transformed into as many dining rooms. In the one where we are led, only one other table is occupied. Our waiter is an old man who drags his feet a bit, but who doesn't stop smiling. He attracts compassion, and Ramón del Valle-Inclán would have liked him a lot.

TIKAL, *27 December*

We had arrived at the airport before six-thirty in the morning in vain; our plane was unable to take off for another two hours. It seemed Tikal was encased in fog. Our little plane—it has only twenty-four seats—flies over mountains covered with forests, then it begins a sharp descent and lands on a miniscule landing strip on the edge of the jungle, hardly a few hundred meters from the Jungle Lodge, where we are to spend the night. No sooner have we penetrated under the many varied tropical trees—palm trees, mahoganies, *chicozapote,* cedars—and their tanglings of lianas, than I experience a strange sensation, melancholy mixed with euphoria: I feel myself transported fifty years into the past, to December 1928, the date of my first contact with the jungle, that of Ceylon, a few kilometers from Colombo. I listen with delight to the cries and squawking of exotic birds, and I manage to catch sight of some, all the way at the top of the trees. I can even identify certain species: parrots, *Chatilla tropical, Paurake* (or "*Pucuyo*").

We leave our bags at the hotel and immediately go see the ruins. Our guide is a young American woman, probably a student in anthropology, very nice. She walks while holding a very long and very thin stick, like the shepherds of the ancient Orient, which she uses to indicate certain details on the monuments. She expresses herself with clarity, without exaggerating, and even with a certain humor. We advance slowly between giant trees, on paths invaded by grass and liana, all the while listening to the "general introduction" quite tactfully provided by our guide. She doesn't know us and hasn't yet discovered what is most likely to interest us. To her, we are just "American tourists" like any others.

She tells us that Tikal was already inhabited in the sixth century B.C., although not one building from that time has been preserved. The Mayans had the custom of demolishing old constructions to build new ones in their place. At the beginning of the Christian era, what is today called the Plaza Mayor already had the look it would keep for many centuries, with its so characteristic platforms and steps. The classic period, says our student, goes from 290 to 900. It is followed by a postclassic period. As some among us showed signs of impatience, our guide hurries to conclude: Most of the buildings date from the classic period, and more precisely from its second half, between 550 and 900. It is also the time when Copán and Palenque knew their hour of glory. Then something happened, undoubtedly an event that no archaeologist has yet brought to light, and the creativity of Tikan culture abruptly dried up. Part of the population, however, remained where they were and continued to celebrate traditional cults in the temples and on the altars of the Plaza Mayor.

But the group begins to wander off. Our guide waves her stick around in a signal to regroup, and leads us to the Plaza Mayor. We pass in front of diverse monuments and only stop once we are at the foot of the temple called "of the Great Jaguar," or Temple Number One, according to the guides. Its presence is extraordinary! It was built out of limestone during the first century of our era. A pyramidal foundation at nine degrees—because for the Mayans the number nine was considered to be sacred—supports a platform on which stands a temple comprised of three rooms. At the top of the temple, at fifty meters above the plaza, is a multicolored edifice, unfortunately in ruins, in the form of a throne. One reaches the door of the temple by an impressively steep stone staircase.

The Plaza Mayor is formed in fact by a great number of diverse temples and monuments, grouped one next to the other around the temple of the Great Jaguar. I have never seen so many constructions in such a restricted space. The impression one has is all the more intense as this "dead city" is surrounded on all sides by a thick, high jungle in a tangled mass of trees, liana, and wild vines.

The history of this ceremonial center is still not well known. Certain scholars even doubt that it ever will be. A residential site perhaps existed not far from here, but that hypothesis itself is very controversial. All around, in a radius of four kilometers, there have indeed been platforms discovered that could have served as foundations for stone or wooden houses, and authors have suggested that some fifty thousand inhabitants must have lived in this area of a few square kilometers. If not, how could these pyramids and temples have been built? Who would have carried the stones needed to build them? And where would the artisans who sculpted and decorated the facades have lived? They would, moreover, have needed several thousand people to furnish food, cultivate the fields, and raise livestock and fowl.

We are told that one can't take a step without walking on vestiges of dwellings in ruin and other monuments buried under the ground for centuries. Excavations will last another eighty years. The smallest pyramid, once cleared of the vegetation that covers and penetrates it, must be restored and strengthened with concrete. And it must still be protected permanently against the jungle, the rain, and earthquakes. At present a good hundred thousand different objects have been uncovered: tools, axes, cult objects and ornaments, and perhaps a million fragments of pottery and ceramics, indispensable material for reconstructing chronology.

I knew in advance that we would need at least three full days to visit the most important monuments. We put off until later visiting some of them. Today we limit ourselves, after having seen in passing innumerable other ruins, to contemplating at leisure the Acropolis of the North. Of all the monuments uncovered up to now, it is the one whose construction is the most complex. Its terminal platform is located about fifteen meters above the plaza. One is all the more impressed in seeing it when one knows that this is only the last dated of the acropolises which have succeeded each other on the same site, a good dozen of which have been counted. Vestiges of a hundred earlier constructions have been discovered under the mass of this architectural ensemble, the oldest dating from the second century B.C. We have time to admire a few stelae covered with hieroglyphics.

We return to the Jungle Lodge at the end of the evening. We are deafened by the cries of the birds. We walk along under the trees, our noses in the air so we can see them take flight. To both Christinel's and my great regret we have not yet seen those extraordinary little creatures called ''spider monkeys.''

After having dinner—quite bad, by the way—at the hotel restaurant, we await nightfall seated on big, hard wooden chairs prodigiously uncomfortable, on the threshhold of the ''straw hut'' where we will sleep. It is in fact a sort of barn about twenty meters long, with a roof made of boughs tied together with wicker. The rooms are separated from each other by thin trellis walls.

TIKAL, *28 December*
 Unforgettable night (at least for me!). It's the first I spend in the heart of the jungle in fifty years. I also remember my *kutiar* on the banks of the Ganges in Rishikesh in the Himalayas, where I stayed from the autumn of 1930 to the spring of 1931.
 ''Se oía la respiración de la noche, enorme, feminina'' [One hears the breathing of the night, enormous, feminine]. I reread this sentence by Octavio Paz (*Arenas movedizas*) three days ago on the plane.
 We get up early in order to visit some of the monuments we saw yesterday, as well as the little, but very precious, museum built on the

edge of the jungle, where we spend an hour. I take note upon note in my little book, mainly bibliographical points.

Paul gave me a gift, *The Birds of Tikal* by Frank B. Smith. In the little plane to Guatemala City, I passed the time leafing through it, with as much delight as regret. Of the two hundred species shown in the book, and which are reproduced in color, I've only been able to see twelve or fifteen at most. Of course, I didn't have binoculars like that old American woman we saw yesterday at twilight who was lying in wait for the birds perched at the summit of the highest and densest trees, and who murmured their names under her breath each time she identified one of them.

In any event, my vision has considerably deteriorated in the last two years. The onset of cataracts, said the specialist I saw in Paris. He tried to arrest their progress by prescribing drops and medication which I take regularly, but without appreciable results. He assured me, however, that I could read without too much harm. "It's what is most important to you," he told me with a smile. I would have seemed ungrateful had I told him he was wrong. And here I am now, forced to open my eyes wide to be able to see the pictures of the birds in Frank Smith's book, the very ones whose cries and squawking I heard just yesterday in the jungle, and which I, too, could have seen if to the myopia of my adolescence had not been added these early cataracts . . .

ANTIGUA, *29 December*

Serene and luminous morning. From our car we can see the volcano constantly. One would say it's smoking, but that is only an impression. In reality, the summit is covered with a thin wreath of clouds.

Upon our arrival in Antigua Guatemala, we go visit the ruins of the monastery of Los Capuchinos, three-quarters of which was demolished during the earthquake of 29 July 1773 which destroyed the city. In 1775 the king of Spain had a new city built, away from the volcano. This was

Guatemala de Asunción, which since then has remained the country's capital.

Rare are the cities that have had as tragic a destiny as that of Santiago de los Caballeros de Guatemala, founded by Pedro de Alvarado at the foot of the volcano Agua. During the night of 15 September 1541, fourteen years after the founding of the city and shortly after it was known that Pedro was dead in Mexico and that his widow, Doña Beatriz, who had proclaimed herself regent in his place, had ordered that the interior and exterior walls of the governor's palace be painted black, fires broke out in several places in the city. Then torrential rains crashed down for three days. They were followed by a terrible earthquake that shook the city and opened the volcano's crater. The waters that had accumulated in it overflowed into the plain. Santiago de los Caballeros disappeared. Many of those who hadn't perished under the rubble died by drowning. Doña Beatriz was among the victims. Her body was found, her hands gripping a crucifix. She had ruled only two days.

The city council nevertheless decided to build a new Santiago, not far from the first. The city was officially founded on 16 March 1543, and a new cathedral was erected. The blood daughter of Alvarado, Doña Leonor Alvarado Xicotenati, who by miracle had escaped the cataclysm, ordered two sarcophagi in which to bury the remains of her father and stepmother, and had them walled up in one of the aisles of the new cathedral. But some time later the wall crumbled and the bones disappeared, lost in the dust of the ruins.

We wander sadly in what was once the famous monastery of Los Capuchinos. Luckily the sun makes the bougainvillea shine with all their fire. They are like clusters of light, some of of them scarlet, others mauve. We go into a circular patio and look quickly at the monks' cells (''the old monks,'' our guide specifies . . .). Then we go down into the cellar, which was used as storerooms for flour, wine, and oil, and we also visit the crypt. We finally return to the light between clusters of those flamboyant flowers called *Pasqua* [poinsettia], and have a final look at the display cases that house objects discovered in the ruins: old pottery originating in Spain, France, and China.

When we get to the plaza, surrounded by ancient colonial dwellings and restaurants in the shade of big trees, we finally discover what creates the charm of Antigua. I now understand why so many artists and writers have chosen to live here. Antigua is perhaps one of the rare old cities of Central America where the light, the luxuriant vegetation, and the beauty of the houses make one forget the sadness of the ruins and the proximity of the volcano. We have lunch under the arcades, then go see the plaza again. Sitting on a bench, near what is called the Siren's Fountain, I think that I would very much like to stay here several days and especially several nights, if only to contemplate this very fountain in the moonlight . . .

In the afternoon we go visit San Carlos Borromeo, the former university which was turned into the Colonial Museum. Large, very cool rooms whose walls are covered with baroque paintings. Admirable portrait of a saint I wasn't familiar with, Saint Clarisse. We go across the cloisters, whose flower garden is embellished with the traditional fountain, and go into the room where the oldest printing press in the city is preserved. In the display cases are exhibited books printed here three hundred years ago. The letters are clearer, and the paper in better condition than that of many books printed in Europe in the last century.

A walk of a few kilometers through the forest takes us to the workshops of San Felipe de Jesús, where artisans craft objects out of silver. We watch them work. As everywhere else, they are delighted to know they are being admired and photographed. In the courtyard, shaded by venerable and majestic trees, American tourists compare their purchases.

Then, on a road ravaged by the last earthquake, we go to San Antonio Aguas Calientes, a small village inhabited almost entirely by weavers. Shawls, dresses, cloths of violent colors, which, however, don't clash. The little church was destroyed in the earthquake of 1977. In the twilight it seems to signal us to approach its ruins and guess their message. But how might we decipher it? We only know that it has to do with an omen.

COPÁN, *30 December*

    I'm writing these lines in all haste, seated on a large rock, while the guide tells our group the history of the excavations. We left Guatemala this morning at six o'clock, and after driving four hours through mountains and forests, we arrived at the border of Honduras. No sooner had our guide disappeared into the border station to have our passports checked than they came to carry out the ritual disinfection of our bus, inside it as well as out. We were riding for an hour on a completely destroyed road, but what followed surpassed our most pessimistic expectations. It was a miracle that our bus was still able to go on under such conditions. It took us more than an hour to cover the fifteen kilometers that separated us from Copán.

    And yet, no sooner had we arrived than fatigue and nerves disappeared as if by magic. The forest in which the ruins are found resembles that of a fairy tale. We are first greeted by three enormous parrots splashed with blue, red, and yellow, then we continue through gigantic trees, the very ones that, after having buried the ruins under their branches, force them to rise up to the surface, but all broken up. Since the Copán site has remained three-quarters unexplored, one may wonder how many of these trees will survive the archeological digs. Their roots, after having broken or split the foundations of the monuments, have brought their stones to the surface where they've rolled into the valley. Not one of the edifices still more than half-buried in the ground will be able to be unearthed and restored—or more precisely "rebuilt"—without first sacrificing the trees that assault it.

    The temple with seven tiers is the first we see since we've entered the forest. Its two anthropomorphic figures—but I give up copying over the notes from my notebook. Huge, round stone engraved with signs and astronomical calculations, and bearing the chronology of the eclipses. The guide tells us that this monument would summarize the conclusions of the "First Mayan Congress on Astronomy." Altars of stone in the form of huge drums. We climb the slopes on difficult paths that wind in between the trees in order to see other monuments, other bas-relief stelae. Then we go back down on paths that are just as steep, for the whole area has been eroded by water and is now only a succession of ravines. The torrential rains considerably impede the exploration of the site. "Too much water! Too much water!" repeats the guide.

We make a stop in front of a stele raised in honor of the only woman who ever reigned over a Mayan population (I'll have to verify this in Chicago). And, of course, the ball court. Then I come across a construction a few meters high which is quite intriguing. One sees on it, in profile, a truly enigmatic animal. Some authors have believed to see in it an elephant and its trunk. But there have never been elephants on the American continent. This figure, asserted the proponents of "diffusionism," according to whom Mesoamerican civilization was of Asian origin, was proof that the Mayans had kept the remembrance—rather confused, to tell the truth—of their first fatherland, Asia . . . At the foot of the statue, a tree whose trunk measures two or three meters in diameter. It is always the same problem: The trees brought the monuments back up above ground, but it was they who had first destroyed them.

We returned at nightfall. Before our bus began its descent into the valley, we had perceived the lights of Guatemala City in the distance. While riding along, I remembered that afternoon in the summer of 1930 at the Imperial Library in Calcutta when I was reading *Elephants and Anthropologists* by George Eliott-Smith, a book whose title is deliberately aggressive and had been suggested to him by the monument we had just seen. Indeed, George Eliott-Smith used the existence of the Copán "elephant" as an argument in support of his diffusionist theory. The book was absurd, but wonderfully written. At the same time, other Indian memories came back to mind. Much too tired to note them down.

CHICHICASTENANGO, *31 December*

Three-hour bus ride, but on good roads this time. As soon as we leave Guatemala City the landscape changes abruptly. Large hills alternate with deep valleys, then one sees the three volcanos in the distance. One of them, the Agua, the most dangerous of the three, emits a thin wreath of smoke. In this limpid air and luminous sky it seems almost unreal, especially when it is suddenly seen as one is coming out of the forest . . .

We arrive in Chichicastenango a little before noon and go directly to visit the church of Santo Tomás. On the square in front of the church, clusters of Indians burn incense and recite prayers to gods and ancestors. High mass is celebrated here only on the occasion of certain festivals. On Sunday only one mass is celebrated, at seven o'clock in the morning. Today is Sunday, and until sunset the church remains at the disposal of the natives who are not yet converted, or whose conversion remains very superficial. Men and widows alone are allowed to participate in the ritual. In the large space that separates the rows of benches, in front of lit candles, a few men and two widows holding their children by the hands recite prayers out loud, just as if they were alone, for their dead and their "protecting saints." They rarely express themselves in Spanish, but most often in their own language, *Quiché*.

The other evening I took some notes, written down elsewhere than in my usual notebook, on this little city, nevertheless famous in its genre. Even today Chichicastenango is still the seat of a "separate Indian government" whose only function is to defend the interests of the indigenous community. In addition to this government there exists a religious organization shared by the *cofradías,* or brotherhoods, each one dedicated to a saint. These brotherhoods, just like the "prayer specialists," the *chuchkajan,* have a more important place in the religious life of the community than the Catholic church. Children are baptized in the church, but at weddings and funerals it is the *chuchkajan* who officiate. Of the fourteen *cofradías* in the city the biggest is that of Santo Tomás, patron saint of the city. At the time of the feast day of each of the patron saints, its statue is carried in a procession through the city, then placed as a sentinel in front of the home of the new head of the brotherhood. The latter must then offer a feast that often costs more than he would earn in an entire year.

But it is the role devolved on the "prayer specialists" that gives religious syncretism all its meaning. They serve as intermediaries between individuals and their saints or "idols." Ceremonies take place at the church. The saints and idols, in other words, the indigenous divinities, are believed to show more solicitude for all that concerns daily life than God Himself, and to carry out the wishes of everyone insofar as possible. This example in itself illustrates one of the most important aspects of the history of religions.

The Chichicastenango market, already famous before the arrival of the Spanish, is in full swing. Dozens of pathways have surged up among makeshift tents and shelters, behind shelves displaying a continuous wall of shirts, dresses, shawls, handkerchiefs, all of them flapping in the wind and waving from one end to the other as soon as a tourist reaches out to touch a fabric. This reminds me of an Oriental bazaar, especially when we go in under a cloth or a tent canvas between two *negocios* to be sheltered from the sun.

We make our way with difficulty through the compact groups of tourists. They come from everywhere, from the United States, of course, but also from South America, Europe, and even Asia. Next to the textile *negocios,* other displays are right on the ground. The vendors sell fruit, lemonade, tortillas, roasted ears of corn, and many other comestibles we're unfamiliar with. From time to time a display proposes awful color prints of vaguely—or aggressively—religious subjects.

After a half hour, I can't take any more. I separate myself from the group and head towards the section where ceramics and more or less decorative objects are sold. It only extends over a few dozen square meters, covered entirely with pottery, plates, and all sorts of vases. Right nearby I discover a little park with a fountain in the middle of it, and a giant palm tree where many, many birds are hopping about. Their song is interrupted by the sharp grunts of pigs being carried under the arms of their buyers, or on their backs, tied up in a net.

We have lunch at the Tulkah Hotel. The rooms on the main floor are packed with tourists. There are other rooms upstairs that are reached by a very picturesque wooden staircase with a flowered balustrade. A local band plays on the patio, and a few vendors have been allowed to display their wares on the grass in the sunlight. Two hours later we return to the market. Simone and Paul return from it, their arms filled with gifts for their children and friends: straw hats, fabric, shawls, all of it stuffed into two enormous net bags.

I'm writing these lines seated at a table at the hotel, for the moment empty of tourists, while waiting for the bus that is to take us to Los Encuentros.

PANAJACHEL, *1 January 1979*

Yesterday afternoon we took the five o'clock bus. Stop in Los Encuentros, where we see, far below us, Lake Atitlan. Then a taxi takes us on the road to Sololá. We go across coffee plantations while watching the setting sun. At seven o'clock we are in Panajachel, a little city on the very edge of Lake Atitlan. We get out at the Riva Bella ''mini-motel.'' In fact it is comprised of a half dozen two-room bungalows in the middle of luxuriant vegetation, trees covered with flowers, and bunches of bougainvillea and hibiscus that I only discovered this morning.

We had dinner in a picturesque and amusing restaurant, La Laguna, run by two young Englishwomen. Not far from there the explosions of firecrackers follow one another and become more and more frequent as midnight approaches. Back at our mini-motel around eleven o'clock, the real fiesta begins: fireworks (which we watch from our window), innumerable firecrackers, and the sirens of firetrucks. There wasn't a fire, but such is the local custom: In all celebrations, motorcyclists and firemen are part of the festivities.

After waking up to the singing of the birds, we have breakfast under the trees and flowers. Panajachel, founded in 1547, has only four thousand inhabitants, all more or less dependent on the coffee plantations or market-gardening. Tourism could, however, easily become their chief industry. The street where our motel-restaurant-garden is located has eight or nine analogous establishments, and others are under construction.

Then we go to see the lake. I've learned from the guide that in *Nahuatl* the word Atitlan means ''place where there is a lot of water.''

The lake is only a few hundred meters from our motel, but it is hidden by the rich villas that line either side of the street that leads to it. The detonations start up again even more strongly, as does the backfiring of the motorcycles. Transistors also join in. Their owners are in general "local people" who speak *Nahuatl* and seem very proud to have such an apparatus. It will take no more than a generation for the din to invade the world. I even wonder whether a government will ever have the *courage* to put an end to it. A "socialist" regime, perhaps . . .

And suddenly the lake is revealed in all its beauty. Where we are standing the beach is already invaded by tourists from the lakeshore hotels, as well as by some local people. The women still wear the traditional red *huipil* and blue petticoats. A few men wear a sort of jacket cut out of a blanket, and white pants.

We don't tire of looking at the lake. We will see it again later in the afternoon, but from other vantage points, and away from the crowds. We see little boats on it, and a larger craft that crosses from one end of the lake to the other twice a day. But the excursion lasts six hours, and we decide against it.

Aldous Huxley claimed that Lake Atitlan is the most beautiful in the world. At twilight we contemplate it again, seated in a garden, under clumps of bougainvillea. I write these notes so I won't give in to the sadness I feel in having to tear myself from my enchantment, for in an hour a taxi will come to take us back to Guatemala City.

GUATEMALA CITY, *2 January*

In my file of notes and cards on Mesoamerican religions, I discover photocopies of certain pages from *Incidents of Travel in Central America, Chiapas and Yucatan* (10th ed., vol. 1 [London: John Murray, 1842]) in which the author, John L. Stephens, tells of his arrival in the village of Copán: "We inquired immediately for the ruins, but none of the villagers could direct us to them, and all advised us to go to the hacienda of Don Gregorio . . ." [p. 91]. After interminable discussions, Stephens ended up acquiring the whole part of the forest that contained the ruins, then half-buried under the earth, or broken up by the trees and their roots, as hearty as they were destructive. And Stephens continues: "I paid fifty dollars for Copán. There was never any difficulty about price. I offered that sum, for which Don Jose Maria thought me only a fool; if I had offered more he would probably have considered me something worse" [p. 128].

And here is the passage [pp. 119–20] where he speaks of the discovery and his exploration of the ruins: "The ground was entirely new; there were no guide-books or guides; the whole was a virgin soil. We could not see ten yards before us, and never knew what we should stumble upon next. At one time we stopped to cut away branches and vines which concealed the face of a monument, and then to dig around and bring to light a fragment, a sculptured corner of which protruded from the earth. I leaned over with breathless anxiety while the Indians worked, and an eye, an ear, a foot, or a hand was disentombed; and when the machete rang against the chiselled stone, I pushed the Indians away, and cleared out the loose earth with my hands. The beauty of the sculpture, the solemn stillness of the woods, disturbed only by the scrambling of monkeys and the chattering of parrots, the absolute solitude of the site, and the mystery that hung over it, all created an interest higher, if possible, than I had ever felt among the ruins of the Old World . . ."

I have just learned, according to chronological facts deciphered from stelae and altars, that the history of Copán is entirely contained between the years 465 and 800, a period during which the calendar was perfected and astronomy made considerable progress, not to mention the splendid decorative art that transfigured certain monuments and made them resemble flowers of stone. Then suddenly, for yet unknown reasons, monuments built after the year 800 cease to be dated, as was previously the custom. From that time, the civilization of Copán fell into decadence, then disappeared.

This scenario, in which the birth, ascension, period of glory, then an abrupt and enigmatic decadence, and finally the disappearance of a civilization are successively witnessed, is apparently repeated everywhere in Central America.

GUATEMALA CITY, *3 January*

I had a strange dream during the night. An unknown person, whom I can hardly distinguish for I am in a dark and narrow hallway, shows me a large bucket filled with dirty water, and states that he is going to place it in my path. Then he blindfolds me. A useless precaution, for while I was listening to him my eyes had become clouded over, and I could see almost nothing at all. The walls, the bucket, the mysterious person himself are lost in the fog. But this person, who was he? Apparently someone important to me, to whom I felt increasingly attached, as to a teacher or to an unknown friend. He had told me to continue walking straight in front of me, rapidly, but with little steps, without stopping to feel the ground under my feet. It was of course an initiatory trial, for to knock over the bucket or simply to put my foot into it would have meant my "being lost." But I didn't know how this "loss" was translated for me.

I remember he clapped his hands and cried, "Go!" My heart beating, I started to advance as he had told me, with rapid little steps. I don't remember what happened next.

In Chicago, a snowstorm has been raging for several days. The airport must surely be closed. I have just learned of the death of Roger Caillois. A cerebral hemorrhage struck him down at the age of sixty-five. It was from his little book, *L'Homme et le sacré*, that I learned about him for the first time, in Lisbon in 1942, then from his articles on "Les démons de midi" in the *Revue de l'histoire des religions*. I was to meet him at Georges Dumézil's in 1946. I envied his encyclopedic knowledge, and especially his courage to deal with all subjects: the religious role of the executioner, fantastic literature, detective novels, crystals and minerals, etc. . . . He was the first translator of Borges, whose work he, more than anyone else, introduced in Europe.

I remember our meeting in Rome in 1955 during the history of religions meetings. One evening when we were all four having dinner in a restaurant, he told me how he felt both confused and amused by my obstinacy in using the term "history and phenomenology of religions." In the French university milieu, he said, the expression "history— comparative or not—of religions" has bad press. It would be better to use other terms, such as "sociology of religions," or "religious anthropology," and from then on many doors would open for me.

A fervent entomologist, he cultivated a true passion for butterflies. It was from his wife that we learned what had happened one day when Roger Caillois was attending, as a representative of UNESCO, the inauguration of an institute in an Asian country. In the park of the new establishment, while a band played the national anthem in the presence of officials and the entire diplomatic corps, a butterfly flew right in front of his eyes. Since it was of a rare species which was still missing from his collection, Roger Caillois, leaving the dignitaries flabbergasted, hurried off in pursuit of it . . .

GUATEMALA CITY, *4 January*

I spend almost the whole day in my room transcribing my notes, many of which, written in haste with a pencil stub, have already become almost illegible.

Next Saturday we will be back in Chicago. The airport is closed, but we still have two days before us. On Tuesday evening I will continue my seminar with Wendy O'Flaherty on the *Shah Namah* (the Book of Kings) of Firdausi. As usual, instead of immersing myself in the *Shah Namah* file which I had had the foresight to bring with me, I give myself up to remembrances (let those who can resist the temptation to relive the great discoveries of their youth and adolescence throw the first stone!). It was at the time of my first trip to Italy, organized by my lycée in the spring of 1926. A specially chartered sleeper-car had taken us from Bucharest to Naples and back, by two different routes. It was in Venice that I discovered in a secondhand bookshop the eight volumes of *Il Libro dei Rei* [the *Shah Namah*] in the translation by Italio Pizzi. During our tour I read the first two volumes with delight, but also with much difficulty, for the translation was in verse. Back home, I started reading it again, but I don't think I completed volume 4. I would reread the *Shah Namah* in its entirety five or six years later, in the French translation by Jules Mohl.

And what can be said about that *Manuale di Lingua Persiana* by Pizzi! I praised it one day in front of Lucian Bogdanov, and even succeeded in making him laugh, he who laughed so rarely.

"How can you," he exclaimed, "so enthusiastically praise the grammar of a language of which you have only the most rudimentary knowledge?"

I replied with embarrassment, arguing with the fervor, with the passionate delight I had felt while reading the book. That afternoon, in that room in the library of the Asiatic Society of Calcutta, Bogdanov proposed to teach me Persian "quickly and well." He could only do so for two months. Some time after that I had to go back to Rumania.

It's truly strange that I suddenly remember Bogdanov and his Persian lessons, not much of which has stayed with me. Of course, forty-seven years have passed since then . . . But it is even stranger that these memories are not accompanied by the slightest melancholy. Everything that's happened to me since, everything I've been able to learn, but also to forget, everything I could wish for, everything I've dreamt of, has remained engraved somewhere inside me, not in my memory, but in a much deeper part of myself.

And this is perhaps why I'm writing these lines without the least bitterness. *Everything that truly matters to me,* I've been able to keep. Nothing has been lost. Without the least bitterness, undoubtedly, but not without a certain fear. Indeed, it would suffice—I've been told—for a little electrode to penetrate into a certain part of my brain for a whole realm of my past to come back to me, intact, *in the most infinite detail.* And if that were to happen. . . .

Index